THE ESSENTIAL ROSA LUXEMBURG

THE ESSENTIAL ROSA LUXEMBURG

Reform or Revolution
&
The Mass Strike

EDITED BY HELEN SCOTT

Haymarket
Books

CHICAGO, ILLINOIS

First published in 2008 by Haymarket Books
P.O. Box 180165
Chicago, IL 60618
773-583-7884
info@haymarketbooks.org
www.haymarketbooks.org

Introductions © 2008 Helen Scott
Reform or Revolution (1898) was translated by Integer
and first published in English in 1937 by Three Arrows Press.
The Mass Strike (1906) was translated by Patrick Lavin and
first published in English in 1925 by the Marxian Educational Society, Detroit.

Trade distribution:
In the U.S. through Consortium Book Sales and Distribution, www.cbsd.com
In Canada, Publishers Group Canada, www.pgcbooks.ca
In the UK, Turnaround Publisher Services, www.turnaround-psl.com
In Australia, Palgrave Macmillan, www.palgravemacmillan.com.au
All other countries, Publishers Group Worldwide, www.pgw.com

This book was published with the generous support of
the Wallace Global Fund and the Lannan Foundation.

Cover design by Ragina Johnson

ISBN 978-1931859-36-3
CIP Data is available
Entered into digital printing May, 2020.

CONTENTS

A NOTE ON THE TEXT

These versions of *Reform or Revolution* and *The Mass Strike* have been reproduced from the original English editions. Minor changes have been made to bring the text up to date with common usage of grammar, spelling, capitalization, and so on. In a very few places, where the original German was mistranslated or there was an error in the original English edition, those have been corrected.

ROSA LUXEMBURG

Even taking into account the distortion and exaggeration to which all revolutionary figures are subject, the contradictions surrounding Rosa Luxemburg are extreme. She was denounced by the rulers of her day as the ruthless terrorist "Bloody Rosa" or "Red Rosa." Yet the biographical film by Margarethe von Trotta, which draws heavily on Luxemburg's letters and speeches, creates a portrait of a sensitive and introspective woman, inclined to pacifism and only reluctantly a revolutionary. She has been cast as an anti-Leninist who denounced the allegedly antidemocratic actions of the Bolsheviks in the Russian Revolution. Yet Luxemburg and Lenin were close allies for many years, and of the Bolsheviks in 1917 Luxemburg wrote: "Their October uprising was not only the actual salvation of the Russian Revolution; it was also the salvation of the honor of international socialism."[1] In turn, Lenin said of Luxemburg that "she was and is an eagle, and not only will she be dear to the memory of Communists in the whole world, but her biography and the *complete* edition of her works . . . will be a very useful lesson in the education of many generations of Communists."[2] She has been portrayed as a "spontaneist" who eschewed the vanguard party or any centralized leadership organization; but in many of her most celebrated essays she repeats the fundamental lesson of *The Mass Strike*, where she writes that socialists "are the most enlightened, most class-conscious vanguard of the proletariat. They cannot and dare not wait, in a fatalist fashion, with folded arms for the advent of the 'revolutionary situation.'"[3]

Although in part these contradictions are the result of deliberate misappropriation of Luxemburg's ideas for political reasons, there is something else at play, too. As you might expect of someone Georg

Lukács called "a genuine dialectician," Luxemburg was a figure who held together sharp and complex, and often opposing, realities.[4] As Marx put it in *The Poverty of Philosophy*: "What constitutes dialectical movement is the coexistence of two contradictory sides, their conflict and their fusion into a new category."[5] The contradictions constitute what is remarkable about Luxemburg, and to downplay or overemphasize one dynamic at the expense of others is to simplify and reduce the whole. She faced the discrimination waged against women, Jews, and Poles, but she drew on the experience to sharpen her sense of solidarity with others facing oppression. She was physically weak and prone to ill health, but fought all the harder because of this, and never shied from an argument even when it opened her to attack. The more you read of her and by her, the more clearly you get a portrait of a real person with weaknesses and flaws, but also outstanding qualities: she was principled, brave, fiercely intelligent, quick-witted and funny, articulate (in several languages), deeply compassionate, and above all, thoroughly committed to socialist revolution.

She was also very much of her era: the decades of her too-short life were marked by the intense antagonisms and dramatic shifts brought by revolution, war, and social upheaval. During her lifetime history could have swung in any number of directions; world socialist revolution was a real possibility. But instead capitalism reasserted itself and ushered in one of the grimmest periods in history. Luxemburg was a product of these times, but also to an unusual degree acted upon them, fighting for socialism and against barbarism. And she left a rich legacy for others who have taken up the struggle.

LUXEMBURG'S LIFE IN POLAND

Poland at the time of Rosa Luxemburg's birth in 1871 was a land divided and occupied by foreign powers that were all themselves undergoing transformation: Austria (part of the ever-changing Hapsburg Empire, and after 1867 the dual monarchy of Austria-Hungary); Prussia (which was a powerful kingdom in the eighteenth and early nineteenth centuries, integrated with the German Empire in 1871); and tsarist Russia, the dominant and most hated of the three empires, and which "for nearly all of Europe . . . was throughout the whole of the nineteenth century, the symbol of obscure, rigid, and ever less effective reaction."[6]

The occupied Poland where Luxemburg spent her youth was a country of stark divisions and conflicts. Mass Polish resistance in the mid-nineteenth century had been met with harsh repression—an estimated ten thousand were exiled—and an intensive campaign of "Russification" restricted Polish language and culture. Economically, while some regions were industrialized and at the forefront of Europe's capitalist development, large rural areas were still effectively feudal and undeveloped. The Lublin border district where Rosa Luxemburg was born had the worst of both worlds, according to Luxemburg's contemporary and main biographer, Paul Frölich:

> [T]he dependence, sufferings, and difficulties of the lower strata of the population from the days of serfdom lingered on. The penetration of the monetary system into this district, remote as it was from the industrial centers, brought only the hardships attendant on the destruction of an old order of society, and not the advantages of the new.[7]

Conditions for working-class Poles in the economically advanced regions were differently harsh, but no less so, replicating the horrors of industrialization that had swept England half a century earlier.[8] Life for the Jewish population was even worse, sharing as they did class oppression, the national oppression of the Polish people, and the added persecution that denied Jews basic civil rights and excluded them from many institutions and professions.

While not politically active, Luxemburg's parents opposed tsarism and Russian imperialism, and also rejected the narrow religious orthodoxy of some Jewish communities in favor of liberal secularism. They were relatively well off, but this did not exclude periods of real hardship. Because of mistreatment of a hip disease in early childhood, Rosa had a lifelong disability. The youngest of five, she was encouraged to read and write from an early age, and was given support and encouragement from her parents and siblings throughout her life. The family moved to the city of Warsaw when Rosa was a young child, at least in part to gain access to better educational opportunities for the children.

Many schools were reserved exclusively for the offspring of Russian administrators; those that admitted Poles had quotas for Jews, and of course there was rigid gender segregation. In the school Rosa attended, the Second Girls' High School in Warsaw, use of the Polish language was forbidden, and a rigid set of rules impinged on every area of life. Luxemburg became active in the school opposition and, despite her obvious academic excellence, was denied the standard reward of a gold medal because of "her 'rebellious attitude' towards the authorities," as her report card put it.[9] Luise Kautsky, wife of German socialist Karl Kautsky, and one of Luxemburg's most enduring intimate friends, wrote of the sixteen-year-old Rosa:

> [S]he already occupied her mind with the most difficult problems— not only with the origins of humanity, with the right to motherhood, the history of tribes and clans, but also and especially with all problems associated with the modern labor movement, with the history of revolutions, the theory of surplus value, etc. Morgan, Bachofen, Lubbock, Kowalewski, and other sociologists, besides Marx and Engels, constituted her chief reading.[10]

As Luxemburg was growing up, Russian oppression affected every aspect of life: "The yoke of oppression weighed on her threefold: she belonged to the Russian people enchained by tsarism, the Polish people suppressed by foreign rule, and to the downtrodden Jewish minority."[11] In addition, she was a woman at a time when politics was overwhelmingly a male domain. And all these experiences contributed to her lifelong hatred of all forms of oppression.

During this time, "socialism," "communism," and "social democracy" were used interchangeably to describe organizations based on working-class struggle and informed by theories systematized by Karl Marx and Friedrich Engels. The working-class association founded in the 1860s that subsequently became known as the First International brought together such organizations from different countries. From its founding in 1889 until the outbreak of the First World War, the Second International continued to function as a global body made up of representatives from the major socialist parties.[12] Throughout this period representatives of the parties making up the International met regularly at party congresses held in various nations; similarly, the many socialist parties held their own congresses in towns or cities in their respective nations.

The socialist movement in Poland developed in the context of struggles against Russian occupation, which were widespread, particularly among the youth: "[T]he secondary schools were hotbeds of political conspiracy . . . and what began as Polish national opposition to the Russianization attempts in the schools often led into the revolutionary socialist movement, whose supporters in those days were almost exclusively the intellectual youth."[13] Jewish workers in Poland were the first to take up Plekhanov's call for them to agitate around political and economic demands; Poland was thus ahead of the rest of

Russia in terms of working-class organization and socialism.[14] As early as the late 1870s groups of socialist workers organized Marxist reading circles and built illegal unions and strikes.[15] These groups were brutally suppressed, but survived and returned in 1882 as the revolutionary socialist party Proletariat. Luxemburg joined Proletariat in the 1880s and was involved in the factory circles—small groups of socialist workers reading literature by Marx and Engels smuggled into the country. In 1888 the Polish Workers League was founded amid renewed working-class struggle, and in 1893 fused with Proletariat and other small groups to form the Polish Socialist Party (Polska Partia Socjalistyczna, PPS).

Threatened with deportation to Siberia when the authorities found out about her activities, Luxemburg went into exile.[16] She lived first in Zurich, Switzerland, which was at that time the center of European socialist activity, and joined the university, which was known as "the alma mater of young revolutionaries." She took courses in philosophy, the natural sciences, and economics, and was a gifted student, but also keenly alert to the limitations of academia. Luxemburg captured the contradictory role of formal education:

> The social, historical, philosophical, and natural sciences are today the ideological products of the bourgeoisie and expressions of its needs and class tendencies. But on a certain level of its development the working class recognizes that for it also "knowledge is power"— not in the tasteless sense of bourgeois individualism and its preachings of "industriousness and diligence" as a means of achieving "happiness," but in the sense of knowledge as a lever of class struggle, as the revolutionary consciousness of the working masses.[17]

She described the university's German chair of economics as a

> ...theorizing bureaucrat who plucks apart the living material of social reality into the most minute fibers and particles, rearranges and categorizes them according to bureaucratic procedure, and delivers them in this mangled state as scientific material for the administrative and legislative activity of Privy Councillors.[18]

Her own doctoral thesis, *The Industrial Development of Poland*, in contrast eschewed obscure specialization in favor of the informed overview of a macroeconomic study. It was recognized and published at the time as an original and insightful work, and "already showed her particular gift for enlivening accurate economic history with striking illustrations—a combination of statistics and social imagery which was peculiarly hers."[19]

In addition to formal academia, Luxemburg was studying in the alternative university of revolutionary politics. Frölich captures something of the heady circles she was part of:

> These students did not squander their time in drinking bouts. Their discussions were tireless and never ending: about philosophy; Darwinism; the emancipation of women; Marx; Tolstoy; the fate of the *obshchina*, the last remnant of Russian agrarian communism; the prospects and the historical significance of capitalist development in Russia; the upshot of the terrorism of *Narodnaya Volya*; Bakunin, Blanqui and the methods of revolutionary struggle; the demoralization of the Western bourgeoisie; Bismarck's fall and the victorious struggle of German Social Democracy against the Anti Socialist Laws (*Ausnahmegesetze*); the liberation of Poland; the teachings of Lavrov and Chernyshevsky, and the "treachery" committed by Turgenev in his novel *Fathers and Sons*; Spielhagen and Zola; a thousand "questions" and always the same theme—revolution.[20]

Another member of these Zurich circles was Leo Jogiches (known most often by the pseudonym Tyszka) who became the most significant personal and political partner of Luxemburg's life. Jogiches was of an age with her—born in Vilna in 1867 to a wealthy Jewish family—and also involved from his youth in the revolutionary circles of the early working-class movement. He was arrested and imprisoned twice before fleeing to Zurich in 1890, where he too became an important figure in the exile political networks and met many of the primary leaders of the international socialist movement.

Luxemburg and Jogiches organized a group of Polish revolutionaries, most notably Feliks Dzierzhinski, Julian Marchlewski, and Adolf Warszawski, around the paper *Sprawa Robotnicza* (The Workers' Cause), which after 1894 broke away from the PPS to build the Social Democracy of the Kingdom of Poland. The break was primarily in opposition to what they saw as the national chauvinism of the PPS, which placed the restoration of Poland above international working-class solidarity. In exile this group successfully built and maintained the clandestine Social Democracy of the Kingdom of Poland and Lithuania (SDKPiL—after merging with Lithuanian socialists in 1899), even in the face of fierce repression.[21]

At the turn of the twentieth century the international socialist movement looked to an organizational model that was most advanced in Germany: a mass, working-class party representing a range of political positions and advocating both immediate social reforms and the ultimate goal of revolution. The Erfurt program, named after the German town where it was drafted in 1891, explicitly declared these as the minimum and maximum platforms of the German party of Social Democracy, the SPD (the initials are from its German name, Sozialdemokratische Partei Deutschlands).

In Germany socialism was legal after the lifting of the antisocialist "Exceptional Laws" in 1890. Elsewhere, however, socialists were forced to work in secret and often in exile. In Russia, which was to become the center of world socialism, Vladimir Ilich Lenin over a period of time developed in practice a different model of a tightly organized vanguard (or leading body) of revolutionary workers. The Russian socialist party, the Russian Social Democratic Labor Party (RSDLP) was famously to split into the revolutionary Bolsheviks (from the Russian word for "majority") and the reformist Mensheviks ("minority"). But up until the outbreak of World War One even Lenin assumed that the SPD was the ideal organizational model.

The Polish party, although ostensibly following the Erfurt program, in practice functioned much like the Bolsheviks. Luxemburg was intimately involved in this project while also, later, building the legal, increasingly established SPD, and this dual experience goes a long way to explaining her unique position on organizational issues. In 1903 she, like Leon Trotsky, who was later to become a key Bolshevik leader, was sharply critical of Lenin's conception of organization in Russia; her 1904 "Organizational Questions of Russian Social Democracy" was an explicit critique of Lenin's *One Step Forward, Two Steps Back*. Yet, as Paul Le Blanc has argued, this polemic was primarily crafted for the German context, and was based on a mistaken concept of Lenin's actual position:

> [W]e should take note of the common ground shared by the two revolutionaries, which is far more considerable than is generally acknowledged. In fact, much of what Luxemburg has written seems like an elaboration of the Leninist conception of the party. Even in her 1904 polemic, she stresses the need for "a proletarian vanguard, conscious of its class interests and capable of self-direction in political activity."[22]

At key moments, particularly after the 1905 Russian Revolution, Luxemburg was closer to Lenin and the Bolsheviks, even while others in the German SPD supported the Mensheviks. She was quite aware of the reformist dangers of social democracy well before Lenin, yet her firm faith in working-class self-activity led her to overestimate the ability of struggle alone, without an independent centralized revolutionary party, to overcome these dangers. For this reason she paid less attention to organizational matters; her primary role in Germany was that of propagandist, and only World War One and the Russian Revolution led her explicitly to revise her position and come out for an independent revolutionary organization.

Luxemburg's experience as an exiled Polish socialist also shaped her distinctive approach to the national question, which was a matter of much debate among socialists from the International Congress in London in 1896. Marx and Engels had appraised struggles for national liberation against oppression by the great empires on the basis of their objective consequence for the democratic revolution in Europe. As tsarist Russia was the bastion of reaction, they argued that socialists should support nationalist movements that challenged but oppose those that aided the empire. With her typical independence of mind, even when it came to established Marxist principles, Luxemburg maintained that conditions within Europe had changed considerably since Marx and Engels developed their position, which should therefore be revisited. She further argued that nationalism in Poland had no progressive basis:

> In Poland, the national movement, right from the beginning, took on a completely different character from that of Western Europe . . . With us Poles the national idea was a class idea of the nobility, never of the *bourgeoisie*. The material base of Polish national aspirations was determined not as in Central Europe in the nineteenth century, by modern capitalist development, but, on the contrary, by the nobility's idea of its social standing, rooted in the natural-feudal economy.
>
> The national movements of Poland vanished together with these feudal relations; whereas the bourgeoisie, as the historical spokesman of capitalistic development, was with us, from the very beginning, a clearly anti-national factor.[23]

Luxemburg argued that a call for national self-determination for Poland could only be reactionary, and thus objected to the inclusion of support for national self-determination in the program of the Russian party:

> The formula of the "right of nations" is inadequate to justify the position of socialists on the nationality question, not only because it fails to take into account the wide range of historical conditions (place and time) existing in each given case and does not reckon with the general current of the development of global conditions, but also because it ignores completely the fundamental theory of modern socialists—the theory of social classes.[24]

This passage points to the three main strands of Luxemburg's argument: The idea of abstract, unchanging "rights" is a bourgeois myth that should be rejected by socialists; global conditions had in many cases supplanted nationalism, as the major capitalist powers went beyond their boundaries to conquer other regions; and working-class internationalism supercedes the idea of a national identity uniting all classes.

She did not universally oppose calls for national liberation.[25] But the Polish question exhibited, in the words of Tony Cliff, "her tendency to generalize too readily from her immediate experiences to the labor movement elsewhere."[26] Furthermore, her correct objection to the PPS led her to seek a material basis for rejecting Polish nationalism, rather than, as was usually her practice, starting from an honest evaluation of circumstances and developing policy from there. In fact, as many Marxists at the time and subsequently have pointed out, in Poland as in other oppressed nations, struggles for independence are not opposed to but rather part of the larger struggle for socialism. As Lenin was to write in 1916: "The dialectics of history is such that small nations, powerless as an independent factor in the struggle against imperialism, play a part as one of the ferments, one of the bacilli which help the real anti-imperialist force, the socialist proletariat, to make its appearance on the scene."[27]

Lenin agreed that *Polish* socialists should not raise the banner of independence, but held that nonetheless the *International* had to defend the *right* of Polish national liberation, or that of any oppressed nation, and that Russian socialists had to include this right in their platform. When he crystallized his position in 1916, he did so largely in opposition to Luxemburg. He argued that she was right to reject the chauvinist PPS, but wrong to generalize from the specific experience of the SDKPiL, in the process ignoring the greater danger of the reactionary nationalism of the oppressor nation, Russia. Lenin instead emphasized strategic flexibility for socialists in the oppressor and the oppressed nations:

> [T]here is a way out in which all participants would remain internationalists: the Russian and German Social-Democrats by demanding for Poland unconditional "freedom to secede"; the Polish Social-Democrats by working for the unity of the proletarian struggle in both small and big countries without putting forward the slogan of Polish independence for the given epoch or the given era.[28]

Luxemburg and her Polish comrades never accepted this solution, and the issue repeatedly became a sticking point for the RSDLP and the SDKPiL, although the Russian and Polish parties were united on many questions for most of the period. Luxemburg's position only hardened after 1914, when the opportunist leaders of German Social Democracy justified support for "their own" nation in the imperialist war in terms of fighting the greater enemy, Russian tsarism, and she criticized the Bolsheviks for granting liberation to oppressed nationalities during the 1917 revolution.

LUXEMBURG IN GERMANY

After Zurich Luxemburg made the decision to go to Germany, where she believed she could make the most significant contribution to international socialism.[29] In exile she continued to be a leader of Polish social democracy—her first significant political document for the International was a report from Poland to the Third Congress in Zurich in 1893—while she also quickly won leadership in the International, and in Germany, home to the largest party.

In the latter decades of the nineteenth century Germany was an important and growing capitalist state, but the old landowning class, known as the Prussian Junkers, still held onto their power; the German bourgeois revolution was incomplete in that it left this old power structure intact even while the new parliamentary system, the Reich, was established in 1871. In the words of historian of German social democracy, Carl Schorske: "[T]he middle-class leaders of the Revolution of 1848 recoiled from the revolution they had conjured up, and, leaving political power in the hands of the aristocracy, placed their hope for the achievement of a constitutional order in legal methods."[30]

A famous conference in Gotha in 1875 brought together different political forces to form the Socialist Labor Party of Germany, which became the Social Democratic Party.[31] In the face of brutal suppression from Bismarck's regime, the SPD became more revolutionary and more Marxist, while the antisocialist laws in place between 1878 and 1890 forced it to work under conditions of illegality.[32] At the first congress—in exile in Switzerland in 1880—they declared themselves revolutionary, with "no illusions" in achieving their goals through parliament. In 1891 they forged the Erfurt program. Pierre Broué describes the platform as conceptualized by one of its authors, Karl Kautsky, who was also the editor of the party's journal, *Neue Zeit*:

> Kautsky did not renounce the maximum program, the socialist revolution, which the expansion of capitalism had made a distant prospect, but laid down that the party could and must fight for the demands of a minimum program, partial aims, and political, economic and social reforms, and must work to consolidate the political and economic power of the workers' movement.[33]

This dichotomy, and the drive to suppress the ensuing contradictions and competing currents, became central to the SPD.

In 1890 the antisocialist laws were repealed and the SPD became legal. Socialism had a mass appeal among the German working class, described by Broué as it looked by the end of the nineteenth century:

> Relatively well-educated, familiar with technology and machines, with a sense of collective work and responsibility, with a taste for organization, the German proletarians were modern workers, able to defend their immediate interests, to devote themselves to militant activity, and to become conscious of a society which treated them merely as tools, and also aware that their solidarity made them into a force which could change their lives and that of the petty bourgeoisie, who capitalist concentration crushed, and who they judged, with some reason, could become their allies in struggle.[34]

Against this background, over the next two decades the SPD became a "state within a state," as Max Weber famously described it in 1907.[35] From 1881, when they won just over 6 percent, the SPD steadily gained votes in the Reichstag (the German House of Representatives), winning more than 30 percent in 1903.

Paradoxically, this very success had a conservatizing effect, as increasingly the party leaders oriented on competition with the capitalist parties and hesitated to take positions likely to open them to attack in the bourgeois press. The party apparatus was "'created during a long period of social stability and economic expansion, [and] it was hired to run election campaigns, handle finances, disseminate the press, and do everything possible to attract new voters.'" This led to a "moderate, easy-to-sell program appealing to the widest possible audience."[36] In 1907 for the first time the SPD lost seats in the Reichstag, in an election dominated by a unified ruling-class campaign of pro-imperialist chauvinism. While the radicals stressed the necessity of responding with a sharper attack on war and nationalism, the reformists drew the opposite conclusion, and blamed the radicals for the electoral disappointment.[37]

This description by American socialist Mary-Alice Waters captures the scale of the party's growth:

> In 1912 . . . the SPD won four and a quarter million votes, or 34.7 percent of the total, making it the largest party in the Reichstag, with 110 deputies. By the beginning of 1914, SPD membership had passed the one million mark. The party published ninety daily papers which reached 1.4 million subscribers. It also had a large women's movement, a youth section, cooperatives, sports and cultural organizations, and several million workers in social-democratic-led trade unions. The capital assets of the SPD's various branches and activities were worth 21.5 million marks and some 3,500 people were employed in the party, trade union, and related apparatuses.[38]

When Luxemburg arrived in Berlin the SPD was already a formidable organization.[39]

Despite the relative social weight of the SPD, it would be wrong to suppose that in 1898 Luxemburg was joining an establishment party. The ruling class at best tolerated the socialists and at worst attacked and harassed them. Many of the leaders, including Luxemburg, endured repeated prison sentences and threats of deportation in addition to vituperative attacks from the bourgeois press. In fact, many of Luxemburg's most important writings were composed in prison and smuggled out to be printed and distributed. Nor were her labors solely intellectual: Her very first task on arriving in Germany was to go to Upper Silesia to organize among the mostly Polish mine workers. She had remarkable success there, speaking in bars and town halls, winning mass support, and establishing herself as a major force in the working-class movement. From this moment on, Luxemburg was to play a vital role within the SPD: "When the German revolutionary movement began to get under way in the new century, Luxemburg was in the van, giving it theoretical structure and tactical leadership, and spurring it on with her eloquence."[40]

Her life in Berlin was initially strange and lonely, and she faced the daunting task of winning leadership among the recognized socialist greats while battling a hostile dominant culture and establishing herself in a new land and language. Anti-Semitism, anti-Polish discrimination, and sexism pervaded the broader society. Luxemburg constantly fought all these forms of oppression; she was particularly conscious of the centrality of the struggle for women's liberation to the socialist project. In 1902 she wrote in the newspaper *Leipziger Volkszeitung*:

"[W]ith the political emancipation of women a strong fresh wind must also blow into its [Social-Democracy's] political and spiritual life, dispelling the suffocating atmosphere of the present philistine family life which so unmistakably rubs off on our party members too, the workers as well as the leaders."[41]

In this as in all things, she consistently challenged convention and shook up institutional patterns.

She soon settled into her new life, and quickly won respect and friendship from a wide range of people. She formed a deep intellectual alliance with Kautsky, especially after she became assistant editor of *Neue Zeit*, and developed a close personal relationship with the entire family, especially Karl's wife, Luise.[42] She also became intimate with Clara Zetkin, a fellow revolutionary who was longtime editor of the journal *Gleichheit* (Equality) and active in organizing women workers. She remained at all times in contact through letters with Leo Jogiches and other Polish comrades, and Jogiches often visited and lived with her for periods of time, especially before their romantic relationship ended in 1907.

Luxemburg made it her life's work to build the revolutionary socialist movement and counter the destructive influence of the SPD's parliamentarianism. Her first and most lasting critique was made in a series of articles that ran in *Neue Zeit*, and were later published as the short book *Reform or Revolution* reproduced here. Luxemburg wrote in response to Eduard Bernstein, one of the main spokespeople for the new reformism, also known as "revisionism" or "opportunism" by its detractors. It is an astonishing achievement that a woman in her twenties, newly arrived in a strange country, was able to have an enormous political impact, exposing the reactionary implications of some of the party's most respected figures, and forcing others, who had previously tolerated Bernstein's attacks on Marxism, to take a stand against them.

Luxemburg saw dull, mechanical writing as symptomatic of dry and disconnected politics, and strove instead to convey in words the living, feeling component of socialism. She described this connection in a letter to friends in 1898, not long after her arrival in Germany:

> I'm not satisfied with the way in which people in the party usually write articles. They are all so conventional, so wooden, so cut-and-dry. . . .
> Our scribblings are usually not lyrics, but whirrings, without color or resonance, like the tone of an engine wheel. I believe that the cause lies in the fact that when people write, they forget for the most part to dig deeply into themselves and to feel the whole import and truth of what

they are writing. I believe that every time, every day, in every article you must live through the thing again, you must feel your way through it, and then fresh words—coming from the heart and going to the heart—would occur to express the old familiar thing. But you get so used to a truth that you rattle off the deepest and greatest things as if they were the "Our Father." I firmly intend, when I write, never to forget to be enthusiastic about what I write and to commune with myself.[43]

Figuratively and emotionally powerful writing was one of Luxemburg's trademarks. Frölich describes her gift of oratory:

> She was economical in the use of grand words and gestures; she achieved her effect purely by the content of her speeches, though in this she was assisted by a silver toned, rich and melodious voice which could fill, without effort, a great hall. She never spoke from notes, and preferred to walk casually up and down the platform because she felt closer to her audience this way. She could establish contact within a few sentences, and from then onwards she kept her audience completely under her spell.[44]

She was also a daunting foe in political arguments, never ducking a fight no matter how unpopular her position. The Austrian socialist Max Adler (1873–1937) described the "revolutionary force" that enlivened her during political debates:

> [D]espite the many mockers and haters with whom she too had to contend, it brought listeners at party congresses under the spell of her fiery temperament, and moved even her opponents to join in the noisy applause. It was characteristic of her, however, that her intellect never lost control of her temperament, so that the revolutionary fire with which she always spoke was also mingled with cool headed reflectiveness, and the effect of this fire was not destructive, but warming and illuminating.[45]

At the front of the radical wing described by Schorske as "the revolutionary goad of the party" Luxemburg frequently faced opposition not only from the ruling class, but also from the conservative and bureaucratic reformists within the SPD.[46] After 1905 the paid, permanent, formal administrative roles came to wield more influence than political positions. Due to a bizarre system of representation, rural and small town branches, which tended to be more conservative due to the weight of parochialism and the lack of large concentrations of workers, acquired more influence than those in urban centers with higher numbers of organized workers and party members with a more radical orientation.[47] This conservatism was most evident in southern Germany. The SPD maintained a policy of "not a man nor a farthing for this system," which entailed, among other things, unconditional refusal to endorse any budget that used working-class taxes to sustain the capitalist state. But in numerous southern provincial legislatures social democratic delegates violated this policy, and they were able to continue doing so because the right wing of the party blocked passage of an explicit ban on voting for provincial or local budgets.

The rightward trajectory of the SPD was temporarily interrupted by one of the most significant events of Luxemburg's life: the 1905 revolution in Russia, which fueled a concurrent upsurge in working-class activity across Europe. Luxemburg threw herself into agitation throughout Germany, and in December crossed the border to take part in the revolution itself, perilously traveling incognito, the only civilian in a train full of counterrevolutionary soldiers.[48] The SDKPiL, with its exile leaders now returned to take the helm, met the challenge of the revolutionary moment, growing in size from 1,500 in 1904 to 40,000 by 1906, and winning effective mass leadership in those years.[49] The firsthand experience of revolution taught Luxemburg two vital lessons, which she explained in her "What Next?" pamphlets of May 1905. First, that revolution depends on the sustained mass activity of the working class themselves:

> In popular revolutions it is not the party committee under the all powerful and brilliant leader or the little circle calling itself a fighting organization which counts, but only the broad masses shedding their blood. The "socialists" may imagine that the masses of the working people must be trained under their orders for the armed struggles, but, in reality, in every revolution it is the masses themselves who find the means of struggle best suited to the given conditions.[50]

While violence will inevitably be a necessary part of this mass struggle, Luxemburg scorned individual adventurism:

> Throwing a bomb is about as dangerous to the government as killing a gnat.. . . Only people incapable of thinking believe that terrorist acts of bombings can make anything more than a momentary impression. Just by themselves, mass actions as a disorganizing tactic are a danger to absolutism. Not only do they disorganize the ruling system, but they also organize at the same time the political forces which will overthrow absolutism and create a new order.[51]

The second lesson was that the primary task for socialists is political agitation among the broadest sections of the peasantry and working-class population, and especially among the soldiers:

This is the only course for Social Democracy. Agitation will win over the countryside. It will undermine discipline in the army; call the broadest masses into open struggle; and generate the forces to build barricades, procure weapons, win victories here and others there, and finally collect and pull everyone into the struggle.[52]

The 1905 revolution, the "great dress rehearsal" for 1917, was defeated by the tsarist counteroffensive by March 1906. Luxemburg and Jogiches were both arrested in Warsaw, and when her alias was broken, Luxemburg was confined to the police prison in the Warsaw Town Hall and then transferred to the infamous Pavillion X of the Warsaw Citadel. She revealed something of the conditions there much later in a letter to Sonia Liebknecht. Here she describes a scene soon after she was at last allowed family visitors:

> [S]ince the meeting took place right after a 6-day hunger strike, I was so weak that the captain of the fortress nearly had to carry me into the visiting room, and in the cage I had to hold on to the wire with both hands, which probably reinforced the impression of a wild animal in a zoo.
> The cage stood in a fairly dark corner of the room, and my brother pressed his face very close to the wire: "Where are you?" he asked over and over again, wiping from his pince-nez the tears which kept him from seeing me.[53]

Her health suffered in the harsh conditions, but she nonetheless showed exceptional resilience, politically engaging her fellow prisoners, and writing letters to reassure her friends. To the Kautskys she wrote from her first prison:

> Taken as a whole, the situation is serious, but after all, we are living in agitated times where "whatever exists deserves to perish."[54] So, be of good cheer and thumb your noses at everything. On the whole, while I was alive our work has gone superbly. I am proud of that; ours was the only oasis in all of Russia where, despite the storm and stress, the work and the struggle continued as energetically and advanced as merrily as during the time of the very freest of "constitutions." Amongst other things, the notion of resistance, which will be the model for future times throughout Russia, is our work.[55]

After her alias was broken and she heard of the transfer she wrote: "Long live the revolution! Be happy and of good cheer, otherwise I will be seriously angry with you. The work outside is going well. I have already read some new issues of the paper. Hurrah!"[56] She was released in July ostensibly on medical grounds but also due to pressure exerted by the social democrats in Germany and Poland on her behalf.[57]

A shared understanding of the centrality of independent working-class initiative and socialist leadership in a revolutionary situation now brought Luxemburg and Lenin together. They spent that summer in Finland (she using the pseudonym Felicia Budelovich due to continued police surveillance) engaged in political discussion with other Bolshevik leaders whom she impressed greatly: Gregory Zinoviev (1883–1936) called her "'the first Marxist who was able to evaluate the Russian revolution correctly and as a whole.'"[58] Luxemburg drew out the lessons of the revolution in *The Mass Strike, the Political Party, and the Trade Unions*, published as a pamphlet in 1906 and reproduced here.

These close personal connections were mirrored in strengthened organizational ties: the SDKPiL joined the RSDLP, newly and temporarily reunited at the 1906 congress in Stockholm; Jogiches and Adolf Warski (1868–1937) were elected to the united central committee; and the SDKPiL leaders frequently were aligned with Lenin and the Bolsheviks.[59] The close collaboration and mutual respect between Lenin and Luxemburg continued for the next five years, despite famous differences on major questions. As Broué puts it, "before the First World War they were the figureheads of the international social-democratic Left."[60]

Nonetheless, on her return to Germany, Luxemburg did not forge a distinct revolutionary organization akin to Lenin's. She regarded separation from the mass party as tantamount to isolation from the working class, and so continued her role as revolutionary antagonist within the SPD. Her reasoning can be seen in the advice she gave in a 1908 letter to a friend, Henrietta Roland-Holst, who was considering leaving the Dutch social democratic party with which she was deeply frustrated: "We cannot stand outside the organization, outside contact with the masses. The worst of workers' parties is better than nothing!"[61] Luxemburg remained part of a network of revolutionary allies within an increasingly hostile and conservative mass reformist party.

From 1906 until 1914 every winter Luxemburg taught at the SPD's Party School in Berlin. She greatly enjoyed her teaching and her classes were very popular. Her wonderful "What Is Economics?" gives a taste of the humor and inspired examples that must have enlivened her lessons. As Mary-Alice Waters writes: "Any student who has suffered through a course in economics, and tried to understand the dry, humorless, and intentionally obscure explanations of professors like those Rosa Luxemburg ridicules, will wish they could have been in her classes."[62] The teaching also gave rise to her most significant contribution to Marxist economics, *Accumulation of Capital*, published in 1913 with the subtitle *A Contribution to an Explanation of Imperialism*.[63]

The study was provoked by her identification of a problem in Volume II of Marx's *Capital* regarding capitalist reproduction. Luxemburg argues that "Marx's diagram of enlarged reproduction cannot explain the actual and historical process of accumulation," and his model assumes "universal and exclusive domination of the capitalist mode of production," although in reality capitalism "depends in all respects on non-capitalist strata and social organizations existing side by side with it."[64] This was the essence of her polemic: that capitalism needs to constantly expand into noncapitalist areas in order to access new supply sources, markets for surplus value, and reservoirs of labor. This compulsion leads to imperialism, the competition between capitalist powers for control over the rest of the world, which in this period predominantly took the colonial form.

In the course of the book Luxemburg explicates and critiques Marx's economic theories, and those of a dizzying range of capitalist and Marxist economists. Her devastating portrait of the centrality of imperialism and war to capitalist development, and the human suffering this produces, remains descriptive of global capitalism today. While dominant ideology separates the realm of economics from "foreign policy," Luxemburg writes:

> In reality, political power is nothing but a vehicle for the economic process. The conditions for the reproduction of capital provide the organic link between these two aspects of the accumulation of capital. The historical career of capitalism can only be appreciated by taking them together. "Sweating blood and filth with every pore from head to toe" characterizes not only the birth of capital but also its progress in the world at every step, and thus capitalism prepares its own downfall under ever more violent contortions and convulsions.[65]

Luxemburg wrongly supposed that capitalism could only continue to grow by gobbling up noncapitalist areas, while the twentieth century showed that capitalism is able to accumulate and expand within its own system.[66] But her apprehension of the significance of global capitalist expansion formed the bedrock of Luxemburg's consistent opposition to imperialism, nationalism, and war, and is invaluable for understanding the interdependence of economic and political forces. As

Paul Le Blanc writes: "The aggressive expansionism and growing militarism would, as Luxemburg so correctly predicted, result in violent catastrophes (colonial wars, world wars, and more) in which the masses of people would pay the price, for the benefit of wealthy and powerful elites."[67]

Luxemburg articulated the anti-imperialist and antimilitarist position within the SPD, as these questions formed the central fault line of the International. Although the 1900 conference in Mainz had debated foreign policy and passed an anticolonial resolution, the party had not otherwise taken up militarism and colonialism in any systematic way, although the revolutionary Karl Liebknecht and revisionist Kurt Eisner had both urged antimilitarist mobilization throughout this period. The situation changed with the International Congress of 1907, in Stuttgart, which in the face of global upheaval sought to forge clear policies on war and colonialism.

On both questions the SPD's official position was a right-wing reversal of the International's principled opposition to colonialism and imperialist war. At the Stuttgart Congress, Luxemburg, as a delegate from Poland, helped compose an antiwar resolution; Lenin assisted, and so trusted Luxemburg to represent his position that he did not speak during the discussion.[68] The resolution asserted that "[i]f the outbreak of war threatens, it is the duty of the workers and their parliamentary representatives in the countries involved, with the aid of the International bureau, to exert all their efforts to prevent the war by means of coordinated action."[69] In her supporting speech Luxemburg expressed what would become the central principle of the revolutionary left in the next decade: "Our agitation in case of war is not only aimed at ending that war, but at using the war to hasten the general collapse of class rule."[70]

The resolution passed, but this seeming victory for antiwar forces only temporarily disguised an actual schism in the International and a shift rightward in the SPD, which resisted taking a stand against war and militarism and increasingly condoned colonialism. The racism of the reformists' position on colonialism can be seen in the congress reports. This is Eduard Bernstein:

> We must get away from the utopian notion of simply abandoning the colonies. The ultimate consequence of such a view would be to give the United States back to the Indians (Commotion). The colonies are there; we must come to terms with that. Socialists too should acknowledge the need for civilized peoples to act somewhat like

guardians of the uncivilized. Lasalle [sic] and Marx recognized this.... Our economics are based, in large measure, on the extraction from the colonies of products that the native peoples had no idea how to use.[71]

The right wing consolidated through a period of top-down reorganization of the party that strengthened the professional bureaucracy and marginalized Luxemburg and other radicals. One of the main architects of the realignment was Friedrich Ebert (1871–1925). Schorske calls Ebert "the archetype of the new Social Democratic functionary [who] seems always to have been in the van of the new, practical activities which slowly sapped the revolutionary *élan* of the German labor movement." This man, "the Stalin of Social Democracy," would have an inordinate and destructive impact on the fate of Luxemburg and international socialism.[72]

The rightward shift continued while the Reichstag was dominated by a united coalition of conservative and liberal political forces called the "Bülow bloc" (named for Prince Bernhard von Bülow) and working-class activity was in a lull. In the context of the breakup of the Bülow bloc in 1909 and a revival of working-class struggle in 1910— mass demonstrations across Prussia, a record number of work stoppages, militant strikes in coal and building industries—the latent conflict erupted, and the party realigned into distinct political groupings. In the face of mass demonstrations for suffrage, Luxemburg, along with many of the most militant workers, advocated a mass political strike, but the Party Executive, following the lead of the conservative trade union leaders, refused to call one.[73]

Recognizing the significance of the mass movement, Luxemburg took two months off from teaching in order to agitate: she toured the country, speaking to large crowds on suffrage and the mass strike, to enthusiastic response. But reports of her speeches in the party journal *Vorwärts* (Forwards) were censored to remove references to popular support for the mass strike, and the paper also refused to publish her article, "Was Weiter?," elaborating her position.[74] On her return to Berlin, Luxemburg learned that, shockingly, Kautsky also refused to publish the piece in *Neue Zeit*, and he had embarked on a public polemic against her position, which he had previously endorsed. Luxemburg's article was published in smaller chunks in other local papers, including the *Dortmunder Arbeiterzeitung* and the *Leipziger Volkszeitung*, as part of her counteroffensive against the poisonous opportunism of the leadership.[75]

In speeches and articles Luxemburg called on the party to build on the victories won by the mass suffrage movement, to test the mood for a general political mass strike, and to go on the offensive with a call for "the slogan of a republic in Germany" as "a practical war cry against militarism, navalism, colonialism, world politics, Junker domination, and the Prussianization of Germany; it is the consequence and the drastic summary of our daily struggle against all these various phenomena of the ruling reaction."[76] In contrast, Kautsky and the rest of the party leadership insisted on a defensive, parliamentary strategy of accommodation to the status quo.[77]

This conflict marked the end of a long, if progressively more strained, alliance between Kautsky and Luxemburg, and the beginning of censorship of the left in the major party publications. The party at this point effectively split into three positions: the reformists; the "Marxist center;" and the revolutionaries or "left radicals."[78] Although the left wing certainly started to coalesce at this point, the conservatives still had the monopoly on organization and power. The picture was thus of "the social democratic working-class movement, preaching a revolutionary doctrine, very non-revolutionary in practice, with only a small disorganized minority of radicals noticing the contradiction."[79]

Imperialism again became the wedge issue for the party in 1911, when the German government sent a military cruiser to Morocco to "protect" its colonial interests. The party executive, seeing the looming elections as paramount, opposed a meeting of the International Bureau to formulate a response for fear this would damage the party's chances in the Reichstag. Luxemburg exposed the executive by making public a written exchange between the leadership and the International, and she denounced the contention that the party should focus on domestic questions and not get bogged down in foreign policy:

> [F]inancial policy, the rule of the Junkers, and the stagnation of so-
> cial reform are organically bound up with militarism, naval policy,
> colonial policy, and with personal rule and its foreign policy. Any ar-
> tificial separation of these spheres can only represent an incomplete
> and one-sided picture of the state of our public affairs. Above all we
> should propagate socialist enlightenment in the Reichstag elections,
> but this we cannot do if we restrict our criticism to Germany's do-
> mestic circumstances, if we fail to depict the great international rela-
> tionships, the growing dominance of capitalism in all parts of the

world, the obvious anarchy in every corner of the globe, and the
major role played by colonial and global policy in this process.[80]

Not only the radicals but also many centrists supported Luxemburg,
and this and other events combined to produce reform of the party
structure. However, the ensuing expansion of the executive, adding
conservatives Otto Braun and Philipp Scheidemann and the left centrist Hugo Haase, actually enhanced the control of Ebert's wing. But
these events also precipitated the independent development of the
revolutionaries, which would culminate in the formation of the
Communist Party.[81]

By this time three distinct approaches were apparent within the
party: the right wing effectively accommodated to imperialism; the
center separated imperialism from capitalism; Luxemburg and the
left wing saw imperialism as the deadly apotheosis of capitalism that
could only be countered with revolutionary socialism.[82] In "Peace
Utopias" Luxemburg drew out the connection between reformism
and the idea that peace was achievable within capitalism. This is impossible, she argued: "For the international antagonisms of the capitalist states are but the complement of class antagonisms, and the
world political anarchy but the reverse side of the anarchic system of
production of capitalism. Both can grow only together and be overcome only together."[83] In stressing the inextricable interdependence
of capitalism, imperialism, and war, Luxemburg anticipated Lenin's
Imperialism: The Highest Stage of Capitalism.[84]

THE BREAKUP OF SOCIAL DEMOCRACY AND THE
DEATH OF ROSA LUXEMBURG

The following period of economic recession and sporadic working-class militancy saw deepening divisions within the International
and its national parties. In 1912 the SPD increased its Reichstag vote,
but at a huge cost: suppression of antiwar and anti-imperialist positions ("don't mention the war") and a disastrous pact with the middle-class progressives.[85] The radicals were effectively cut off from the
leadership in the same year that the Bolsheviks formed a separate,
revolutionary party in Russia. At the Chemnitz Conference in 1913,
lengthy debates on the question of war were decided in favor of the
"center," and the Reichstag delegation voted for a tax bill that would
increase military spending, on the grounds that it was a progressive

tax reform. Luxemburg anticipated the logical conclusion of these developments in her response:

> If you take the position of our deputation's resolution, then you will get yourself into the situation where, if war breaks out and this fact can't be altered, and if then the question arises whether the costs should be covered by indirect or direct taxes, you will then logically support the approval of war credits.[86]

She was proved correct on the infamous date of August 4, 1914, when the SPD Reichstag delegates voted to support the war by approving the military budget. Rosa Luxemburg wrote with searing irony:

> For the proletariat there is not one vital rule, as scientific socialism has hitherto proclaimed, but rather there are two such rules: one for peace and one for war. In peacetime the class struggle applies within each country, and international solidarity vis-à-vis other countries; in wartime it is class solidarity within and the struggle between the workers of the various countries without. The global historical appeal of the *Communist Manifesto* undergoes a fundamental revision and, as amended by Kautsky, now reads: proletarians of all countries, unite in peacetime and cut each other's throats in war![87]

The SPD even signed onto the Burgfrieden, an agreement under which political parties vowed not to compete with each other or challenge the government, which acquired special wartime dictatorial powers. The trade-union leadership meanwhile disciplined the labor movement on the behalf of the state.[88] The start of World War One saw the collapse of the International, as in case after case social democratic parties followed the SPD, betrayed the principle of working-class solidarity, and supported the war efforts of their respective national ruling classes. Luxemburg's SDKPiL was among the few parties that held on to the principle of socialist internationalism.[89]

In Germany, Luxemburg was unable to stop the descent into chauvinism within the party and the labor movement, but nonetheless turned to the task of agitation against the war. With Clara Zetkin, Franz Mehring, and others she formed Die Internationale group—named for a new journal that only saw one issue before it was banned—and later the Spartakusbund (Spartacus League), which published the *Spartakusbriefe* (Spartacus Letters).[90] Meanwhile in September 1914 the Bolsheviks called for a new International, the nucleus of which developed at a famous 1915 conference in Zimmerwald, Switzerland. Luxemburg and Liebknecht planned to submit guiding principles to the conference, but conditions prevented them from doing so or attending in person. What they wrote was published instead as an illegal handbill and then appended to the *Juniusbroschüre* (Junius pamphlet), Luxemburg's work written in prison under her pen name Junius.[91]

Luxemburg was arrested soon after the outbreak of the war and was to remain almost continuously imprisoned, other than a break of a few months in 1916, until the 1918 German revolution freed her. She was first held in the Barnimstrasse Military Women's Prison in Berlin, which was "pure hell—eleven cubic meters, filthy, overrun with vermin, messy, and furnished in the most primitive fashion," and about which she later wrote: "The month and a half I spent there left gray hairs on my head and cracks in my nerves from which I shall never recover."[92] Next she was moved to the remote fortress prison in Wronke, where she had access to a yard with flowers and birds, of which she talks lovingly in her letters. Then finally she went to the Breslau prison, where she spent over three years, mostly confined to a small, dark cell.

Even in prison Luxemburg continued to play a leading role in the newly configured revolutionary left, writing for *Die Internationale*, the *Spartakusbriefe*, the "Introduction to Political Economy," which was not published during her life, and "Guiding Principles [or Theses] concerning the Tasks of International Social Democracy." Most famously, she wrote the "Crisis in German Social-Democracy," which came to be known as the *Juniusbroschüre*.

The Junius Pamphlet, which Raya Dunayevskaya calls "the first comprehensive antiwar pamphlet to come out of Germany," offers a scorching indictment that captures not only the horror of the First World War, but of every imperialist war of the ensuing century.[93] Luxemburg reviles the "stinking corpse" of Social Democracy's epic betrayal, and argues, elaborating on Engels's proposition that capitalism offers either an advance to socialism or a reversion to barbarism, that the only alternative to the insanity of war is socialist revolution:

> The soldiers of socialism, the workers of England, of France, of Germany, of Italy, of Belgium are murdering each other at the bidding of capitalism, are thrusting cold, murderous irons into each other's breasts, are tottering over their graves, grappling in each other's death-bringing arms....
> This madness will not stop, and this bloody nightmare of hell will not cease until the workers of Germany, of France, of Russia and of England will wake up out of their drunken sleep; will clasp each others'

hands in brotherhood and will drown the bestial chorus of war agitators and the hoarse cry of capitalist hyenas with the mighty cry of labor,
"Proletarians of all countries, unite!"[94]

In the words of Luise Kautsky, the pamphlet "achieved unparal-
leled success with all opponents of war in Germany and, insofar as it
could pass the frontiers, also abroad. The wealth of ideas, the bold-
ness of speech, the beauty of diction, and the truly revolutionary content characterize this work as one of the weightiest documents
against the crime of war."[95]

Although initially only a few voices publicly opposed the war, the
wave of hysterical patriotism whipped up at its outbreak transformed
into widespread popular opposition as its brutal reality and economic
burden increasingly impacted the working class. In 1915 twenty social
democratic representatives voted against the war budget, and a left
opposition within the party consolidated. May Day 1916 saw the first
major demonstrations against war in Berlin, attended by both Luxemburg and Liebknecht, temporarily out of prison. Demonstrations for
peace broke out sporadically, and against the severe food shortages
that culminated in the grim "Turnip Winter" of 1916–17, when only
the rich could attain many goods on the black market and, in the
words of Schorske, "the opulence of speculators was a standing insult
to the workers' districts and to the emaciated soldiers who emerged
from time to time on leave from the hell of the battlefield."[96]

More and more rank-and-file Social Democrats rallied behind the
left wing, this although a full three-quarters of male SPD activists
were conscripted to war.[97] The Spartacists called on soldiers to fight
against their own ruling class rather than the working classes of the
"enemy" nations, and agitated around the slogans "End the war by
strikes" and "The main enemy is at home!" That they had substan-
tial mass following is evident in the protests and strikes that broke
out when Liebknecht was arrested; many of the leaders were sent to
the front or imprisoned. Yet for all their mass appeal, they were a
small, youthful organization lacking experienced, trained members
and roots in workplaces.

The outbreak of revolution in Russia in 1917 had a huge impact
throughout Germany, and sparked widespread desertion from the
armed forces. Luxemburg began writing *The Russian Revolution*
while in Breslau prison, and although it was never finished, and not
published until 1922, after her death, it is a valuable account of the

revolution and its implications for international socialism. Luxemburg celebrates the monumental achievement of the Russian masses, and sees in it an utter refutation of German social democracy and Russian Menshevism, as well as a vindication of the Bolsheviks:

> [T]he Bolshevik tendency performs the historic service of having proclaimed from the very beginning, and having followed with iron consistency, those tasks which alone could save democracy and drive the revolution ahead. All power exclusively in the hands of the worker and peasant masses, in the hands of the soviets—this was indeed the only way out of the difficulty into which the revolution had gotten; this was the sword stroke with which they cut the Gordian knot, freed the revolution from a narrow blind alley and opened up for it an untrammeled path into the free and open fields.[98]

She also describes the extremely hostile environment in which the revolution now found itself—"the frightful compulsion of the world war, the German occupation and all the abnormal difficulties connected therewith," which she traces in part to "the failure of the German proletariat and the occupation of Russia by German imperialism," both objectively assisted by the perfidy of German social democracy.[99] This defense of the revolution included strong criticism of the Bolsheviks' agrarian policies, advocacy of national self-determination, and dissolution of the Constituent Assembly, all of which she saw as symptomatic of the daunting conditions facing a national revolution that had not internationalized.[100]

Within the SPD the formal leaders were for war and against revolution, the centrists were against war and against revolution, Luxemburg and the left were against war and for revolution. Following a conference of Spartacists and left radicals in January 1917, the SPD expelled the opposition, both leftists and centrists, who three months later formed the Independent Social Democrats, the USPD, while the official leadership became the majority SPD or M-SPD.[101] Although some left radicals objected (importantly the radical group located in Bremen), the Spartacists joined the USPD, and the revolutionaries did not develop an independent organization.

When in the summer of 1917 a revolutionary wave spontaneously erupted in the navy, its leaders disastrously turned to the USPD for guidance and ended up being crushed by the authorities. Broué writes:

> The approaching tragedy in Germany was summed up in this drama, in the contrast between the readiness of the young workers in uniform to act, and the impotence of leaders crushed by responsibilities, and

convinced that the future of humanity could be settled in terms of sub-scriptions, local branches and speeches in parliamentary assemblies.[102]

Nevertheless, the masses proceeded to build revolutionary steam, and in November 1918 workers and soldiers toppled the old regime through mass strikes and mass actions, and established worker and soldier councils. But on the resignation of the Emperor Wilhelm it was the right wing of social democracy who opportunistically took charge: Friedrich Ebert became the chancellor of the Reich, and Philipp Scheidemann declared the new "Democratic Republic," of which Ebert also became people's commissar, to preempt Liebknecht's proclamation of the "German Socialist Republic" soon after. The USPD accepted an offer to share rule in the new government, even as the ruling class turned to a Constituent Assembly as a way to *avoid* socialist revolution.

The ruling class effectively looked to the M-SPD for its survival, and the key social democratic leaders—Friedrich Ebert, Gustav Noske, Karl Legien, Philipp Scheidemann, Otto Landsberg—consciously opposed the revolution from its start.[103] The government proceeded to give verbal support to the workers while actually defending the ruling class: collaborating with the army chiefs; allowing the bourgeois functionaries and ministers to maintain their positions; enabling the bourgeois press to retain its dominance. At each step not only were the revolutionaries disorganized themselves, but they were also constantly undermined by the official champions of socialism, Ebert and his henchmen. So for example, when workers developed a security force to defend the revolution, Gustav Noske, a right-winger who had been chairman of the Brandenburg SPD, created the Freikorps (Free Corps), a private counterrevolutionary militia composed of officers and other privileged, highly trained troops, who became known as the "Noske Guards." And the bourgeois press maintained a steady stream of invective against "Red Rosa" and the Spartacists.

When Luxemburg was released from prison on November 8 all the tasks of building a revolutionary party were only in their infancy while the revolution was well under way.[104] The newspaper *Rote Fahne* (Red Flag) was launched the same month, and Luxemburg and the other revolutionaries finally broke with the USPD to form the German Communist Party (KPD) in December. But even then the revolutionaries were not sufficiently organized or unified to function as an effective political force. Those revolutionaries who had initially opposed merger with the USPD now became an ultra-left current within the KPD, arguing against participation in the upcoming Constituent Assembly elections and for a break with the trade unions. Luxemburg failed to avert this disastrous abstentionism. The factory delegates, many of whom supported communist principles, were suspicious of the "adventurist elements" and therefore the new party became isolated from the revolutionary workers, who in turn lacked the political leadership crucially provided by the Bolsheviks between February and October 1917 in Russia.[105]

By late December, following an armed battle between revolutionary sailors and counterrevolutionary soldiers sent in by Ebert, the workers in Berlin recognized the true role of the M-SPD. Mass pressure forced the Independents to resign from the government, and at this point the masses were poised to take over the capital. Broué quotes a communist eyewitness from January 5:

> "What we saw [that day] in Berlin was perhaps the largest proletarian mass action in history. We do not believe that there were demonstrations on this scale in Russia. From the Roland statue to the Siegesallee, the proletarians were marching, rank upon rank. There were marchers far away in the Tiergarten. They had brought their weapons, and they carried their red banners. They were ready to do anything and to give anything, even their lives. It was an army of 200,000 such as no Ludendorff had ever seen."[106]

Armed workers also took over the offices of *Vorwärts* and other newspapers, along with railway and police buildings. At this crucial moment the task of leadership fell to a hastily organized and unwieldy "Revolutionary Committee" consisting of representatives from the Independents, Communists, and Revolutionary Shop Stewards.

After much debate and disagreement, the Revolutionary Committee, including Liebknecht (representing the KPD but unbeknownst to Luxemburg), issued a call to arms.[107] While the revolutionary leadership disagreed on a course of action, the government had no such misgivings, and sent in troops to crush the insurgents. In the face of this violence, factory delegates called for a new government, made up of representatives from the Majority and Independent Social Democrats and the Communist Party. The communists rejected such a move, while the M-SPD cynically capitalized on the desire for unity among socialist workers, and demonized the Spartacists (a label they used at will) as divisive terrorists.

At the same time, the real terrorists, the Noske Guard, set about systematically murdering the revolutionary leaders. On January 15 Luxemburg and Liebknecht were arrested and taken to the Guard headquarters at the Hotel Eden, where they were interrogated, beaten, and dealt blows to the head with rifle butts. Liebknecht was driven away and shot. Luxemburg's body was weighted and thrown into the canal, not to be found for several months. Less than two years earlier, from prison, she wrote to Sonja Liebknecht: "You know that, in spite of it all, I really hope to die at my post, in a street fight or in prison."[108]

With these murders, the KPD lost two vital leaders. Jogiches (who was by this time also in Germany) and most of the other leading communists soon met the same fate. Although the revolution continued for four more years, bereft of an effective leadership, it was to end in decisive defeat. This precipitated counterrevolution in isolated Russia, and the end of hopes for the internationalization of socialist revolution: "The fiasco of Germany's 'failed October' in 1923 was to mark a decisive turn in postwar history. At this pivotal point for Europe, the initiative passed back into the hands of the bourgeoisie, who were not to lose it again."[109]

Luxemburg's final essay, "Order Reigns in Berlin," places the events of January 1919 in the context of revolutionary history, and denounces the violence of counterrevolution. Her description of the massacre of the workers occupying *Vorwärts* is chillingly prescient of her own fate: "The massacred mediators, who wanted to negotiate the surrender of the *Vorwärts* and were beaten beyond recognition by rifle butts, so that their bodies could not even be identified; captives who were put up against the wall and murdered in a way that spattered their skulls and brains all over."[110] The article also reveals the clarity with which she understood the moment, describing the weakness of the revolutionary masses and their leadership in comparison to the ruthless determination of the counterrevolutionary forces arrayed against them. She goes on to draw out the lessons learned from each battle in the ongoing class struggle, including the defeats such as this one:

> The leadership failed. But the leadership can and must be created anew by the masses and out of the masses. The masses are the crucial factor; they are the rock on which the ultimate victory of the revolution will be built. The masses were up to the task. They fashioned this "defeat" into a part of those historical defeats which constitute the pride and power of international socialism. And that is why this "defeat" is the seed of the future triumph.[111]

This long-term perspective resonates with Luxemburg's earlier assertion that "the history of socialism is the school of life. We always derive new stimulation from it."[112] Luxemburg's life work remains richly relevant today. Indeed it is almost impossible not to see the current occupations of Afghanistan and Iraq in her description of a world at war in *The Junius Pamphlet*:

> Business is flourishing upon the ruins. Cities are turned into shambles, whole countries into deserts, villages into cemeteries, whole nations into beggars, churches into stables; popular rights, treaties, alliances, the holiest words and the highest authorities have been torn into scraps.... Shamed, dishonored, wading in blood and dripping with filth, thus capitalist society stands. Not as we usually see it, playing the roles of peace and righteousness, of order, of philosophy, of ethics—but as a roaring beast, as an orgy of anarchy, as a pestilential breath, devastating culture and humanity—so it appears in all its hideous nakedness.[113]

Global capitalism today *is* barbarism for huge sections of humanity, condemned to hunger, homelessness, perpetual war, and occupation. But the other side of globalization, the struggle for social justice, can also be seen: in the rebellion against neoliberalism in Latin America; in the mass May Day protests of immigrant workers in cities across the United States; in the continuing Palestinian resistance to Israeli occupation; in the growing antiwar sentiment of U.S. soldiers who return "home to find need and misery while billions are heaped up in the hands of a few capitalists."[114] And this is Luxemburg's most important lesson for today: "In this moment of armament lunacy and war orgies, only the resolute will to struggle of the working masses, their capacity and readiness for powerful mass actions, can maintain world peace and push away the menacing world conflagration."[115]

Helen Scott
September 2007

NOTES

1   Rosa Luxemburg, "The Russian Revolution," in Mary-Alice Waters, ed., *Rosa Luxemburg Speaks* (New York: Pathfinder, 1970), 290.
2   V. I. Lenin, "From 'Notes of a Publicist,'" in ibid., 440. Lenin wrote this in 1922, in response to what he saw as a misrepresentation through selective publication of Luxemburg's work by Paul Levi. Lenin acknowledges mistakes in some of Luxemburg's positions, but insists that her overall achievement was far greater than these errors.

3   Rosa Luxemburg, "The Mass Strike, the Political Party, and the Trade Unions," in ibid., 200.

4   Georg Lukács (1885–1971), Hungarian Communist, active in the Hungarian Commune of 1919 and exiled after its defeat. He is widely recognized for his theoretical contribution to dialectics in *History and Class Consciousness: Studies in Marxist Dialectics* (1922), trans. Rodney Livingstone (Cambridge, MA: MIT Press, 1971), 182.

5   Karl Marx, "The Poverty of Philosophy" (1847), in David McLellan, ed., *Karl Marx: Selected Writings* (Oxford: Oxford University Press, 1977), 195–213.

6   J. P. Nettl, *Rosa Luxemburg*, vol. I (London: Oxford University Press, 1966), 41.

7   Paul Frölich, *Rosa Luxemburg: Ideas in Action*, trans. Joanna Hoornweg (London: Pluto, 1972), 21.

8   Nettl, *Rosa Luxemburg*, vol. I, 43.

9   Waters, *Rosa Luxemburg Speaks*, 2; Frölich, *Rosa Luxemburg*, 25.

10 Luise Kautsky, "Remembering Rosa Luxemburg," in Paul Le Blanc, ed., *Rosa Luxemburg: Reflections and Writings* (Amherst, MA: Humanity Books, 1999), 34.

11 Frölich, *Rosa Luxemburg*, 28.

12 The Marxism of the *Communist Manifesto* and the First International differed from earlier varieties of socialism, such as the reformism of Lassalle and the utopianism of the Fabians: it developed a scientific method, historical materialism, that understood history as successive class struggles and analyzed social forms in terms of their underlying economic systems and class relationships. It identified the working class as the social force with not only the motive but also the power to wage a revolution that would replace capitalism with socialism.

13 Frölich, *Rosa Luxemburg*, 25.

14 George Plekhanov (1856–1918), often referred to as "the father of Russian Marxism," translated the *Communist Manifesto* into Russian, formed the Emancipation of Labor Group in Geneva, and pioneered Marxism throughout the Russian Empire.

15 Frölich, *Rosa Luxemburg*, 34.

16 Luxemburg's comrades smuggled her out with the help of a Catholic priest. They convinced him that "a Jewish girl had a burning desire to become a Christian, but could only do so abroad because of the vehement resistance of her relatives. Rosa Luxemburg played her part in the pious deception so adroitly that the priest rendered the necessary assistance. Hidden under straw in a peasant's cart, Rosa Luxemburg crossed the border to freedom" (Frölich, *Rosa Luxemburg*, 28; see also Nettl, *Rosa Luxemburg*, vol. I, 59).

17 Rosa Luxemburg, "The National Question and Autonomy," http://www.marxists.org/archive/luxemburg/1909/nationalquestion/ch05.htm.

18 Quoted in Frölich, *Rosa Luxemburg*, 30.

19 Nettl, *Rosa Luxemburg*, vol. I, 106.

20 Frölich, *Rosa Luxemburg*, 29.

21 Nettl, *Rosa Luxemburg*, vol. I, 78.

22 Paul Le Blanc, "Luxemburg and Lenin on Organization," in *Rosa Luxemburg: Reflections and Writings* (Amherst, NY: Humanity Books, 1999), 93.

23 Luxemburg, "The Nation State and the Proletariat," http://www.marxists.org/archive/luxemburg/1909/national-question/ch02.htm.

24 Luxemburg, "The Right of Nations to Self-Determination." http://www.marxists.org/archive/luxemburg/1909/nationalquestion/ch01.htm.

25 For example, she supported the national movement of the South Slavs against Turkish domination; Marx, on the other hand, had condemned the movement of the Slavs because in attacking Russia's lesser competitors it objectively strengthened the greater empire.

26 Tony Cliff, *Rosa Luxemburg* (London: Bookmarks, 1959, 1986), 61.

27 V. I. Lenin, "The Irish Rebellion of 1916," *Questions of National Policy and Proletarian Internationalism* (Moscow: Progress Publishers, 1964), 161.

28 V. I. Lenin, "The Specific and the General in the Position of the Dutch and Polish Social-Democrat Internationalists," ibid., 155.

29 It was difficult for foreign socialists, regarded by the German authorities as "little better than criminals," to obtain residency permits. Luxemburg thus entered into an arranged marriage with Gustav Lübeck, son of her friends Karl and Olympia, in 1897. The marriage was in name only, and they divorced five years later, but sometimes Luxemburg signed her name "Frau Gustav Lübeck." (Nettl, *Rosa Luxemburg*, vol. I, 109–110).

30 Carl E. Schorske, *German Social Democracy, 1905–1917: The Development of the Great Schism* (Cambridge, MA: Harvard University Press), 1.

31 The Lassalleaner—the General German Workers' Association of Ferdinand Lassalle, who believed socialism could be achieved through democratic reform and workers' cooperatives—and the Eisenacher—named for the 1869 meeting in Eisenach that had united August Bebel's Verband der Deutschen Arbeitervereine (German Workers' Association) and the social-democratic party of Wilhelm Liebknecht (father of Rosa Luxemburg's future ally Karl Liebknecht).

32 Otto von Bismarck, chancellor of the German empire from 1871–1890, sought to achieve and maintain Prussian supremacy within Europe, and the dominance of the Junkers within the German empire.

33 Pierre Broué, *The German Revolution 1917–1923*, 1971 trans. John Archer (Chicago: Haymarket Books, 2006), 17. Karl Kautsky (1854–1938) was considered the leading Marxist of the Second International, and for a long time was the defender of "orthodox" Marxism against revisionists.

34 Ibid., 7.

35 For further elaboration of this development, Schorske recommends the

work of Weber's student, sociologist Robert Michels's *Zur Soziologie des Parteiwesens in der modernen Demokratie* (Leipzig, 1910).

36 Le Blanc, *Rosa Luxemburg*, 15

37 Schorske, *German Social Democracy*, 64.

38 Waters, Introduction, *Rosa Luxemburg Speaks*, 5–6.

39 Ibid., 5.

40 Schorske, *German Social Democracy*, 21.

41 Quoted in Raya Dunayevskaya, *Rosa Luxemburg, Women's Liberation, and Marx's Philosophy of Revolution* (Urbana: University of Illinois Press, 1991), 90.

42 Frölich, *Rosa Luxemburg*, 57.

43 Quoted in Frölich, *Rosa Luxemburg*, 56–7.

44 Frölich, *Rosa Luxemburg*, 204.

45 Quoted in Frölich, *Rosa Luxemburg*, 205.

46 Schorske, *German Social Democracy*, 195.

47 Ibid., 122–145.

48 Nettl, *Rosa Luxemburg*, 304.

49 Frölich, *Rosa Luxemburg*, 126; Le Blanc, "Luxemburg and Lenin," 98.

50 Quoted in Frölich, *Rosa Luxemburg*, 117.

51 Quoted in ibid., 118.

52 Quoted in ibid.

53 Stephen E. Bronner, ed., *The Letters of Rosa Luxemburg* (Boulder, CO: Westview Press, 1978), 180.

54 The quotation is from *The Eighteenth Brumaire*, Marx's account, first published in 1852, of the rise of Louis Bonaparte. Its relevance for Luxemburg can be seen in Marx's account of his purpose in writing: to "demonstrate how the class struggle in France created circumstances and relationships that made it possible for a grotesque mediocrity to play a hero's part," Quoted in Robert C. Tucker, ed., *The Marx-Engels Reader*, 2nd ed. (New York: Norton, 1978), 594.

55 Bronner, *Letters of Rosa*, 116.

56 Ibid., 117.

57 Frölich, *Rosa Luxemburg*, 129; Nettl, *Rosa Luxemburg*, 349.

58 Quoted in Nettl, *Rosa Luxemburg*, 357.

59 Luxemburg here was out of line with the SPD leadership, who endorsed the Mensheviks; Luxemburg had in fact even before this raised some questions while formally supporting Bebel and Kautsky's anti-Bolshevik position.

60 Broué, *German Revolution*, 33.

61 Quoted in Dunayevskaya, *Rosa Luxemburg*, 61.

62 Waters, *Rosa Luxemburg Speaks*, 219. "What Is Economics?" is

reprinted in Waters, *Rosa Luxemburg Speaks*, 219–249.

63 She responded to criticisms of her work in the 1915 *Anti-Critique*, published in 1921, which usefully elaborates the central theoretical elements more clearly than the original.

64 Rosa Luxemburg, *The Accumulation of Capital* (1913), trans. Agnes Schwarzschild (London: Routledge, 2003), 328–329, 345.

65 Ibid., 433. The quotation is from the description of capitalism's beginnings in the chapter "The Genesis of the Industrial Capitalist" in Karl Marx, *Capital* , vol. I (1867) (New York: Vintage, 1977), 926. The full quote reads: "If money, according to Augier, 'comes into the world with a congenital blood-stain on one cheek,' capital comes dripping from head to toe, from every pore, with blood and dirt."

66 For a helpful summary of Luxemburg's argument and subsequent debates, see Anthony Brewer, *Marxist Theories of Imperialism: A Critical Survey* (London: Routledge, 1980), 61–76.

67 Paul Le Blanc, "The Challenge of Revolutionary Democracy in the Life and Thought of Rosa Luxemburg," MRZine.org (March 14, 2006) http://mrzine.monthlyreview.org/leblanc140306.html.

68 Nettl, *Rosa Luxemburg*, 398–9.

69 Quoted in Schorske, *German Social Democracy*, 83; Nettl, *Rosa Luxemburg*, 399.

70 Quoted in Nettl, *Rosa Luxemburg*, 399.

71 John Riddell, ed., *The Communist International in Lenin's Time: Lenin's Struggle for a Revolutionary International, Documents: 1907–1917; The Preparatory Years* (New York: Monad Press, 1984), 10–11.

72 Schorske, *German Social Democracy*, 123–4.

73 Increasing trade-union hegemony over SPD political positions played a significant role in the party's conservatization, as will be discussed in the introduction to *The Mass Strike*.

74 Reprinted in English as "The Next Step" in Robert Looker, ed., *Rosa Luxemburg: Selected Political Writings* (New York: Grove Press, 1974), 148–159. It has also been translated variously as "What Further?," "What More?," and "What Now?" See Dunayevskaya, *Rosa Luxemburg*, 29, n4.

75 Dunayevskaya, *Rosa Luxemburg*, 20–21.

76 Quoted in Frölich, *Rosa Luxemburg*, 181.

77 Lenin at the time sided with Kautsky, but subsequently acknowledged Luxemburg's perspicacity in identifying the depth of corruption within the party in general and with Kautsky in particular. In a letter of October 1914 he wrote "Rosa Luxemburg was right. She realized long ago that Kautsky was a time-serving theorist, serving the majority of the party, serving opportunism in short." Quoted in Nettl, *Rosa Luxemburg*, 626.

78 The leaders of the revolutionaries were Luxemburg, Clara Zetkin, Franz Mehring, Karl Liebknecht, Karski (Julian Marchlewski), Karl Radek, and Anton Pannekoek. See Frölich, *Rosa Luxemburg*, 182.

79 Chris Harman, *The Lost Revolution: Germany 1918–1923* (London: Bookmarks, 1982), 20.

80 Rosa Luxemburg, "Concerning Morocco," in Robert Looker, *Rosa Luxemburg,* 166.

81 Schorske, *German Social Democracy,* 198.

82 Brewer, *Marxist Theories,* 123.

83 Rosa Luxemburg, "Peace Utopias," in Waters, *Rosa Luxemburg Speaks,* 252.

84 Lenin's work of 1916 refuted Kautsky's theory of "ultra-imperialism," a systematization of the centrist idea that capitalism could dispense with imperialist wars. Kautsky's argument was published shortly before the outbreak of World War One. V. I. Lenin, *Imperialism: The Highest Stage of Capitalism, a Popular Outline* (1916) (New York: International Publishers, 1939), and Karl Kautsky, *Ultra Imperialism* (1914), *New Left Review* 59 (January–February 1970).

85 Frölich, *Rosa Luxemburg,* 183; see also Schorske, *German Social Democracy,* 263–4.

86 Quoted in Schorske, *German Social Democracy,* 266–7.

87 Luxemburg, "Rebuilding the International," in Le Blanc, *Rosa Luxemburg,* 202.

88 Schorske, *German Social Democracy,* 293.

89 Social-democratic parties in Poland, Russia, Serbia, Italy, Bulgaria, and the United States were the exception to the rule: they all renounced chauvinism and upheld the principle of international class solidarity.

90 Named after Spartacus, the legendary leader of a slave rebellion against the Roman Empire in the first century BC.

91 Junius was the pen name used by the anonymous critic of King George III whose letters, published in the 1760s and 1770s, famously attacked the corruption of the English regime. It is assumed that the author took the name from Lucius Junius Brutus, known as the founder of the Roman Republic.

92 Quoted in Frölich, *Rosa Luxemburg,* 234.

93 Dunayevskaya, *Rosa Luxemburg,* 68.

94 Rosa Luxemburg, *Junius Pamphlet,* in Waters, 257–331, 328.

95 Quoted in Paul Le Blanc, "Remembering Rosa Luxemburg," *Rosa Luxemburg: Reflections and Writings,* 50.

96 Schorske, *German Social Democracy,* 90.

97 Harman, *Lost Revolution,* 27.

98 Rosa Luxemburg, *The Russian Revolution,* in Peter Hudis and Kevin B. Anderson, eds., *The Rosa Luxemburg Reader* (New York: Monthly Review Press, 2004), 287.

99 Ibid., 309.

100 However, when the question of the Constituent Assembly arose during the German Revolution, Luxemburg reassessed her judgment on this

issue. See Frölich, *Rosa Luxemburg*, 252.

101 Broué points out that the split was not between reformists and revolutionaries but rather between different reformists, with the revolutionaries on the expelled side: 170,000 stayed with the M-SPD and 120,000 left. The USPD now contained radically different political figures, including Liebknecht, Luxemburg, Kautsky, Hilferding, and Bernstein.

102 Broué, *German Revolution*, 100.

103 Frölich, *Rosa Luxemburg*, 267.

104 Frölich, *Rosa Luxemburg*, 269.

105 Lenin's *"Left Wing" Communism, an Infantile Disorder* (1920) (London: Bookmarks, 1993), explains why the German communists' abstention from the Constituent Assembly and the unions was disastrous, and contrasts the behavior of the German communists with that of the Bolsheviks.

106 Quoted in Broué, *German Revolution*, 241. Erich Ludendorff (1865–1937) was chief of staff under General Paul von Hindenburg (1847–1934) during World War One. In "What Does the Spartacus League Want?" Luxemburg names both as "chief criminals responsible for starting and prolonging the war" (in Hudis and Anderson, *Rosa Luxemburg Reader*, 349–356). Forced out of the country during the revolution, he returned and became the first Nazi party member of the Reichstag in 1924.

107 On hearing that Liebknecht put his signature to the call to arms, Luxemburg, according to Paul Levi, "said that it would no longer be possible to go on working [with him] in future." (Broué, *German Revolution*, 253). Nettl reports that "Rosa taxed Liebknecht with the following reproach when he returned to the party offices after one meeting of the Revolutionary Executive: 'But Karl, how could you, and what about our programme?'" (Nettl, *Rosa Luxemburg*, vol. II, 767).

108 Repr. in Hudis and Anderson, *Rosa Luxemburg Reader*, 390.

109 Broué, *German Revolution*, 899.

110 Rosa Luxemburg, "Order Reigns in Berlin," in Hudis and Anderson, *Rosa Luxemburg Reader*, 374.

111 Ibid., 378.

112 Speech to the Nürnberg Congress (1908), in Dick Howard, *Selected Political Writings of Rosa Luxemburg* (New York: Monthly Review Press, 1971), 279–282.

113 Rosa Luxemburg, *Junius Pamphlet*, in Waters, *Rosa Luxemburg Speaks*, 262.

114 Rosa Luxemburg, "To the Proletarians of All Countries," first published *Rote Fahne*, November 25, 1918, in Howard, *Selected Political Writings of Rosa Luxemburg* (New York: Monthly Review Press, 1971), 352–356.

115 Rosa Luxemburg, "The Idea of May Day on the March," first published *Leipziger Volkszeitung*, April 30, 1913, in Howard, *Selected Political Writings*, 317–321.

INTRODUCTION TO
REFORM OR REVOLUTION

The debate around reformism was named for its primary spokesperson, and the main target of Luxemburg's *Reform or Revolution*, Eduard Bernstein.[1] Born in 1850, Bernstein joined the Eisenacher in 1872 and edited the illegal paper *Sozialdemokrat* during the period of the antisocialist laws.[2] Exiled in England, he developed a close relationship with Friedrich Engels, and was also influenced by leaders of the Fabians and trade unions.[3] From 1896 to 1898 Bernstein wrote a series of articles that were published in *Neue Zeit* under the title "Problems of Socialism," and then, in 1899, a book, *Die Voraussetzungen des Sozialismus und die Aufgaben der Sozialdemokratie* (The Presuppositions of Socialism and the Tasks of Social Democracy), published in English as *Evolutionary Socialism*.[4]

Bernstein did not explicitly launch an assault on Marx, rather he claimed to be updating him for a new period in which capitalism offered peace, prosperity, and ever-widening democracy to the working class, and obviated revolution. Acting as one of the literary executors after his death, Bernstein yoked Engels into the reformist project. Engels's final work was an introduction to Marx's *Class Struggles in France*, which argued for a changed tactic in revolutionary struggle: "Future insurrections would have to take on a very different character, and be carried out by large masses of the people in a stormy offensive against the military forces of the enemy."[5] The SPD executive, worried that the essay would provoke repression from the German government, secretly edited out all references to revolutionary violence, and this was to become "the 'Testament of Friedrich Engels': a condemnation of all forms of violence and of all future revolutions, and a glorification of legality."[6]

In keeping with the habit of the SPD to compromise, balance, and avoid open disagreements, the party leadership, even those who did not endorse his ideas, were content to leave Bernstein unchallenged. Parvus launched a series of articles against him in *Sächsische Arbeiterzeitung*.[7] But otherwise, "[t]he task of clarifying the relationship between the reformist tactic and the revolutionary goal of the party fell to a newcomer to German Social Democracy: Rosa Luxemburg."[8] Fresh from the mines and factories of Upper Silesia, Luxemburg saw that Bernstein was out of touch with the real conditions of workers, and also that his theories represented a fundamental and pernicious challenge to socialism that had to be confronted and rejected. She published two series of articles in *Leipziger Volkszeitung* in September 1898 and April 1899, which were collected as Part I of *Social Reform or Revolution* in 1899; Part II consisted of a response to Bernstein's book. A second, single edition of *Reform or Revolution* was published in 1908; this work, translated into English by Integer in 1937, is reproduced here.

When Luxemburg spoke out against Bernstein in the 1898 party congress, some in the establishment disparaged her for being young and a woman. One critic opened an assault with the sarcastic phrase, "One should always be polite to ladies."[9] Luxemburg pointed out that ad hominem attacks are the last resort of indefensible positions. Her response to Georg von Vollmar, ex-army officer, leader of the Bavarian party, and spokesperson for southern reformism, is typical: "If . . . Vollmar comes with the specious argument—'you greenhorn . . . I could be your grandfather,' then we can only take this as evidence that he must be on his last legs for more concrete arguments (laughter)."[10]

Luxemburg won the argument with Bernstein: resolutions against reformism passed at the congresses of 1899, 1901, and 1903, and at the International Congress of 1904. Even Bernstein voted against his position! But this victory only masked the growing dominance of revisionism within the SPD establishment. After the electoral success of 1903 Bernstein and other revisionists recommended a policy of appealing to the middle class and cooperating with Liberals in the Reichstag.[11] And in many ways Bernstein was correct in arguing that his position was in keeping with the *practice* of the SPD.[12] The leadership became dominated by the unprincipled advocates of what Luxemburg called "practical politics."[13] The opposition between revolutionaries and reformists formed the backdrop of party debates over the mass strike, the weight of the trade unions, the Russian revolution of 1905, and beyond, to the questions of militarism and imperialism that split the party in 1914.

Bernstein returned to Germany in 1901 and was elected to Parliament in 1902. He voted for war credits on August 4, 1914, joined the USPD in 1917, and reverted to the SPD at the end of the war, living until 1932.[14] Luxemburg became a key leader of the revolutionary wing of social democracy that was to become the German Communist Party (KPD), until she was murdered on the order of reformists in January 1919. Her *Reform or Revolution* has been an inspiring document for generations of revolutionaries, and continues to offer a devastating critique of the idea that capitalism can be reformed to provide global peace and prosperity.

Helen Scott

NOTES

1   Luxemburg also names Konrad Schmidt (1865–1932), who was another leading reformist and editor of the revisionist journal *Sozialistische Monatshefte*.

2   See footnote 31 of the general introduction.

3   The Fabians from 1884 (and to the present time: the Fabians are still active in the UK) advocated democratic socialism through debate, education, and persuasion of capitalist politicians. They are named for the Roman general nicknamed "the delayer," who argued against direct military confrontation in favor of gradual attrition.

4   Eduard Bernstein, *Evolutionary Socialism*, trans. Edith C. Harvey (New York: Schocken, 1961).

5   Frölich, *Rosa Luxemburg*, 63.

6   Ibid.

7   Parvus was the pseudonym of Alexander Helphand (1867–1924), a Russian revolutionary who was with the left wing of German social democracy and for many years an ally of Luxemburg. After Parvus and Julian Marchlewski were expelled by the royal government of Saxony, Luxemburg took up the editorship of *Sächsische Arbeiterzeitung*. Luxemburg broke with Parvus when he declared his support for Germany at the outbreak of World War One.

8   Schorske, *German Social Democracy*, 21.

9   Quoted in Nettl, *Rosa Luxemburg*, vol. I, 153.

10 Quoted in ibid., 152.

11 Schorske, *German Social Democracy*, 23.

12 Hudis and Anderson, *Rosa Luxemburg Reader*, 11.

13 Robert Looker, Introduction, *Selected Political Writings of Rosa Luxemburg* (New York: Grove Press, 1974), 36–7.

14 Howard, *Selected Political Writings*, 420.

REFORM OR REVOLUTION

INTRODUCTION

A t first view the title of this work may be found surprising. Can the social democracy be against reforms? Can we counterpose the social revolution, the transformation of the existing order, our final goal, to social reforms? Certainly not. The daily struggle for reforms, for the amelioration of the condition of the workers within the framework of the existing social order, and for democratic institutions, offers to the social democracy the only means of engaging in the proletarian class war and working in the direction of the final goal—the conquest of political power and the suppression of wage labor. Between social reforms and revolution there exists for the social democracy an indissoluble tie. The struggle for reforms is its means; the social revolution, its aim.

It is in Eduard Bernstein's theory, presented in his articles on "Problems of Socialism," *Neue Zeit* of 1897–98, and in his book *Die Voraussetzungen des Sozialismus and die Aufgaben der Sozialdemokratie* [The Preconditions of Socialism and the Tasks of Social Democracy—in English published under the title *Evolutionary Socialism*—Ed.] that we find for the first time, the opposition of the two factors of the labor movement. His theory tends to counsel us to renounce the social transformation, the final goal of the social democracy and, inversely, to make of social reforms, the means of the class struggle, its aim. Bernstein himself has very clearly and characteristically formulated this viewpoint when he wrote: "The final goal, no matter what it is, is nothing; the movement is everything."

But since the final goal of socialism constitutes the only decisive factor distinguishing the social democratic movement from bourgeois democracy and from bourgeois radicalism, the only factor transforming the entire labor movement from a vain effort to repair the capitalist order into a class struggle against this order, for the suppression of this order—the question: "Reform or revolution?" as it is posed by Bernstein, equals for the social democracy the question: "To be or not to be?" In the controversy with Bernstein and his followers, everybody in the party ought to understand clearly it is not a question of this or that method of struggle, or the use of this or that set of tactics, but of the very existence of the social democratic movement.

Upon a casual consideration of Bernstein's theory, this may appear like an exaggeration. Does he not continually mention the social democracy and its aims? Does he not repeat again and again, in very explicit language, that he too strives toward the final goal of socialism, but in another way? Does he not stress particularly that he fully approves of the present practice of the social democracy?

That is all true, to be sure. It is also true that every new movement, when it first elaborates its theory and policy, begins by finding support in the preceding movement, though it may be in direct contradiction with the latter. It begins by suiting itself to the forms found at hand and by speaking the language spoken hereto. In time, the new grain breaks through the old husk. The new movement finds its forms and its own language.

To expect an opposition against scientific socialism at its very beginning, to express itself clearly, fully, and to the last consequence on the subject of its real content; to expect it to deny openly and bluntly the theoretic basis of the social democracy—would amount to underrating the power of scientific socialism. Today he who wants to pass as a socialist, and at the same time declare war on Marxian doctrine, the most stupendous product of the human mind in the century, must begin with involuntary esteem for Marx. He must begin by acknowledging himself to be his disciple, by seeking in Marx's own teachings the points of support for an attack on the latter, while he represents this attack as a further development of Marxian doctrine. On this account, we must, unconcerned by its outer forms, pick out the sheathed kernel of Bernstein's theory. This is a matter of urgent necessity for the broad layers of the industrial proletariat in our party.

No coarser insult, no baser aspersion, can be thrown against the workers than the remark: "Theoretic controversies are only for academicians." Some time ago Lassalle* said: "Only when science and the workers, these opposite poles of society, become one, will they crush in their arms of steel all obstacles to culture." The entire strength of the modern labor movement rests on theoretical knowledge.

But doubly important is this knowledge for the workers in the present case, because it is precisely they and their influence in the movement that are in the balance here. It is their skin that is being brought to market. The opportunist theory in the party, the theory formulated by Bernstein, is nothing else than an unconscious attempt to assure predominance to the petty bourgeois elements that have entered our party, to change the policy and aims of our party in their direction. The question of reform and revolution, of the final goal and the movement, is basically, in another form, but the question of the petty bourgeois or proletarian character of the labor movement.

It is, therefore, in the interest of the proletarian mass of the party to become acquainted, actively and in detail, with the present theoretical controversy with opportunism. As long as theoretical knowledge remains the privilege of a handful of "academicians" in the party, the latter will face the danger of going astray. Only when the great mass of workers take the keen and dependable weapons of scientific socialism in their own hands will all the petty bourgeois inclinations, all the opportunistic currents, come to naught. The movement will then find itself on sure and firm ground. "Quantity will do it."

PART I

THE OPPORTUNIST METHOD

If it is true that theories are only the images of the phenomena of the exterior world in the human consciousness, it must be added, concerning Eduard Bernstein's system, that theories are sometimes inverted images. Think of a theory of instituting socialism by means of social reforms in the face of the complete stagnation of the reform

---

* Ferdinand Lassalle (1825–1864) was the founder in 1863 of Germany's first socialist party, the General Association of German Workers, which merged with Bebel and Liebknecht's Eisenach group to form the SPD at Gotha in 1875. —H.S.

movement in Germany. Think of a theory of trade-union control over production in face of the defeat of the metal workers in England. Consider the theory of winning a majority in Parliament, after the revision of the constitution of Saxony and in view of the most recent attempts against universal suffrage. However, the pivotal point of Bernstein's system is not located in his conception of the practical tasks of the social democracy. It is found in his stand on the course of the objective development of capitalist society, which, in turn, is closely bound to his conception of the practical tasks of the social democracy.

According to Bernstein, a general decline of capitalism seems to be increasingly improbable because, on the one hand, capitalism shows a greater capacity of adaptation, and, on the other hand, capitalist production becomes more and more varied.

The capacity of capitalism to adapt itself, says Bernstein, is manifested first in the disappearance of general crises, resulting from the development of the credit system, employers' organizations, wider means of communication, and informational services. It shows itself secondly in the tenacity of the middle classes, which hails from the growing differentiation of the branches of production and the elevation of vast layers of the proletariat to the level of the middle class. It is furthermore proved, argues Bernstein, by the amelioration of the economic and political situation of the proletariat as a result of its trade-union activity.

From this theoretic stand is derived the following general conclusion about the practical work of the social democracy. The latter must not direct its daily activity toward the conquest of political power, but toward the betterment of the condition of the working class within the existing order. It must not expect to institute socialism as a result of a political and social crisis, but should build socialism by means of the progressive extension of social control and the gradual application of the principle of cooperation.

Bernstein himself sees nothing new in his theories. On the contrary, he believes them to be in agreement with certain declarations of Marx and Engels. Nevertheless, it seems to us that it is difficult to deny that they are in formal contradiction with the conceptions of scientific socialism.

If Bernstein's revisionism merely consisted in affirming that the march of capitalist development is slower than was thought before, he would merely be presenting an argument for adjourning the conquest of power by the proletariat, on which everybody agreed up to now. Its only consequence would be a slowing up of the pace of the struggle.

But that is not the case. What Bernstein questions is not the rapidity of the development of capitalist society, but the march of the development itself and, consequently, the very possibility of a change to socialism.

Socialist theory up to now declared that the point of departure for a transformation to socialism would be a general and catastrophic crisis. We must distinguish in this outlook two things: the fundamental idea and its exterior form.

The fundamental idea consists of the affirmation that capitalism, as a result of its own inner contradictions, moves toward a point when it will be unbalanced, when it will simply become impossible. There were good reasons for conceiving that juncture in the form of a catastrophic general commercial crisis. But that is of secondary importance when the fundamental idea is considered.

The scientific basis of socialism rests, as is well known, on three principal results of capitalist development. First, on the growing anarchy of capitalist economy, leading inevitably to its ruin. Second, on the progressive socialization of the process of production, which creates the germs of the future social order. And third, on the increased organization and consciousness of the proletarian class, which constitutes the active factor in the coming revolution.

Bernstein pulls away from the first of the three fundamental supports of scientific socialism. He says that capitalist development does not lead to a general economic collapse.

He does not merely reject a certain form of the collapse. He rejects the very possibility of collapse. He says textually: "One could claim that by collapse of the present society is meant something else than a general commercial crisis, worse than all others, that is a complete collapse of the capitalist system brought about as a result of its own contradictions." And to this he replies: "With the growing development of society a complete and almost general collapse of the present system of production becomes more and more improbable, because capitalist development increases on the one hand the capacity of adaptation and, on the other—that is at the same time, the differentiation of industry." (*Neue Zeit*, 1897–98, vol. 18, 555)

But then the question arises: why and how, in that case, shall we attain the final goal? According to scientific socialism, the historic necessity of the socialist revolution manifests itself above all in the growing anarchy of capitalism, which drives the system into an impasse. But if one admits with Bernstein that capitalist development does not move in the direction of its own ruin, then socialism ceases to be objectively necessary. There remain the other two mainstays of the scientific explanation of socialism, which are also said to be consequences of capitalism itself: the socialization of the process of production and the growing consciousness of the proletariat. It is these two matters that Bernstein has in mind when he says: "The suppression of the theory of collapse does not in any way deprive socialist doctrine of the power of persuasion. For, examined closely, what are all factors enumerated by us that make for the suppression or the modification of the former crises? Nothing else, in fact, than the conditions, or even in part the germs of the socialization of production and exchange." (Ibid., 554)

Very little reflection is needed to understand that here, too, we face a false conclusion. Where lies the importance of all the phenomena that are said by Bernstein to be the means of capitalist adaptation—cartels, the credit system, the development of means of communication, the amelioration of the situation of the working class, etc.? Obviously, in that they suppress or, at least, attenuate the internal contradictions of capitalist economy, and stop the development or the aggravation of these contradictions. Thus the suppression of crises can only mean the suppression of the antagonism between production and exchange on the capitalist base. The amelioration of the situation of the working class, or the penetration of certain fractions of the class into the middle layers, can only mean the attenuation of the antagonism between capital and labor. But if the aforementioned factors suppress the capitalist contradictions and consequently save the system from ruin, if they enable capitalism to maintain itself—and that is why Bernstein calls them "means of adaptation"—how can cartels, the credit system, trade unions, etc., be at the same time "the conditions and even, in part, the germs" of socialism? Obviously only in the sense that they express most clearly the social character of production.

But by presenting it in its capitalist form, the same factors render superfluous, inversely, in the same measure, the transformation of this socialized production into socialist production. That is why they can be the germs or conditions of a socialist order only in a theoretical sense and not in a historic sense. They are phenomena which, in the light of our conception of socialism, we know to be related to socialism but which, in fact, not only do not lead to a socialist revolution but render it, on the contrary, superfluous.

There remains one force making for socialism—the class consciousness of the proletariat. But it, too, is in the given case not the
simple intellectual reflection of the growing contradictions of capitalism and its approaching decline. It is now no more than an ideal
whose force of persuasion rests only on the perfection attributed to it.

We have here, in brief, the explanation of the socialist program by
means of "pure reason." We have here, to use simpler language, an
idealist explanation of socialism. The objective necessity of socialism,
the explanation of socialism as the result of the material development
of society, falls to the ground.

Revisionist theory thus places itself in a dilemma. Either the socialist transformation is, as was admitted up to now, the consequence
of the internal contradictions of capitalism, and with the growth of
capitalism will develop its inner contradictions, resulting inevitably,
at some point, in its collapse (in that case the "means of adaptation"
are ineffective and the theory of collapse is correct); or the "means of
adaptation" really will stop the collapse of the capitalist system and
thereby enable capitalism to maintain itself by suppressing its own
contradictions. In that case socialism ceases to be a historic necessity.
It then becomes anything you want to call it, but it is no longer the
result of the material development of society.

The dilemma leads to another. Either revisionism is correct in its
position on the course of capitalist development, and therefore the
socialist transformation of society is only a utopia, or socialism is not
a utopia, and the theory of "means of adaptation" is false. There is
the question in a nutshell.

THE ADAPTATION OF CAPITAL

According to Bernstein, the credit system, the perfected means of
communication, and the new capitalist combines are the important
factors that forward the adaptation of capitalist economy.

Credit has diverse applications in capitalism. Its two most important
functions are to extend production and to facilitate exchange. When the
inner tendency of capitalist production to extend boundlessly strikes
against the restricted dimensions of private property, credit appears as a

means of surmounting these limits in a particular capitalist manner. Credit, through shareholding, combines in one magnitude of capital a large number of individual capitals. It makes available to each capitalist the use of other capitalists' money—in the form of industrial credit. As commercial credit it accelerates the exchange of commodities and therefore the return of capital into production, and thus aids the entire cycle of the process of production. The manner in which these two principal functions of credit influence the formation of crises is quite obvious. If it is true that crises appear as a result of the contradiction existing between the capacity of extension, the tendency of production to increase, and the restricted consumption capacity of the market, credit is precisely, in view of what was stated above, the specific means that makes this contradiction break out as often as possible. To begin with, it increases disproportionately the capacity of the extension of production and thus constitutes an inner motive force that is constantly pushing production to exceed the limits of the market. But credit strikes from two sides. After having (as a factor of the process of production) provoked overproduction, credit (as a factor of exchange) destroys, during the crisis, the very productive forces it itself created. At the first symptom of the crisis, credit melts away. It abandons exchange where it would still be found indispensable, and appearing instead ineffective and useless, there where some exchange still continues, it reduces to a minimum the consumption capacity of the market.

Besides having these two principal results, credit also influences the formation of crises in the following ways. It constitutes the technical means of making available to an entrepreneur the capital of other owners. It stimulates at the same time the bold and unscrupulous utilization of the property of others. That is, it leads to speculation. Credit not only aggravates the crisis in its capacity as a dissembled means of exchange, it also helps to bring and extend the crisis by transforming all exchange into an extremely complex and artificial mechanism that, having a minimum of metallic money as a real base, is easily disarranged at the slightest occasion.

We see that credit, instead of being an instrument for the suppression or the attenuation of crises, is on the contrary a particularly mighty instrument for the formation of crises. It cannot be anything else. Credit eliminates the remaining rigidity of capitalist relationships. It introduces everywhere the greatest elasticity possible. It renders all capitalist forces extensible, relative, and mutually sensitive to the highest degree. Doing this, it facilitates and aggravates crises, which are nothing more or less than the periodic collisions of the contradictory forces of capitalist economy.

That leads us to another question. Why does credit generally have the appearance of a "means of adaptation" of capitalism? No matter what the relation or form in which this "adaptation" is represented by certain people, it can obviously consist only of the power to suppress one of the several antagonistic relations of capitalist economy, that is, of the power to suppress or weaken one of these contradictions, and allow liberty of movement, at one point or another, to the other fettered productive forces. In fact, it is precisely credit that aggravates these contradictions to the highest degree. It aggravates the antagonism between the mode of production and the mode of exchange by stretching production to the limit and at the same time paralyzing exchange at the smallest pretext. It aggravates the antagonism between the mode of production and the mode of appropriation by separating production from ownership, that is, by transforming the capital employed in production into "social" capital and at the same time transforming a part of the profit, in the form of interest on capital, into a simple title of ownership. It aggravates the antagonism existing between the property relations (ownership) and the relations of production by putting into a small number of hands immense productive forces and expropriating a large number of small capitalists. Lastly, it aggravates the antagonism existing between the social character of production and private capitalist ownership by rendering necessary the intervention of the state in production.

In short, credit reproduces all the fundamental antagonisms of the capitalist world. It accentuates them. It precipitates their development and thus pushes the capitalist world forward to its own destruction. The prime act of capitalist adaptation, as far as credit is concerned, should really consist in breaking and suppressing credit. In fact, credit is far from being a means of capitalist adaptation. It is, on the contrary, a means of destruction of the most extreme revolutionary significance. Has not this revolutionary character of credit actually inspired plans of "socialist" reform? As such, it has had some distinguished proponents, some of whom (Isaac Pereira in France),* were, as Marx put it, half prophets, half rogues.

---

* Isaac Péreira (1806–1880) was a French bourgeois economist. —H.S.

Just as fragile is the second "means of adaptation": employers' organizations. According to Bernstein, such organizations will put an end to anarchy of production and do away with crises through their regulation of production. The multiple repercussions of the development of cartels and trusts have not been considered too carefully up to now. But they represent a problem that can only be solved with the aid of Marxist theory.

One thing is certain. We could speak of a damming up of capitalist anarchy through the agency of capitalist combines only in the measure that cartels, trusts, etc., become, even approximately, the dominant form of production. But such a possibility is excluded by the very nature of cartels. The final economic aim and result of combines is the following. Through the suppression of competition in a given branch of production, the distribution of the mass of profit realized on the market is influenced in such a manner that there is an increase of the share going to this branch of industry. Such organization of the field can increase the rate of profit in one branch of industry at the expense of another. That is precisely why it cannot be generalized, for when it is extended to all important branches of industry, this tendency suppresses its own influence.

Furthermore, within the limits of their practical application the result of combines is the very opposite of suppression of industrial anarchy. Cartels ordinarily succeed in obtaining an increase of profit in the home market by producing at a lower rate of profit for the foreign market, thus utilizing the supplementary portions of capital that they cannot utilize for domestic needs. That is to say, they sell abroad cheaper than at home. The result is the sharpening of competition abroad—the very opposite of what certain people want to find. That is well demonstrated by the history of the world sugar industry.

Generally speaking, combines, treated as a manifestation of the capitalist mode of production, can only be considered a definite phase of capitalist development. Cartels are fundamentally nothing else than a means resorted to by the capitalist mode of production for the purpose of holding back the fatal fall of the rate of profit in certain branches of production. What method do cartels employ for this end? That of keeping inactive a part of the accumulated capital. That is, they use the same method that in another form is employed in crises. The remedy and the illness resemble each other like two drops of water. Indeed the first can be considered the lesser evil only up to a certain point. When the outlets of disposal begin to shrink, and the world market has been extended to its limit and has become exhausted through the competition of the capitalist countries—and sooner or later that is bound to come—then the forced partial idleness of capital will reach such dimensions that the remedy will become transformed into a malady, and capital, already pretty much "socialized" through regulation, will tend to revert again to the form of individual capital. In the face of the increased difficulties of finding markets, each individual portion of capital will prefer to take its chances alone. At that time, the large regulating organizations will burst like soap bubbles and give way to aggravated competition.*

In a general way, cartels, just like credit, appear therefore as a determined phase of capitalist development, which in the last analysis aggravates the anarchy of the capitalist world and expresses and ripens its internal contradictions. Cartels aggravate the antagonism existing between the mode of production and exchange by sharpening the struggle between the producer and consumer, as is the case especially in the United States. They aggravate, furthermore, the antagonism existing between the mode of production and the mode of appropriation by opposing, in the most brutal fashion, to the working class the superior force of organized capital, and thus increasing the antagonism between capital and labor.

---

* In a note to the third volume of *Capital*, Engels wrote in 1894: "Since the above was written (1865), competition on the world-market has been considerably intensified by the rapid development of industry in all civilized countries, especially in America and Germany. The fact that the rapidly and enormously growing productive forces grow beyond the control of the laws of the capitalist mode of exchanging commodities, inside of which they are supposed to move, this fact impresses itself nowadays more and more even on the minds of the capitalists. This is shown especially by two symptoms. First, by the new and general mania for a protective tariff, which differs from the old protectionism especially by the fact that now the articles which are capable of being exported are the best protected. In the second place it is shown by the trusts of manufacturers of whole spheres of production for the regulation of production, and thus of prices and profits. It goes without saying that these experiments are practicable only so long as the economic weather is relatively favorable. The first storm must upset them and prove, that, although production assuredly needs regulation, it is certainly not the capitalist class which is fitted for that task. Meanwhile the trusts have no other mission but to see to it that the little fish are swallowed by the big fish still more rapidly than before." —R.L.

Finally, capitalist combinations aggravate the contradiction existing between the international character of capitalist world economy and the national character of the state—insofar as they are always accompanied by a general tariff war, which sharpens the differences among the capitalist states. We must add to this the decidedly revolutionary influence exercised by cartels on the concentration of production, technical progress, etc.

In other words, when evaluated from the angle of their final effect on capitalist economy, cartels and trusts fail as "means of adaptation." They fail to attenuate the contradictions of capitalism. On the contrary, they appear to be an instrument of greater anarchy. They encourage the further development of the internal contradictions of capitalism. They accelerate the coming of a general decline of capitalism.

But if the credit system, cartels, and the rest do not suppress the anarchy of capitalism, why have we not had a major commercial crisis for two decades, since 1873? Is this not a sign that, contrary to Marx's analysis, the capitalist mode of production has adapted itself—at least, in a general way—to the needs of society? Hardly had Bernstein rejected, in 1898, Marx's theory of crises when a profound general crisis broke out in 1900, while seven years later, a new crisis, beginning in the United States, hit the world market. Facts proved the theory of "adaptation" to be false. They showed at the same time that the people who abandoned Marx's theory of crisis only because no crisis occurred within a certain space of time merely confused the essence of this theory with one of its secondary exterior aspects—the ten-year cycle. The description of the cycle of modern capitalist industry as a ten-year period was to Marx and Engels, in 1860 and 1870, only a simple statement of facts. It was not based on a natural law but on a series of given historic circumstances that were connected with the rapidly spreading activity of young capitalism.

The crisis of 1825 was, in effect, the result of extensive investment of capital in the construction of roads, canals, and gas works, which took place during the preceding decade, particularly in England, where the crisis broke out. The following crisis of 1836–1839 was similarly the result of heavy investments in the construction of means of transportation. The crisis of 1847 was provoked by the feverish building of railroads in England (from 1844 to 1847, in three years, the British Parliament gave railway concessions to the value of 15 billion dollars). In each of the three mentioned cases, a crisis came after new bases for capitalist development were established. In 1857, the same result was brought by the abrupt opening of new markets for European industry in America and Australia, after the discovery of the gold mines, and the extensive construction of railway lines especially in France, where the example of England was then closely imitated. (From 1852 to 1856, new railway lines to the value of 1,250 million francs were built in France alone.) And finally we have the great crisis of 1873—a direct consequence of the first boom of large industry in Germany and Austria, which followed the political events of 1866 and 1871.

So that up to now, the sudden extension of the domain of capitalist economy, and not its shrinking, was each time the cause of the commercial crisis. That the international crises repeated themselves precisely every ten years was a purely exterior fact, a matter of chance. The Marxist formula for crises as presented by Engels in *Anti-Dühring* and by Marx in the first and third volumes of *Capital*, applies to all crises only in the measure that it uncovers their international mechanism and their general basic causes.

Crises may repeat themselves every five or ten years, or even every eight or twenty years. But what proves best the falseness of Bernstein's theory is that it is in the countries having the greatest development of the famous "means of adaptation"—credit, perfected communications, and trusts—that the last crisis (1907–1908) was most violent.

The belief that capitalist production could "adapt" itself to exchange presupposes one of two things: either the world market can spread unlimitedly, or on the contrary, the development of the productive forces is so fettered that it cannot pass beyond the bounds of the market. The first hypothesis constitutes a material impossibility. The second is rendered just as impossible by the constant technical progress that daily creates new productive forces in all branches.

There remains still another phenomenon that, says Bernstein, contradicts the course of capitalist development as it is indicated above. In the "steadfast phalanx" of middle-size enterprises, Bernstein sees a sign that the development of large industry does not move in a revolutionary direction, and is not as effective from the angle of the concentration of industry as was expected by the "theory" of collapse. He is here, however, the victim of his own lack of understanding. For to see the progressive disappearance of the middle-sized enterprise as a necessary result of the development of large industry is to misunderstand sadly the nature of this process.

According to Marxist theory, small capitalists play in the general course of capitalist development the role of pioneers of technical change. They possess that role in a double sense. They initiate new methods of production in well-established branches of industry; they are instrumental in the creation of new branches of production not yet exploited by the big capitalist.

It is false to imagine that the history of the middle-size capitalist establishments proceeds rectilinearly in the direction of their progressive disappearance. The course of this development is on the contrary purely dialectical and moves constantly among contradictions. The middle capitalist layers find themselves, just like the workers, under the influence of two antagonistic tendencies, one ascendant, the other descendant. In this case, the descendant tendency is the continued rise of the scale of production, which overflows periodically the dimensions of the average size parcels of capital and removes them repeatedly from the terrain of world competition. The ascendant tendency is, first, the periodic depreciation of the existing capital, which lowers again, for a certain time, the scale of production, in proportion to the value of the necessary minimum amount of capital. It is represented, besides, by the penetration of capitalist production into new spheres. The struggle of the average size enterprise against big Capital cannot be considered a regularly proceeding battle in which the troops of the weaker party continue to melt away directly and quantitatively. It should be rather regarded as a periodic mowing down of the small enterprises, which rapidly grow up again, only to be mowed down once more by large industry. The two tendencies play ball with the middle capitalist layers. The descending tendency must win in the end. The very opposite is true about the development of the working class.

The victory of the descending tendency must not necessarily show itself in an absolute numerical diminution of the middle-sized enterprises. It must show itself, first in the progressive increase of the minimum amount of capital necessary for the functioning of the enterprises in the old branches of production; second, in the constant diminution of the interval of time during which the small capitalists conserve the opportunity to exploit the new branches of production. The result as far as the small capitalist is concerned is a progressively shorter duration of his stay in the new industry and a progressively more rapid change in the methods of production as a field for investment. For the average capitalist strata, taken as a whole, there is a process of more and more rapid social assimilation and dissimilation. Bernstein knows this perfectly well. He himself comments on this. But what he seems to forget is that this very thing is the law of the movement of the average capitalist enterprise. If one admits that small capitalists are pioneers of technical progress, and if it true that the latter is the vital pulse of the capitalist economy, then it is manifest that small capitalists are an integral part of capitalist development, and they will disappear only with capitalist development. The progressive disappearance of the middle-sized enterprise—in the absolute sense considered by Bernstein—means not, as he thinks, the revolutionary course of capitalist development, but precisely the contrary, the cessation, the slowing up of development. "The rate of profit, that is to say, the relative increase of capital," said Marx, "is important first of all for new investors of capital, grouping themselves independently. And as soon as the formation of capital falls exclusively into a handful of big capitalists, the revivifying fire of production is extinguished. It dies away."

THE REALIZATION OF SOCIALISM
THROUGH SOCIAL REFORMS

Bernstein rejects the "theory of collapse" as a historic road toward socialism. Now what is the way to a socialist society that is proposed by his "theory of adaptation to capitalism"? Bernstein answers this question only by allusion. Konrad Schmidt,* however, attempts to deal with this detail in the manner of Bernstein. According to him, "the trade-union struggle for hours and wages and the political struggle for reforms will lead to a progressively more extensive control over the conditions of production," and "as the rights of the capitalist proprietor will be diminished through legislation, he will be reduced in time to the role of a simple administrator." "The capitalist will see his property lose more and more value to himself" till finally "the direction and administration of exploitation will be taken from him entirely" and "collective exploitation" instituted.

---

* Konrad Schmidt (1865–1932) was a German social democratic economist and ally of Bernstein, one of the founders of the revisionist journal *Sozialistische Monatshefte.* (Interestingly, he was the brother of the radical artist Käthe Kollwitz, who produced the print that memorialized Liebknecht's death.) —H.S.

Therefore trade unions, social reforms, and, adds Bernstein, the political democratization of the state are the means of the progressive realization of socialism.

But the fact is that the principal function of trade unions (and this was best explained by Bernstein himself in *Neue Zeit* in 1891) consists in providing the workers with a means of realizing the capitalist law of wages, that is to say, the sale of their labor power at current market prices. Trade unions enable the proletariat to utilize, at each instant, the conjuncture of the market. But these conjunctures—(1) the labor demand determined by the state of production, (2) the labor supply created by the proletarianization of the middle strata of society and the natural reproduction of the working classes, and (3) the momentary degree of productivity of labor—remain outside of the sphere of influence of the trade unions. Trade unions cannot suppress the law of wages. Under the most favorable circumstances, the best they can do is to impose on capitalist exploitation the "normal" limit of the moment. They have not, however, the power to suppress exploitation itself, not even gradually.

Schmidt, it is true, sees the present trade-union movement in a "feeble initial stage." He hopes that "in the future" the "trade union movement will exercise a progressively increased influence over the regulation of production." But by the regulation of production we can only understand two things: intervention in the technical domain of the process of production and fixing the scale of production itself. What is the nature of the influence exercised by trade unions in these two departments? It is clear that in the technique of production, the interest of the capitalist agrees, up to a certain point, with the progress and development of capitalist economy. It is his own interest that pushes him to make technical improvements. But the isolated worker finds himself in a decidedly different position. Each technical transformation contradicts his interests. It aggravates his helpless situation by depreciating the value of his labor power and rendering his work more intense, more monotonous, and more difficult. Insofar as trade unions can intervene in the technical department of production, they can only oppose technical innovation. But here they do not act in the interest of the entire working class and its emancipation, which accords rather with technical progress and, therefore, with the interest of the isolated capitalist. They act here in a reactionary direction. And in fact, we find efforts on the part of workers to intervene in the technical part of production not in the future, where Schmidt looks for it, but in the past of the trade-union movement. Such efforts characterized the old phase of English trade unionism (up to 1860), when the British organizations were still tied to medieval "corporative" vestiges and found inspiration in the outworn principle of "a fair day's wage for a fair day's labor," as expressed by Webb in his *History of Trade Unionism*.*

On the other hand, the effort of the labor unions to fix the scale of production and the prices of commodities is a recent phenomenon. Only recently have we witnessed such attempts—and again in England. In their nature and tendencies, these efforts resemble those dealt with above. What does the active participation of trade unions in fixing the scale and cost of production amount to? It amounts to a cartel of the workers and entrepreneurs in a common stand against the consumer and especially rival entrepreneurs. In no way is the effect of this any different from that of ordinary employers' associations. Basically we no longer have here a struggle between labor and capital, but the solidarity of capital and labor against the total consumers. Considered for its social worth, it is seen to be a reactionary move that cannot be a stage in the struggle for the emancipation of the proletariat because it connotes the very opposite of the class struggle. Considered from the angle of practical application, it is found to be a utopia, which, as shown by a rapid examination, cannot be extended to the large branches of industry producing for the world market.

So that the scope of trade unions is limited essentially to a struggle for an increase of wages and the reduction of labor time, that is to say, to efforts at regulating capitalist exploitation as they are made necessary by the momentary situation of the world market. But labor unions can in no way influence the process of production itself. Moreover, trade-union development moves—contrary to what is asserted by Konrad Schmidt—in the direction of a complete detachment of the labor market from any immediate relation to the rest of the market.

That is shown by the fact that even attempts to relate labor contracts to the general situation of production by means of a system of sliding wage scales have been outmoded with historic development. The British labor unions are moving farther and farther away from such efforts.

---

* Sydney Webb (1859–1947) and Beatrice Potter-Webb (1858–1943), who were founders of the English Fabian Society in 1889, coauthored this and many other works. —H.S.

Even within the effective boundaries of its activity the trade-union movement cannot spread in the unlimited way claimed for it by the theory of adaptation. On the contrary, if we examine the large factors of social development, we see that we are not moving toward an epoch marked by a victorious development of trade unions, but rather toward a time when the hardships of labor unions will increase. Once industrial development has attained its highest possible point and capitalism has entered its descending phase on the world market, the trade-union struggle will become doubly difficult. In the first place, the objective conjuncture of the market will be less favorable to the sellers of labor power, because the demand for labor power will increase at a slower rate and labor supply more rapidly than is the case at present. In the second place, the capitalists themselves, in order to make up for losses suffered on the world market, will make even greater efforts than at present to reduce the part of the total product going to the workers (in the form of wages). The reduction of wages is, as pointed out by Marx, one of the principal means of retarding the fall of profit. The situation in England already offers us a picture of the beginning of the second stage of trade-union development. Trade-union action is reduced of necessity to the simple defense of already realized gains, and even that is becoming more and more difficult. Such is the general trend of things in our society. The counterpart of this tendency should be the development of the political side of the class struggle.

Konrad Schmidt commits the same error of historic perspective when he deals with social reforms. He expects that social reforms, like trade-union organizations, will "dictate to the capitalists the only conditions under which they will be able to employ labor power." Seeing reform in this light, Bernstein calls labor legislation a piece of "social control," and as such, a piece of socialism. Similarly, Schmidt always uses the term "social control" when he refers to labor-protective laws. Once he has thus happily transformed the state into society, he confidently adds: "That is to say, the rising working class." As a result of this trick of substitution, the innocent labor laws enacted by the German Federal Council are transformed into transitory socialist measures supposedly enacted by the German proletariat.

The mystification is obvious. We know that the present state is not "society" representing the "rising working class." It is itself the representative of capitalist society. It is a class state. Therefore its reform measures are not an application of "social control," that is, the control of society working freely in its own labor process. They are forms of control applied by the class organization of Capital to the production of Capital. The so-called social reforms are enacted in the interests of capital. Yes, Bernstein and Schmidt see at present only "feeble beginnings" of this control. They hope to see a long succession of reforms in the future, all favoring the working class. But here they commit a mistake similar to their belief in the unlimited development of the trade-union movement.

A basic condition for the theory of the gradual realization of socialism through social reforms is a certain objective development of capitalist property and of the state. Schmidt says that the capitalist proprietor tends to lose his special rights with historic development, and is reduced to the role of a simple administrator. He thinks that the expropriation of the means of production cannot possibly be effected as a single historic act. He therefore resorts to the theory of expropriation by stages. With this in mind, he divides the right to property into (1) the right of "sovereignty" (ownership)—which he attributes to a thing called "society" and which he wants to extend—and (2) its opposite, the simple right of use, held by the capitalist, but which is supposedly being reduced in the hands of the capitalists to the mere administration of their enterprises.

This interpretation is either a simple play on words, and in that case the theory of gradual expropriation has no real basis, or it is a true picture of judicial development, in which case, as we shall see, the theory of gradual expropriation is entirely false.

The division of the right of property into several component rights, an arrangement serving Schmidt as a shelter wherein he may construct his theory of "expropriation by stages," characterized feudal society, founded on natural economy. In feudalism, the total product was shared among the social classes of the time on the basis of the personal relations existing between the feudal lord and his serfs or tenants. The decomposition of property into several partial rights reflected the manner of distribution of the social wealth of that period. With the passage to the production of commodities and the dissolution of all personal bonds among the participants in the process of production, the relation between men and things (that is to say, private property) became reciprocally stronger. Since the division is no longer made on the basis of personal relations but through exchange, the different rights to a share in the social wealth are no longer measured as fragments of property rights having a common interest. They are measured according to the values brought by each on the market.

The first change introduced into juridical relations with the advance of commodity production in the medieval city communes was the development of absolute private property. The latter appeared in the very midst of the feudal juridical relations. This development has progressed at a rapid pace in capitalist production. The more the process of production is socialized, the more the process of distribution (division of wealth) rests on exchange. And the more private property becomes inviolable and closed, the more capitalist property becomes transformed from the right to the product of one's own labor to the simple right to appropriate somebody else's labor. As long as the capitalist himself manages his own factory, distribution is still, up to a certain point, tied to his personal participation in the process of production. But as the personal management on the part of the capitalist becomes superfluous—which is the case in the shareholding societies today—the property of capital, so far as its right to share in the distribution (division of wealth) is concerned, becomes separated from any personal relation with production. It now appears in its purest form. The capitalist right to property reaches its most complete development in capital held in the shape of shares and industrial credit.

So that Konrad Schmidt's historic schema, tracing the transformation of the capitalist "from a proprietor to a simple administrator," belies the real historic development. In historic reality, on the contrary, the capitalist tends to change from a proprietor and administrator to a simple proprietor. What happens here to Schmidt happened to Goethe:*

What is, he sees as in a dream.
What no longer is, becomes for him reality.

Just as Schmidt's historic schema travels, economically, backward from a modern shareholding society to an artisan's shop, so, juridically, he wishes to lead back the capitalist world into the old feudal shell of the Middle Ages.

---

* Johann Wolfgang von Goethe (1749–1832) was Germany's most celebrated poet and dramatist, and author of the play *Faust*. —H.S.

Also from this point of view, "social control" appears in reality under a different aspect than seen by Schmidt. What functions today as "social control"—labor legislation, the control of industrial organizations through share holding, etc.—has absolutely nothing to do with his "supreme ownership." Far from being, as Schmidt believes, a reduction of capitalist ownership, his "social control," is, on the contrary, a protection of such ownership. Or, expressed from the economic viewpoint, it is not a threat to capitalist exploitation, but simply the regulation of exploitation. When Bernstein asks if there is more or less of socialism in a labor protective law, we can assure him that, in the best of labor protective laws, there is no more "socialism" than in a municipal ordinance regulating the cleaning of streets or the lighting of streetlamps.

CAPITALISM AND THE STATE

The second condition of the gradual realization of socialism is, according to Bernstein, the evolution of the state in society. It has become a commonplace to say that the present state is a class state. This, too, like everything referring to capitalist society, should not be understood in a rigorous absolute manner, but dialectically.

The state became capitalist with the political victory of the bourgeoisie. Capitalist development modifies essentially the nature of the state, widening its sphere of action, constantly imposing on it new functions (especially those affecting economic life), making more and more necessary its intervention and control in society. In this sense, capitalist development prepares little by little the future fusion of the state to society. Following this line of thought, one can speak of an evolution of the capitalist state into society, and it is undoubtedly what Marx had in mind when he referred to labor legislation as the first conscious intervention of "society" in the vital social process, a phrase upon which Bernstein leans heavily.

But on the other hand the same capitalist development realizes another transformation in the nature of the state. The present state is, first of all, an organization of the ruling class. It assumes functions favoring social development specifically because, and in the measure that, these interests and social development coincide, in a general fashion, with the interests of the dominant class. Labor legislation is enacted as much in the immediate interest of the capitalist class as in the interest of society in general. But this harmony endures only up to a certain point of capitalist development. When capitalist development has reached a certain level, the interests of the bourgeoisie, as a class, and the needs of economic progress begin to clash even in the capitalist sense. We believe that this phase has already begun. It shows itself in two extremely important phenomena of contemporary social life: on the one hand, the policy of tariff barriers, and on the other, militarism. These two phenomena have played an indispensable, and in that sense a progressive and revolutionary role in the history of capitalism. Without tariff protection the development of large industry would have been impossible in several countries. But now the situation is different.

At present, protection does not serve so much to develop young industry as to maintain artificially certain aged forms of production.

From the angle of capitalist development, that is, from the point of view of world economy, it matters little whether Germany exports more merchandise into England or England exports more merchandise into Germany. From the viewpoint of this development it may be said that the blackamoor has done his work and it is time for him to go his way. Given the condition of reciprocal dependence in which the various branches of industry find themselves, a protectionist tariff on any commodity necessarily results in raising the cost of production of other commodities inside the country. It therefore impedes industrial development. But this is not so from the viewpoint of the interests of the capitalist class. While industry does not need tariff barriers for its development, the entrepreneurs need tariffs to protect their markets. This signifies that at present tariffs no longer serve as a means of protecting a developing capitalist section against a more advanced section. They are now the arm used by one national group of capitalists against another group. Furthermore, tariffs are no longer necessary as an instrument of protection for industry in its movement to create and conquer the home market. They are now indispensable means for the cartelization of industry, that is, means used in the struggle of capitalist producers against consuming society in the aggregate. What brings out in an emphatic manner the specific character of contemporary customs policies is the fact that today not industry, but agriculture plays the predominant role in the making of tariffs. The policy of customs protection has become a tool for converting and expressing the feudal interests in capitalist form.

The same change has taken place in militarism. If we consider history as it was—not as it could have been or as it should have been—we must agree that war has been an indispensable feature of capitalist development. The United States, Germany, Italy, the Balkan States, and Poland all owe the condition or the rise of their capitalist development to wars, whether resulting in victory or defeat. As long as there were countries marked by internal political division or economic isolation that had to be destroyed, militarism played a revolutionary role, considered from the viewpoint of capitalism.

But at present the situation is different. If world politics have become the stage of menacing conflicts, it is not so much a question of the opening of new countries to capitalism. It is a question of already existing *European* antagonisms, which, transported into other lands, have exploded there. The armed opponents we see today in Europe and on other continents do not range themselves as capitalist countries on one side and backward countries on the other. They are states pushed to war especially as a result of their similarly advanced capitalist development. In view of this, an explosion is certain to be fatal to this development, in the sense that it must provoke an extremely profound disturbance and transformation of economic life in all countries.

However, the matter appears entirely different when considered from the standpoint of the *capitalist class*. For the latter militarism has become indispensable. First, as a means of struggle for the defense of "national" interests in competition against other "national" groups. Second, as a method of placement for financial and industrial capital. Third, as an instrument of class domination over the laboring population inside the country. In themselves, these interests have nothing in common with the development of the capitalist mode of production. What demonstrates best the specific character of present-day militarism is the fact that it develops generally in all countries as an effect, so to speak, of its own internal, mechanical motive power, a phenomenon that was completely unknown several decades ago. We recognize this in the fatal character of the impending explosion that is inevitable in spite of the complete indecisiveness of the objectives and motives of the conflict. From a motor of capitalist development militarism has changed into a capitalist malady.

In the clash between capitalist development and the interest of the dominant class, the state takes a position alongside the latter. Its policy, like that of the bourgeoisie, comes into conflict with social development.

It thus loses more and more its character as a representative of the whole of society and is transformed at the same rate, into a pure *class* state. Or, to speak more exactly, these two qualities distinguish themselves more from each other and find themselves in a contradictory relation in the very nature of the state. This contradiction becomes progressively sharper. For, on one hand, we have the growth of the functions of a general interest on the part of the state, its intervention in social life, its "control" over society. But, on the other hand, its class character obliges the state to move the pivot of its activity and its means of coercion more and more into domains that are useful only to the class character of the bourgeoisie and have for society as a whole only a negative importance, as in the case of militarism and tariff and colonial policies. Moreover, the "social control" exercised by this state is at the same time penetrated with and dominated by its class character (see how labor legislation is applied in all countries).

The extension of democracy, which Bernstein sees as a means of realizing socialism by degrees, does not contradict but, on the contrary, corresponds perfectly to the transformation realized in the nature of the state.

Konrad Schmidt declares that the conquest of a social democratic majority in parliament leads directly to the gradual "socialization" of society. Now, the democratic forms of political life are without a question a phenomenon expressing clearly the evolution of the state in society. They constitute, to that extent, a move toward a socialist transformation. But the conflict within the capitalist state, described above, manifests itself even more emphatically in modern parliamentarism. Indeed, in accordance with its form, parliamentarism serves to express, within the organization of the state, the interests of the whole society. But what parliamentarism expresses here is capitalist society, that is to say, a society in which capitalist interests predominate. In this society, the representative institutions, democratic in form, are in content the instruments of the interests of the ruling class. This manifests itself in a tangible fashion in the fact that as soon as democracy shows the tendency to negate its class character and become transformed into an instrument of the real interests of the population, the democratic forms are sacrificed by the bourgeoisie, and by its state representatives. That is why the idea of the conquest of a parliamentary reformist majority is a calculation that, entirely in the spirit of bourgeois liberalism, preoccupies itself only with one side—the formal side—of democracy, but does not take into account the other side, its real content. All in all, parliamentarism is not a directly socialist element gradually impregnating the whole capitalist society. It is, on the contrary, a specific form of the bourgeois class state, helping to ripen and develop the existing antagonisms of capitalism.

In light of the history of the objective development of the state, Bernstein and Schmidt's belief that increased "social control" results in the direct introduction of socialism is transformed into a formula that finds itself from day to day in greater contradiction with reality.

The theory of the gradual introduction of socialism proposes a progressive reform of capitalist property and the capitalist state in the direction of socialism. But in consequence of the objective laws of existing society, one and the other develop in a precisely opposite direction. The process of production is increasingly socialized, and state intervention, the control of the state over the process of production, is extended. But at the same time, private property becomes more and more the form of open capitalist exploitation of the labor of others, and state control is penetrated with the exclusive interests of the ruling class. The state, that is to say, the *political* organization of capitalism, and property relations, that is to say, the *juridical* organization of capitalism, become more *capitalist* and not more socialist, posing to the theory of the progressive introduction of socialism two insurmountable difficulties.

Fourier's* scheme of changing, by means of a system of phalansteries, the water of all the seas into tasty lemonade was surely a fantastic idea. But Bernstein, proposing to change the sea of capitalist bitterness into a sea of socialist sweetness, by progressively pouring into it bottles of social reformist lemonade, presents an idea that is merely more insipid but no less fantastic.

The production relations of capitalist society approach more and more the production relations of socialist society. But on the other hand, its political and juridical relations established between capitalist society and socialist society a steadily rising wall. This wall is not overthrown, but is on the contrary strengthened and consolidated, by the development of social reforms and the course of democracy. Only

---

* Francois Marie Charles Fourier (1772–1837) was a French utopian socialist who developed a theory of social change through cooperative agricultural and industrial communities, known as "phalansteries." —H.S.

the hammer blow of revolution, that is to say, *the conquest of political power by the proletariat, can break down this wall.*

THE CONSEQUENCES OF SOCIAL REFORMISM AND THE GENERAL NATURE OF REFORMISM

In the first chapter we aimed to show that Bernstein's theory lifted the program of the socialist movement off its material base and tried to place it on an idealist base. How does this theory fare when translated into practice?

Upon the first comparison, the party practice resulting from Bernstein's theory does not seem to differ from the practice followed by the social democracy up to now. Formerly, the activity of the Social Democratic Party consisted of trade-union work, of agitation for social reforms, and the democratization of existing political institutions. The difference is not in the *what,* but in the *how.*

At present, the trade-union struggle and parliamentary practice are considered to be the means of guiding and educating the proletariat in preparation for the task of taking over power. From the revisionist standpoint, this conquest of power is at the same time impossible and useless. And therefore, trade-union and parliamentary activity are to be carried on by the party only for their immediate results, that is, for the purpose of bettering the present situation of the workers, for the gradual reduction of capitalist exploitation, for the extension of social control.

So that if we do not consider momentarily the immediate amelioration of the workers' condition—an objective common to our party program as well as to revisionism—the difference between the two outlooks is, in brief, the following. According to the present conception of the party, trade-union and parliamentary activity are important for the socialist movement because such activity prepares the proletariat, that is to say, creates the *subjective* factor of the socialist transformation, for the task of realizing socialism. But according to Bernstein, trade-union and parliamentary activity gradually reduce capitalist exploitation itself. They remove from capitalist society its capitalist character. They realize *objectively* the desired social change.

Examining the matter closely, we see that the two conceptions are diametrically opposed. Viewing the situation *from the current standpoint of our party*, we say that as a result of its trade-union and parliamentary struggles, the proletariat becomes convinced of the impossibility of accomplishing a fundamental social change through such activity and arrives at the understanding that the conquest of power is unavoidable. Bernstein's theory, however, begins by declaring that this conquest is impossible. It concludes by affirming that socialism can only be introduced as a result of the trade-union struggle and parliamentary activity. For as seen by Bernstein, trade-union and parliamentary action has a socialist character because it exercises a progressively socializing influence on capitalist economy.

We tried to show that this influence is purely imaginary. The relations between capitalist property and the capitalist state develop in entirely opposite directions, so that the daily practical activity of the present social democracy loses, in the last analysis, all connection with work for socialism. From the viewpoint of a movement for socialism, the trade-union struggle and our parliamentary practice are vastly important insofar as they make socialistic the *awareness*, the consciousness, of the proletariat and help to organize it as a class. But once they are considered as instruments of the direct socialization of capitalist economy, they lose not only their usual effectiveness but cease being means of preparing the working class for the conquest of power. Eduard Bernstein and Konrad Schmidt suffer from a complete misunderstanding when they console themselves with the belief that even though the program of the party is reduced to work for social reforms and ordinary trade-union work, the final objective of the labor movement is not thereby discarded, for each forward step reaches beyond the given immediate aim and the socialist goal is implied as a tendency in the supposed advance.

That is certainly true about the present procedure of the German social democracy. It is true whenever a firm and conscious effort for the conquest of political power impregnates the trade-union struggle and the work for social reforms. But if this effort is separated from the movement itself and social reforms are made an end in themselves, then such activity not only does not lead to the final goal of socialism but moves in a precisely opposite direction.

Schmidt simply falls back on the idea that an apparently mechanical movement, once started, cannot stop by itself, because "one's appetite grows with eating," and the working class will not supposedly content itself with reforms till the final socialist transformation is realized.

Now the last-mentioned condition is quite real. Its effectiveness is guaranteed by the very insufficiency of capitalist reforms. But the conclusion drawn from it could only be true if it were possible to construct an unbroken chain of augmented reforms leading from the capitalism of today to socialism. This is, of course, sheer fantasy. In accordance with the nature of things as they are, the chain breaks quickly, and the paths that the supposed forward movement can take from that point on are many and varied.

What will be the immediate result should our party change its general procedure to suit a viewpoint that wants to emphasize the practical results of our struggle, that is, social reforms? As soon as "immediate results" become the principal aim of our activity, the clear-cut, irreconcilable point of view, which has meaning only insofar as it proposes to win power, will be found more and more inconvenient. The direct consequence of this will be the adoption by the party of a "policy of compensation," a policy of political trading, and an attitude of diffident, diplomatic conciliation. But this attitude cannot be continued for a long time. Since the social reforms can only offer an empty promise, the logical consequence of such a program must necessarily be disillusionment.

It is not true that socialism will arise automatically from the daily struggle of the working class. Socialism will be the consequence of (1) the growing contradictions of capitalist economy and (2) the comprehension by the working class of the unavailability of the suppression of these contradictions through a social transformation. When, in the manner of revisionism, the first condition is denied and the second rejected, the labor movement finds itself reduced to a simple cooperative and reformist movement.* We move here in a straight line toward the total abandonment of the class viewpoint.

This consequence also becomes evident when we investigate the general character of revisionism. It is obvious that revisionism does not wish to concede that its standpoint is that of the capitalist apologist. It does not join the bourgeois economists in denying the existence of the contradictions of capitalism. But, on the other hand, what precisely constitutes the fundamental point of revisionism and

---

* The cooperative movement in Germany started in 1903 under Adolf von Elm's leadership and grew exponentially in the next decade, drawing on the traditions developed by Robert Owen in England and Charles Fourier in France. —H.S.

distinguishes it from the attitude taken by the social democracy up to now, is that it does not base its theory on the belief that the contradictions of capitalism will be suppressed as a result of the logical inner development of the present economic system.

We may say that the theory of revisionism occupies an intermediate place between two extremes. Revisionism does not expect to see the contradictions of capitalism mature. It does not propose to suppress these contradictions through a revolutionary transformation. It wants to lessen, to attenuate, the capitalist contradictions. So that the antagonism existing between production and exchange is to be mollified by the cessation of crises and the formation of capitalist combines. The antagonism between capital and labor is to be adjusted by bettering the situation of the workers and by the conservation of the middle classes. And the contradiction between the class state and society is to be liquidated through increased state control and the progress of democracy.

It is true that the present procedure of the social democracy does not consist in waiting for the antagonisms of capitalism to develop and in passing on, only then, to the task of suppressing them. On the contrary, the essence of revolutionary procedure is to be guided by the direction of this development, once it is ascertained, and inferring from this direction what consequences are necessary for the political struggle. Thus the social democracy has combated tariff wars and militarism without waiting for their reactionary character to become fully evident. Bernstein's procedure is not guided by a consideration of the development of capitalism, by the prospect of the aggravation of its contradictions. It is guided by the prospect of the attenuation of these contradictions. He shows this when he speaks of the "adaptation" of capitalist economy.

Now when can such a conception be correct? If it is true that capitalism will continue to develop in the direction it takes at present, then its contradictions must necessarily become sharper and more aggravated instead of disappearing. The possibility of the attenuation of the contradictions of capitalism presupposes that the capitalist mode of production itself will stop its progress. In short, the general condition of Bernstein's theory is the cessation of capitalist development.

This way, however, his theory condemns itself in a twofold manner.

In the first place, it manifests its *utopian* character in its stand on the establishment of socialism. For it is clear that a defective capitalist development cannot lead to a socialist transformation.

In the second place, Bernstein's theory reveals its *reactionary* character when it is referred to the rapid capitalist development that is taking place at present. Given the development of real capitalism, how can we explain, or rather state, Bernstein's position? We have demonstrated in the first chapter the baselessness of the economic conditions on which Bernstein builds his analysis of existing social relationships. We have seen that neither the credit system nor cartels can be said to be "means of adaptation" of capitalist economy. We have seen that not even the temporary cessation of crises nor the survival of the middle class can be regarded as symptoms of capitalist adaptation. But even though we should fail to take into account the erroneous character of all these details of Bernstein's theory we cannot help but be stopped short by one feature common to all of them. Bernstein's theory does not seize these manifestations of contemporary economic life as they appear in their organic relationship with the whole of capitalist development, with the complete economic mechanism of capitalism. His theory pulls these details out of their living economic context. It treats them as *disjecta membra* (separate parts) of a lifeless machine.

Consider, for example, his conception of the adaptive effect of *credit*. If we recognize credit as a higher natural stage of the process of exchange and, therefore, of the contradictions inherent in capitalist exchange, we cannot at the same time see it as a mechanical means of adaptation existing outside of the process of exchange. It would be just as impossible to consider money, merchandise, capital as "means of adaptation" of capitalism.

However, credit, like money, commodities, and capital, is an organic link of capitalist economy at a certain stage of its development. Like them, it is an indispensable gear in the mechanism of capitalist economy, and at the same time, an instrument of destruction, since it aggravates the internal contradictions of capitalism.

The same thing is true about cartels and the new, perfected means of communication.

The same mechanical view is presented by Bernstein's attempt to describe the promise of the cessation of crises as a symptom of the "adaptation" of capitalist economy. For him, crises are simply derangements of the economic mechanism. With their cessation, he thinks, the mechanism could function well. But the fact is that crises are not "derangements" in the usual sense of the word. They are "derangements" without which capitalist economy could not develop at all. For if crises constitute the only method possible in capitalism—and therefore the normal method—of solving periodically the conflict existing between the unlimited extension of production and the narrow limits of the world market, then crises are an organic manifestation inseparable from capitalist economy.

In the "unhindered" advance of capitalist production lurks a threat to capitalism that is much graver than crises. It is the threat of the constant fall of the rate of profit, resulting not from the contradiction between production and exchange, but from the growth of the productivity of labor itself. The fall in the rate of profit has the extremely dangerous tendency of rendering impossible any enterprise for small and middle-sized capitals. It thus limits the new formation and therefore the extension of placements of capital.

And it is precisely crises that constitute the other consequence of the same process. As a result of their periodic *depreciation* of capital, crises bring a fall in the prices of means of production, a paralysis of a part of the active capital, and in time the increase of profits. They thus create the possibilities of the renewed advance of production. Crises therefore appear to be the instruments of rekindling the fire of capitalist development. Their cessation—not temporary cessation, but their total disappearance in the world market—would not lead to the further development of capitalist economy. It would destroy capitalism.

True to the mechanical view of his theory of adaptation, Bernstein forgets the necessity of crises as well as the necessity of new placements of small and middle-sized capitals. And that is why the constant reappearance of small capital seems to him to be the sign of the cessation of capitalist development though, it is, in fact, a symptom of normal capitalist development.

It is important to note that there is a viewpoint from which all the above-mentioned phenomena are seen exactly as they have been presented by the theory of "adaptation." It is the viewpoint of the isolated (single) capitalist, who reflects in his mind the economic facts around him just as they appear when refracted by the laws of competition. The isolated capitalist sees each organic part of the whole of our economy as an independent entity. He sees them as they act on him, the single capitalist. He therefore considers these facts to be simple "derangements" of simple "means of adaptation." For the isolated capitalist, it is true, crises are really simple derangements; the cessation of crises accords him a longer existence. As far as he is concerned, credit is only a means of "adapting" his insufficient productive forces to the needs of the market. And it seems to him that the cartel of which he becomes a member really suppresses industrial anarchy.

Revisionism is nothing else than a theoretic generalization made from the angle of the isolated capitalist. Where does this viewpoint belong theoretically if not in vulgar bourgeois economics?

All the errors of this school rest precisely on the conception that mistakes the phenomena of competition, as seen from the angle of the isolated capitalist, for the phenomena of the whole of capitalist economy. Just as Bernstein considers credit to be a means of "adaptation," so the vulgar economy considers money to be a judicious means of "adaptation" to the needs of exchange. Vulgar economy, too, tries to find the antidote against the ills of capitalism in the phenomena of capitalism. Like Bernstein, it believes that it is possible to regulate capitalist economy. And in the manner of Bernstein, it arrives in time at the desire to palliate the contradictions of capitalism, that is, at the belief in the possibility of patching up the sores of capitalism. It ends up by subscribing to a program of reaction. It ends up in utopia.

The theory of revisionism can therefore be defined in the following way. It is a theory of standing still in the socialist movement, built, with the aid of vulgar economy, on a theory of capitalist standstill.

PART II

ECONOMIC DEVELOPMENT AND SOCIALISM*

The greatest conquest of the developing proletarian movement has been the discovery of grounds of support for the realization of socialism in the *economic condition* of capitalist society. As a result of this discovery, socialism was changed from an "ideal" dream by humanity for thousands of years to a thing of *historic necessity.*

Bernstein denies the existence of the economic conditions for socialism in the society of today. On this count his reasoning has undergone an interesting evolution. At first, in *Neue Zeit*, he simply contested the rapidity of the process of concentration taking place in

---

* A discussion of Bernstein's book, *Die Voraussetzungen des Socialismus und die Aufgaben der Sozialdemokratie.* —R.L.

industry. He based his position on a comparison of the occupational statistics of Germany in 1882 and 1895. In order to use these figures for his purpose, he was obliged to proceed in an entirely summary and mechanical fashion. In the most favorable case, he could not, even by demonstrating the persistence of middle-sized enterprises, weaken in the least the Marxian analysis, because the latter does not suppose, as a condition for the realization of socialism, either a definite rate of concentration of industry—that is, a definite *delay* of the realization of socialism—or, as we have already shown, the *absolute disappearance* of small capitals, usually described as the disappearance of the small bourgeoisie.

In the course of the latest development of his ideas, Bernstein furnishes us in his book a new assortment of proofs: the statistics of *shareholding societies*. These statistics are used in order to prove that the number of shareholders increases constantly, and, as a result, the capitalist class does not become smaller but grows bigger. It is surprising that Bernstein has so little acquaintance with his material. And it is astonishing how poorly he utilizes the existing data in his own behalf.

If he wanted to disprove the Marxian law of industrial development by referring to the condition of shareholding societies, he should have resorted to entirely different figures. Anybody who is acquainted with the history of shareholding societies in Germany knows that their average foundation capital has *diminished* almost constantly. Thus while before 1871 their average foundation capital reached the figure of 10.8 million marks, it was only 4.01 million marks in 1871, 3.8 million marks in 1873, less than a million from 1882 to 1887, 0.52 million in 1891, and only 0.62 million in 1892. After this date the figures oscillated around 1 million marks, falling to 1.78 in 1895 and to 1.19 in the course of the first half of 1897. (Van de Borght: *Handwörterbuch der Staatswissenschaften*, 1)*

These are surprising figures. Using them, Bernstein hoped to show the existence of a counter-Marxian tendency for retransformation of large enterprises into small ones. The obvious answer to his attempt is the following. If you are to prove anything at all by means of your statistics, you must first show that they refer to the *same* branches of industry. You must show that small enterprises really replace large

---

* Van de Borght's *Handwörterbuch der Staatswissenschaften* (*Sourcebook of Economic Statistics*). —H.S.

ones, that they do not, instead, appear only where small enterprises or even artisan industry were the rule before. This, however, you cannot show to be true. The statistical passage of immense shareholding societies to middle-sized and small enterprises can be explained only by referring to the fact that the system of shareholding societies continues to penetrate new branches of production. Before, only a small number of large enterprises were organized as shareholding societies. Gradually shareholding organization has won middle-sized and even small enterprises. Today we can observe shareholding societies with a capital below 1,000 marks.

Now what is the economic significance of the extension of the system of shareholding societies? Economically the spread of shareholding societies stands for the growing socialization of production under the capitalist form—socialization not only of large but also of middle-sized and small production. The extension of shareholding does not therefore contradict Marxist theory but, on the contrary, confirms it emphatically.

What does the economic phenomenon of a shareholding society actually amount to? It represents, on one hand, the unification of a number of small fortunes into a large capital of production. It stands, on the other hand, for the separation of production from capitalist ownership. That is, it denotes that a double victory is being won over the capitalist mode of production—but still on a capitalist base.

What is the meaning, therefore, of the statistics cited by Bernstein, according to which an ever-greater number of shareholders participate in capitalist enterprises? These statistics go to demonstrate precisely the following: at present a capitalist enterprise does not correspond, as before, to a single proprietor of capital but a number of capitalists. Consequently, *the economic notion of "capitalist" no longer signifies an isolated individual. The industrial capitalist of today is a collective person, composed of hundreds and even of thousands of individuals. The category "capitalist" has itself become a social category. It has become "socialized"—within the framework of capitalist society.*

In that case, how shall we explain Bernstein's belief that the phenomenon of shareholding societies stands for the dispersion and not the concentration of capital? Why does he see the extension of capitalist property where Marx saw its suppression?

That is a simple economic error. By "capitalist," Bernstein does not mean a category of production but the right to property. To him, "capitalist" is not an economic unit but a fiscal unit. And "capital" is for him not a factor of production but simply a certain quantity of money. That is why in his English sewing thread trust he does not see the fusion of 12,300 persons with money into a single capitalist unit but 12,300 different capitalists. That is why the engineer Schuze whose wife's dowry brought him a large number of shares from stockholder Mueller is also a capitalist for Bernstein. That is why for Bernstein the entire world seems to swarm with capitalists.*

Here, too, the theoretic base of his economic error is his "popularization" of socialism. For this is what he does. By transporting the concept of capitalism from its productive relations to property relations, and by speaking of simple individuals instead of speaking of entrepreneurs, he moves the question of socialism from the domain of production into the domain of relations of fortune—that is, from the relation between capital and labor to the relation between poor and rich.

In this manner we are merrily led from Marx and Engels to the author of *The Evangel of the Poor Fisherman*. There is this difference, however. Weitling,** with the sure instinct of the proletarian, saw in the opposition between the poor and the rich the class antagonisms in their primitive form, and wanted to make of these antagonisms a lever of the movement for socialism. Bernstein, on the other hand, locates the realization of socialism in the possibility of making the poor rich. That is, he locates it in the attenuation of class antagonisms and, therefore, in the petty bourgeoisie.

---

* Nota bene! Bernstein evidently finds in the great diffusion of small shares a proof that social wealth is beginning to pour shares on all little men. Indeed, who but small bourgeois and even workers could buy shares for the bagatelle of one pound sterling or 20 marks? Unfortunateley his supposition rests on an error of calculation. We are operating here with the nominal value of shares instead of operating with their market value, something entirely different. For example, on the mining market, the South African Rand mine shares are on sale. These shares, like most mining values, are quoted at one pound sterling or 20 paper marks. But already in 1899 they sold at 43 pounds sterling, that is to say, not at 20 but at 860 marks. And it is so in all cases. So that these shares are perfectly bourgeois, and not at all petty bourgeois or proletarian "bonds on social wealth," for that are bought at their nominal value only by a small minority of shareholders. —R.L.

** Wilhelm Weitling (1808–1871) was a significant working-class writer and leader in the early days of German socialism who collaborated with Blanqui, became increasingly utopian, and emigrated to the United States after 1848. —H.S.

True, Bernstein does not limit himself to the statistics of incomes. He furnishes statistics of economic enterprises, especially those of the following countries: Germany, France, England, Switzerland, Austria, and the United States. But these statistics are not the comparative figures of *different periods* in each country but of each period in different countries. We are not therefore offered (with the exception of Germany, where he repeats the old contrast between 1895 and 1882), a comparison of the statistics of enterprises of a given country at different epochs but the *absolute* figures for different countries: England in 1891, France in 1894, the United States in 1890, etc.

He reaches the following conclusion: "Though it is true that large exploitation is already supreme in industry today, it nevertheless represents, including the enterprises dependent on large exploitation, even in a country as developed in Prussia, *only half of the population occupied in production.*" This is also true about Germany, England, Belgium, etc.

What does he actually prove here? He proves not the existence of such or such a *tendency of economic development* but merely the *absolute relation of forces* of different forms of enterprise, or, put in other words, the absolute relation of the various classes in our society.

Now if one wants to prove in this manner the impossibility of realizing socialism, his reasoning must rest on the theory according to which the result of social efforts is decided by the relation of the numerical material forces of the elements in the struggle, that is, by the factor of *violence*. In other words, Bernstein, who always thunders against Blanquism,* himself falls into the grossest Blanquist error. There is this difference, however. To the Blanquists, who represented a socialist and revolutionary tendency, the possibility of the economic realization of socialism appeared quite natural. On this possibility they built the chances of a violent revolution—even by a small minority. Bernstein, on the contrary, infers from the numerical insufficiency of a socialist majority the impossibility of the economic realization of socialism. The social democracy, *does not, however, expect to attain its aim either as a result of the victorious violence of a minority or through the numerical superiority of a majority. It sees socialism come as a result of economic*

---

* The doctrine of socialist revolution through conspiratorial armed insurrection by small groups on behalf of the working class, as opposed to the Marxist concept of mass working-class self-activity. Named for the French revolutionary Louis Auguste Blanqui (1805–1881). —H.S.

*necessity—and the comprehension of that necessity—leading to the
suppression of capitalism by the working masses.* And this necessity
manifests itself above all in the anarchy of capitalism.
What is Bernstein's position on the decisive question of anarchy in
capitalist economy? He denies only the great general crises. He does
not deny partial and national crises. In other words, he refuses to see
a great deal of the anarchy of capitalism; he sees only a little of it. He
is—to use Marx's illustration—like the foolish virgin "who was only
a little bit pregnant." But the misfortune is that in matters like economic anarchy little and much are equally bad. If Bernstein recognizes the existence of a little of this anarchy, we may point out to him
that by the mechanism of market economy this bit of anarchy will be
extended to unheard-of proportions, to end in collapse. But if Bernstein hopes, while maintaining the system of commodity production,
to transform gradually his bit of anarchy into order and harmony, he
again falls into one of the fundamental errors of bourgeois political
economy, according to which the mode of exchange is independent
of the mode of production.

This is not the place for a lengthy demonstration of Bernstein's
surprising confusion concerning the most elementary principles of
political economy. But there is one point—to which we are led by
the fundamental question of capitalist anarchy—that must be clari-
fied immediately.

Bernstein declares that Marx's law of surplus value is a simple abstraction. In political economy a statement of this sort obviously constitutes an insult. But if surplus value is only a simple abstraction, if it
is only a figment of the mind—then every normal citizen who has
done military duty and pays his taxes on time has the same right as
Karl Marx to fashion his individual absurdity, to make his own law
of value. "Marx has as much right to neglect the qualities of commodities till they are no more than the incarnation of quantities of
simple human labor as have the economists of the Böhm-Jevons*
school to make an abstraction of all the qualities of commodities outside of their utility."

---

* Eugen von Böhm-Bawerk (1815–1914) was an Austrian economist and
critic of Marx, leader of the marginal utility school of economics; William
Stanley Jevons (1835–1882) was an English economist and philosopher
who also contributed to the marginal utility school. [cont.]

That is, to Bernstein, Marx's social labor and Menger's* abstract utility are quite similar—pure abstractions. Bernstein forgets completely that Marx's abstraction is not an invention. It is a discovery. It does not exist in Marx's head but in market economy. It has not an imaginary existence, but a real social existence, so real that it can be cut, hammered, weighed, and put in the form of money. The abstract human labor discovered by Marx is, in its developed form, no other than *money*. That is precisely one of the greatest of Marx's discoveries, while to all bourgeois political economists, from the first of the mercantilists to the last of the classicists, the essence of money has remained a mystic enigma.

The Böhm-Jevons abstract utility is, in fact, a conceit of the mind. Or stated more correctly, it is a representation of intellectual emptiness, a private absurdity, for which neither capitalism nor any other society can be made responsible, but only vulgar bourgeois economy itself. Hugging their brainchild, Bernstein, Böhm and Jevons, and the entire subjective fraternity can remain twenty years or more before the mystery of money without arriving at a solution that is different from the one reached by any cobbler, namely that money is also a "useful" thing.

Bernstein has lost all comprehension of Marx's law of value. Anybody with a small understanding of Marxian economics can see that without the law of value, Marx's doctrine is incomprehensible. Or to speak more concretely—for him who does not understand the nature of the commodity and its exchange, the entire economy of capitalism, with all its concatenations, must of necessity remain an enigma.

[cont.] Hitherto capitalist economists shared with Marx a labor theory of value, locating the source of profits in labor. The economists of the marginal utility school moved away from any objective measure of value, and instead argued that value was based on the subjective approximation of the usefulness (utility) derived from extra amounts of the product (marginal increment). They posited an ideal system of supply and demand ensuring that buyers and sellers end up paying and receiving the right amount. As long as the market is free of any impediments, they argued, (such as state-mandated minimum wage or controls on food costs) crises of overproduction were impossible, and workers and capitalists alike would receive the appropriate reward for their product. As a justification for the free market, this model remains dominant in bourgeois economics today. —H.S.

* Karl Menger (1840–1921) was an Austrian economist and a member of the psychological school that contributed to marginalist economics. —H.S.

What precisely was the key that enabled Marx to open the door to the secrets of capitalist phenomena and solve, as if in play, problems that were not even suspected by the greatest minds of classic bourgeois political economy? It was his conception of capitalist economy as historic phenomenon—not merely in the sense recognized in the best of cases by the classic economists, that is, when it concerns the feudal past of capitalism—but also insofar as it concerns the socialist future of the world. The secret of Marx's theory of value, of his analysis of the problem of money, of his theory of capital, of the theory of the rate of profit, and consequently of the entire existing economic system, is found in the transitory character of capitalist economy, the inevitability of its collapse, leading—and this is only another aspect of the same phenomenon—to socialism. It is only because Marx looked at capitalism from the socialist's viewpoint, that is, from the historic viewpoint, that he was enabled to decipher the hieroglyphics of capitalist economy. And it is precisely because he took the socialist viewpoint as a point of departure for his analysis of bourgeois society that he was in the position to give a scientific base to the socialist movement.

This is the measure by which we evaluate Bernstein's remarks. He complains of the "dualism" found everywhere in Marx's monumental *Capital*. "The work wishes to be a scientific study and prove, at the same time, a thesis that was completely elaborated a long time before the editing of the book; it is based on a schema that already contains the result to which he wants to lead. The return to the *Communist Manifesto** proves the existence of vestiges of utopianism in Marx's doctrine."

But what is Marx's "dualism" if not the dualism of the socialist future and the capitalist present? It is the dualism of capitalism and labor, the dualism of the bourgeoisie and the proletariat. It is the scientific reflection of the dualism existing in bourgeois society, the dualism of the class antagonism writhing inside the social order of capitalism.

Bernstein's recognition of this theoretic dualism in Marx as "a survival of utopianism" is really his naive avowal that he denies the historic dualism of bourgeois society, that he denies the existence of class antagonism in capitalism. It is his confession that socialism has become for him only a "survival of utopianism." What is Bernstein's "monism"—Bernstein's unity—but the eternal unity of the capitalist regime, the unity of the former socialist who has renounced his aim

---

* That is the socialist goal! —R.L.

and has decided to find in bourgeois society, one and immutable, the goal of human development?

Bernstein does not see in the economic structure of capitalism the development that leads to socialism. But in order to conserve his socialist program, at least in form, he is obliged to take refuge in an idealist construction, placed outside of all economic development. He is obliged to transform socialism itself from a definite historical phase of social development into an abstract "principle."

That is why the "cooperative principle"—the meager decantation of socialism by which Bernstein wishes to garnish capitalist economy—appears as a concession made not to the socialist future of society, but to Bernstein's own socialist past.

COOPERATIVES, UNIONS, DEMOCRACY

Bernstein's socialism offers to the workers the prospect of sharing in the wealth of society. The poor are to become rich. How will this socialism be brought about? His articles in *Neue Zeit,* "Problems of Socialism," contain only vague allusions to this question. Adequate information, however, can be found in his book.

Bernstein's socialism is to be realized with the aid of these two instruments: labor unions—or as Bernstein himself characterizes them, economic democracy—and cooperatives. The first will suppress industrial profit; the second will do away with commercial profit.

Cooperatives, especially cooperatives in the field of production, constitute a hybrid form in the midst of capitalism. They can be described as small units of socialized production within capitalist exchange.

But in capitalist economy exchange dominates production* (that is, production depends to a large extent on market possibilities). As a result of competition, the complete domination of the process of production by the interests of capital—that is, pitiless exploitation—becomes a condition for the survival of each enterprise. The domination of capital over the process of production expresses itself in the following ways. Labor is intensified. The workday is lengthened or shortened, according to the situation of the market. And, depending on the requirements of the market, labor is either employed or thrown back into the street. In other words, use is made of all methods that enable an enterprise to stand up against its competitors in the market. The workers forming a cooperative in the field of production are thus faced with the contradictory

necessity of governing themselves with the utmost absolutism. They are
obliged to take toward themselves the role of capitalist entrepreneur—a
contradiction that accounts for the failure of production cooperatives,
which either become pure capitalist enterprises or, if the workers' interests continue to predominate, end by dissolving.

Bernstein has himself taken note of these facts. But it is evident
that he has not understood them. For, together with Mrs. Potter-
Webb, he explains the failure of production cooperatives in England
by their lack of "discipline." But what is so superficially and flatly
called here "discipline" is nothing else than the natural absolutist
regime of capitalism, which, it is plain, the workers cannot successfully use against themselves.

Producers' cooperatives can survive within capitalist economy
only if they manage to suppress, by means of some detour, the capi-
talist-controlled contradiction between the mode of production and
the mode of exchange. And they can accomplish this only by removing themselves artificially from the influence of the laws of free competition. And they can succeed in doing the last only when they assure themselves beforehand of a constant circle of consumers, that is,
when they assure themselves of a constant market.

It is the consumers' cooperative that can offer this service to its
brother in the field of production. Here—and not in Oppenheimer's*
distinction between cooperatives that purchase and cooperatives that
sell—is the secret sought by Bernstein: the explanation for the invari-
able failure of producers' cooperatives functioning independently and
their survival when they are backed by consumers' organizations.

If it is true that the possibilities of existence of producers' cooperatives within capitalism are bound up with the possibilities of existence of consumers' cooperatives, then the scope of the former is limited, in the most favorable of cases, to the small local market and to
the manufacture of articles serving immediate needs, especially food
products. Consumers', and therefore producers', cooperatives are excluded from the most important branches of capital production—the
textile, mining, metallurgical, and petroleum industries, machine construction, locomotive, and shipbuilding. For this reason alone (forget-
ting for the moment their hybrid character), cooperatives in the field

---

* Franz Oppenheimer (1864–1943) was a German economist, sociologist,
and reform socialist, favorably regarded by Bernstein. —H.S.

of production cannot be seriously considered as the instrument of a general social transformation. The establishment of producers' cooperatives on a wide scale would suppose, first of all, the suppression of the world market, the breaking up of the present world economy into small local spheres of production and exchange. The highly developed, widespread capitalism of our time is expected to fall back to the merchant economy of the Middle Ages.

Within the framework of present society, producers' cooperatives are limited to the role of simple annexes to consumers' cooperatives. It appears, therefore, that the latter must be the beginning of the proposed social change. But this way the expected reform of society by means of cooperatives ceases to be an offensive against capitalist production. That is, it ceases to be an attack against the principal bases of capitalist economy. It becomes, instead, a struggle against commercial capital, especially small and middle-sized commercial capital. It becomes an attack made on the twigs of the capitalist tree.

According to Bernstein, trade unions too are a means of attack against capitalism in the field of production. We have already shown that trade unions cannot give the workers a determining influence over production. Trade unions can neither determine the dimensions of production nor the technical progress of production.

This much may be said about the purely economic side of the "struggle of the rate of wages against the rate of profit," as Bernstein labels the activity of the trade union. It does not take place in the blue of the sky. It takes place within the well-defined framework of the law of wages. The law of wages is not shattered but applied by trade-union activity.

According to Bernstein, it is the trade unions that lead—in the general movement for the emancipation of the working class—the real attack against the rate of industrial profit. According to Bernstein, trade unions have the task of transforming the rate of industrial profit into "rates of wages." The fact is that trade unions are least able to execute an economic offensive against profit. Trade unions are nothing more than the organized *defense* of labor power against the attacks of profit. They express the resistance offered by the working class to the oppression of capitalist economy.

On the one hand, trade unions have the function of influencing the situation in the labor-power market. But this influence is being constantly overcome by the proletarianization of the middle layers of our society, a process that continually brings new merchandise on the labor market. The second function of the trade unions is to ameliorate the condition of the workers. That is, they attempt to increase the share of the social wealth going to the working class. This share, however, is being reduced with the fatality of a natural process by the growth of the productivity of labor. One does not need to be a Marxist to notice this. It suffices to read Rodbertus's* *In Explanation of the Social Question.*

In other words, the objective conditions of capitalist society transform the two economic functions of the trade unions into a sort of labor of Sisyphus,** which is, nevertheless, indispensable. For as a result of the activity of his trade unions, the worker succeeds in obtaining for himself the rate of wages due to him in accordance with the situation of the labor-power market. As a result of trade-union activity, the capitalist law of wages is applied and the effect of the depressing tendency of economic development is paralyzed, or to be more exact, is attenuated.

However, the transformation of the trade union into an instrument for the progressive reduction of profit in favor of wages presupposes the following social conditions; first, the cessation of the proletarianization of the middle strata of our society; secondly, a stoppage of the growth of productivity of labor. We have in both cases *a return to precapitalist conditions.*

Cooperatives and trade unions are totally incapable of transforming the *capitalist mode of production.* This is basically understood by Bernstein, though in a confused manner. For he refers to cooperatives and trade unions as a means of reducing the profit of the capitalists and thus enriching the workers. In this way, he renounces the struggle against the *capitalist mode of production* and attempts to direct the socialist movement to struggle against "capitalist distribution."*** Again and again, Bernstein refers to socialism as an effort toward a

---

* Johann Karl Rodbertus, also known as Karl Rodbertus-Jagetzow (1805–1875), was an economist and politician who advocated a form of state socialism influential among conservative social democrats. —H.S.

** The mythological king of Corinth who in the lower world was condemned to roll to the top of a hill a huge stone, which constantly rolled back, making his task incessant. —R.L.

*** The term used by Bernstein to describe the allocation of the total social wealth of the several sections of capitalist society. —R.L.

"just, juster, and still more just" mode of distribution. (*Vorwärts*, March 26, 1899)

It cannot be denied that the direct cause leading the popular masses into the socialist movement is precisely the "unjust" mode of distribution characteristic of capitalism. When the social democracy struggles for the socialization of the entire economy, it aspires therewith also to a "just" distribution of the social wealth. But, guided by Marx's observation that the mode of distribution of a given epoch is a natural consequence of the mode of production of that epoch, the social democracy does not struggle against distribution in the framework of capitalist production. It struggles instead for the suppression of capitalist production itself. In a word, the social democracy wants to establish the mode of socialist distribution by suppressing the capitalist mode of production. Bernstein's method, on the contrary, proposes to combat the capitalist mode of distribution in the hope of gradually establishing, in this way, the socialist mode of production.

What, in that case, is the basis of Bernstein's program for the reform of society? Does it find support in definite tendencies of capitalist production? No. In the first place, he denies such tendencies. In the second place, the socialist transformation of production is for him the effect and not the cause of distribution. He cannot give his program a materialist base, because he has already overthrown the aims and the means of the movement for socialism, and therefore its economic conditions. As a result, he is obliged to construct himself an idealist base.

"Why represent socialism as the consequence of economic compulsion?" he complains. "Why degrade man's understanding, his feeling for justice, his will?" (*Vorwärts*, March 26, 1899). Bernstein's superlatively just distribution is to be attained thanks to man's free will, man's will acting not because of economic necessity, since this will itself is only an instrument, but because of man's comprehension of justice, because of man's *idea of justice*.

We thus quite happily return to the principle of justice, to the old warhorse on which the reformers of the earth have rocked for ages, for lack of surer means of historic transportation. We return to that lamentable Rosinate on which the Don Quixotes of history have galloped toward the great reform of the earth, always to come home with their eyes blackened.

The relation of the poor to the rich, taken as a base for socialism, the principle of cooperation as the content of socialism, the "most just distribution" as its aim, and the idea of justice as its only historic legit-imization—with how much more force, more wit, and more fire did Weitling defend that sort of socialism fifty years ago. However, that genius of a tailor did not know scientific socialism. If today the conception torn into bits by Marx and Engels a half century ago is patched up and presented to the proletariat as the last word of social science, that, too, is the art of a tailor, but it has nothing of genius about it.

Trade unions and cooperatives are the economic points of support for the theory of revisionism. Its principal political condition is the growth of democracy. The present manifestations of political reaction are to Bernstein only "displacement." He considers them accidental, momentary, and suggests that they are not to be considered in the elaboration of the general directives of the labor movement.

To Bernstein, democracy is an inevitable stage in the development of society. To him, as to the bourgeois theoreticians of liberalism, democracy is the great fundamental law of historic development, the realization of which is served by all the forces of political life. However, Bernstein's thesis is completely false. Presented in this absolute form, it appears as a petty bourgeois vulgarization of results of a very short phase of bourgeois development, the last twenty-five or thirty years. We reach entirely different conclusions when we examine the historic development of democracy a little closer and consider at the same time the general political history of capitalism.

Democracy has been found in the most dissimilar social formations: in primitive communist groups, in the slave states of antiquity, and in the medieval communes. And similarly absolutism and constitutional monarchy are to be found under the most varied economic orders. When capitalism began, with the first production of commodities, it resorted to a democratic constitution in the municipal communes of the Middle Ages. Later, when it developed to manufacturing, capitalism found its corresponding political form in the absolute monarchy. Finally, as a developed industrial economy, it brought into being in France the democratic republic of 1793, the absolute monarchy of Napoleon I, the nobles' monarchy of the Restoration period (1815–1830), the bourgeois constitutional monarchy of Louis Philippe, then again the democratic republic, and again the monarchy of Napoleon III, and finally, for the third time, the republic.

In Germany, the only truly democratic institution—universal suffrage—is not a conquest won by bourgeois liberalism. Universal suffrage in Germany was an instrument for the fusion of the small states. It is only in this sense that it has any importance for the development of the German bourgeoisie, which is otherwise quite satisfied with a semifeudal constitutional monarchy. In Russia, capitalism prospered for a long time under the regime of oriental absolutism, without having the bourgeoisie manifest the least desire in the world to introduce democracy. In Austria, universal suffrage was above all a safety line thrown to a foundering and decomposing monarchy. In Belgium, the conquest of universal suffrage by the labor movement was undoubtedly due to the weakness of the local militarism, and consequently to the special geographic and political situation of the country. But we have here a "bit of democracy" that has been won not by the bourgeoisie but *against it*.

The uninterrupted victory of democracy, which to our revisionism, as well as to bourgeois liberalism, appears as a great fundamental law of human history and, especially, modern history, is shown upon closer examination to be a phantom. No absolute and general relation can be constructed between capitalist development and democracy. The political form of a given country is always the result of the composite of all the existing political factors, domestic as well as foreign. It admits within its limits all variations of the scale, from absolute monarchy to the democratic republic.

We must abandon, therefore, all hope of establishing democracy as a general law of historical development, even within the framework of modern society. Turning to the present phase of bourgeois society, we observe here, too, political factors that, instead of assuring the realization of Bernstein's schema, lead rather to the abandonment by bourgeois society of the democratic conquests won up to now.

Democratic institutions—and this is of the greatest significance—have completely exhausted their function as aids in the development of bourgeois society. Insofar as they were necessary to bring about the fusion of small states and the creation of large modern states (Germany, Italy), they are no longer indispensable at present. Economic development has meanwhile effected an internal organic cicatrization.

The same thing can be said concerning the transformation of the entire political and administrative state machinery from feudal or semifeudal mechanism to capitalist mechanism. While this transformation has been historically inseparable from the development of democracy, it has been realized today to such an extent that the purely democratic "ingredients" of society, such as universal suffrage and the republican state form, may be suppressed without having the administration, the state finances, or the military organization find it necessary to return to the forms they had before the March Revolution.*

If liberalism as such is now absolutely useless to bourgeois society, it has become, on the other hand, a direct impediment to capitalism from other standpoints. Two factors dominate completely the political life of contemporary states: world politics and the labor movement. Each is only a different aspect of the present phase of capitalist development.

As a result of the development of the world economy and the aggravation and generalization of competition on the world market, militarism and the policy of big navies have become, as instruments of world politics, a decisive factor in the interior as well as in the exterior life of the great states. If it is true that world politics and militarism represent a rising tendency in the present phase of capitalism, then bourgeois democracy must logically move in a descending line.

In Germany, the era of great armament, begun in 1893, and the policy of world politics, inaugurated with the seizure of Kiao-Cheou,** were paid for immediately with the following sacrificial victim: the decomposition of liberalism, the deflation of the Center Party, which passed from opposition to government. The recent elections to the Reichstag of 1907, unrolling under the sign of the German colonial policy, were at the same time the historical burial of German liberalism.

If foreign politics push the bourgeoisie into the arms of reaction, this is no less true about domestic politics—thanks to the rise of the working class. Bernstein shows that he recognizes this when he makes the social democratic "legend," which "wants to swallow everything"—in other words, the socialist efforts of the working class—responsible for the desertion of the liberal bourgeoisie. He advises the proletariat to disavow its socialist aim, so that the mortally frightened liberals might come out of the mouse hole of reaction. Making the suppression of the socialist labor movement an essential condition for the preservation of bourgeois democracy, he proves in a

---

* The German revolution of 1842, which struck an effective blow against the feudal institutions in Germany. —R.L.

** Following its defeat in the war with Japan, European powers pursued a new colonialist offensive in China. Germany controlled the region of Kiao-Cheou from 1898 to 1919. —H.S.

striking manner that this democracy is in complete contradiction with the inner tendency of development of the present society. He proves at the same time that the socialist movement is itself a *direct product* of this tendency.

But he proves, at the same time, still another thing. By making the renouncement of the socialist aim an essential condition of the resurrection of bourgeois democracy, he shows how inexact is the claim that bourgeois democracy is an indispensable condition of the socialist movement and the victory of socialism. Bernstein's reasoning exhausts itself in a vicious circle. His conclusion swallows his premises.

The solution is quite simple. In view of the fact that bourgeois liberalism has given up its ghost from fear of the growing labor movement and its final aim, we conclude that the socialist labor movement is today the *only* support for that which is not the goal of the socialist movement—democracy. We must conclude that democracy can have no other support. We must conclude that the socialist movement is not bound to bourgeois democracy, but that, on the contrary, the fate of democracy is bound with the socialist movement. We must conclude from this that democracy does not acquire greater chances of life in the measure that the working class renounces the struggle for its emancipation, but that, on the contrary, democracy aquires greater chances of survival as the socialist movement becomes sufficiently strong to struggle against the reactionary consequences of world politics and the bourgeois desertion of democracy. He who would strengthen democracy should want to strengthen and not weaken the socialist movement. He who renounces the struggle for socialism renounces both the labor movement and democracy.

CONQUEST OF POLITICAL POWER

The fate of democracy is bound up, we have seen, with the fate of the labor movement. But does the development of democracy render superfluous or impossible a proletarian revolution, that is, the conquest of political power by the workers?

Bernstein settles the question by weighing minutely the good and bad sides of social reform and social revolution. He does it almost in the same manner in which cinnamon or pepper is weighed out in a consumers' cooperative store. He sees the legislative course of historic development as the action of "intelligence," while the revolutionary course of historic development is for him the action of "feeling." Reformist activity he recognizes as a slow method of historic progress, revolution as a rapid method of progress. In legislation he sees a methodical force; in revolution, a spontaneous force.

We have known for a long time that the petty bourgeois reformer finds "good" and "bad" sides in everything. He nibbles a bit at all grasses. But the real course of events is little affected by such combination. The carefully gathered little pile of the "good sides" of all things possible collapses at the first fillip of history. Historically, legislative reform and the revolutionary method function in accordance with influences that are much more profound than the consideration of the advantages or inconveniences of one method or another.

In the history of bourgeois society, legislative reform served to strengthen progressively the rising class till the latter was sufficiently strong to seize political power, to suppress the existing juridical system, and to construct itself a new one. Bernstein, thundering against the conquest of political power as a theory of Blanquist violence, has the misfortune of labeling as a Blanquist error that which has always been the pivot and the motive force of human history. From the first appearance of class societies having the class struggle as the essential content of their history, the conquest of political power has been the aim of all rising classes. Here is the starting point and end of every historic period. This can be seen in the long struggle of the Latin peasantry against the financiers and nobility of ancient Rome, in the struggle of the medieval nobility against the bishops, and in the struggle of the artisans against the nobles in the cities of the Middle Ages. In modern times, we see it in the struggle of the bourgeoisie against feudalism.

Legislative reform and revolution are not different methods of historic development that can be picked out at pleasure from the counter of history, just as one chooses hot or cold sausages. Legislative reform and revolution are different *factors* in the development of class society. They condition and complement each other, and are at the same time reciprocally exclusive, as are the north and south poles, the bourgeoisie and the proletariat.

Every legal constitution is the *product* of a revolution. In the history of classes, revolution is the act of political creation, while legislation is the political expression of the life of a society that has already come into being. Work for reform does not contain its own force, independent from revolution. During every historic period, work for reforms is carried on only in the direction given to it by the impetus of the last revolution, and continues as long as the impulsion of the last revolution continues to make itself felt. Or, to put it more concretely, in each historic period work for reforms is carried on only in the framework of the social form created by the last revolution. Here is the kernel of the problem.

It is contrary to history to represent work for reforms as a long-drawn-out revolution and revolution as a condensed series of reforms. A social transformation and a legislative reform do not differ according to their duration but according to their content. The secret of historic change through the utilization of political power resides precisely in the transformation of simple quantitative modification into a new quality, or to speak more concretely, in the passage of a historic period from one given form of society to another.

That is why people who pronounce themselves in favor of the method of legislative reform *in place and in contradistinction to* the conquest of political power and social revolution do not really choose a more tranquil, calmer, and slower road to the *same* goal, but a *different* goal. Instead of taking a stand for the establishment of a new society they take a stand for surface modifications of the old society. If we follow the political conceptions of revisionism, we arrive at the same conclusion that is reached when we follow the economic theories of revisionism. Our program becomes not the realization of *socialism,* but the reform of *capitalism:* not the suppression of the system of wage labor, but the diminution of exploitation, that is, the suppression of the abuses of capitalism instead of the suppression of capitalism itself.

Does the reciprocal role of legislative reform and revolution apply only to the class struggle of the past? Is it possible that now, as a result of the development of the bourgeois juridical system, the function of moving society from one historic phase to another belongs to legislative reform, and that the conquest of state power by the proletariat has really become "an empty phrase," as Bernstein puts it?

The very opposite is true. What distinguishes bourgeois society from other class societies—from ancient society and from the social order of the Middle Ages? Precisely the fact that class domination does not rest on "acquired rights" but on *real economic relations*—the fact that wage labor is not a juridical relation, but purely an economic relation. In our juridical system there is not a single legal formula for the class domination of today. The few remaining traces of such formulas of class domination are (as that concerning servants) survivals of feudal society.

How can wage slavery be suppressed the "legislative way," if wage slavery is not expressed in laws? Bernstein, who would do away with capitalism by means of legislative reform, finds himself in the same situation as Uspensky's* Russian policeman who says: "Quickly I seized the rascal by the collar! But what do I see? The confounded fellow has no collar!" And that is precisely Bernstein's difficulty.

"All previous societies were based on an antagonism between an oppressing class and an oppressed class" (the *Communist Manifesto*). But in the preceding phases of modern society, this antagonism was expressed in distinctly determined juridical relations and could, especially because of that, accord, to a certain extent, a place to new relations within the framework of the old. "In the midst of serfdom, the serf raised himself to the rank of a member of the town community" (the *Communist Manifest*). How was that made possible? It was made possible by the progressive suppression of all feudal privileges in the environs of the city: the corvee, the right to special dress, the inheritance tax, the lord's claim to the best cattle, the personal levy, marriage under duress, the right to succession, etc., which all together constituted serfdom.

In the same way, the small bourgeoisie of the Middle Ages succeeded in raising itself, while it was still under the yoke of feudal absolutism, to the rank of bourgeoisie (the *Communist Manifesto*). By what means? By means of the formal partial suppression or complete loosening of the corporative bonds, by the progressive transformation of the fiscal administration and of the army.

Consequently, when we consider the question from the abstract viewpoint, not from the historic viewpoint, we can *imagine* (in view of the former class relations) a legal passage, according to the reformist method, from feudal society to bourgeois society. But what do we see in reality? In reality, we see that legal reforms not only did not obviate the seizure of political power by the bourgeoisie, but have, on the contrary, prepared for it and led to it. A formal social-political

---

* Gleb Ivanovich Uspensky (1843–1902) was a Russian populist writer, author of realist novels of peasant life. —H.S.

transformation was indispensable for the abolition of slavery as well as for the complete suppression of feudalism.

But the situation is entirely different now. No law obliges the proletariat to submit itself to the yoke of capitalism. Poverty, the lack of means of production, obliges the proletariat to submit itself to the yoke of capitalism. And no law in the world can give to the proletariat the means of production while it remains in the framework of bourgeois society, for not laws but economic development have torn the means of production from the producers' possession.

And neither is the exploitation inside the system of wage labor based on laws. The level of wages is not fixed by legislation, but by economic factors. The phenomenon of capitalist exploitation does not rest on a legal disposition, but on the purely economic fact that labor power plays in this exploitation the role of merchandise possessing, among other characteristics, the agreeable quality of producing value–*more* than the value it consumes in the form of the laborer's means of subsistence. In short, the fundamental relations of the domination of the capitalist class cannot be transformed by means of legislative reforms, on the basis of capitalist society, because these relations have not been introduced by bourgeois laws, nor have they received the form of such laws. Apparently Bernstein is not aware of this for he speaks of "socialist reforms." On the other hand, he seems to express implicit recognition of this when he writes, on page 10 of his book, that "the economic motive acts freely today, while formerly it was masked by all kinds of relations of domination, by all sorts of ideology."

It is one of the peculiarities of the capitalist order that within it all the elements of the future society first assume, in their development, a form not approaching socialism but, on the contrary, a form moving more and more away from socialism. Production takes on a progressively increasing social character. But under what form is the social character of capitalist production expressed? It is expressed in the form of the large enterprise, in the form of the shareholding concern, the cartel, within which the capitalist antagonisms, capitalist exploitation, the oppression of labor power, are augmented to the extreme.

In the army, capitalist development leads to the extension of obligatory military service, to the reduction of the time of service and, consequently, to a material approach to a popular militia. But all of this takes place under the form of modern militarism, in which the domination of the people by the militarist state and the class character of the state manifest themselves most clearly.

In the field of political relations, the development of democracy brings—in the measure that it finds a favorable soil—the participation of all popular strata in political life and, consequently, some sort of "people's state." But this participation takes the form of bourgeois parliamentarism, in which class antagonism and class domination are not done away with, but are, on the contrary, displayed in the open. Exactly because capitalist development moves through these contradictions, it is necessary to extract the kernel of socialist society from its capitalist shell. Exactly for this reason must the proletariat seize political power and suppress completely the capitalist system.

Of course, Bernstein draws other conclusions. If the development of democracy leads to the aggravation and not to the lessening of capitalist antagonisms, "the social democracy," he answers us, "in order not to render its task more difficult, must by all means try to stop social reforms and the extension of democratic institutions." Indeed, that would be the right thing to do if the social democracy found to its taste, in the petty bourgeois manner, the futile task of picking for itself all the good sides of history and rejecting the bad sides of history. However, in that case, it should at the same time "try to stop" capitalism in general, for there is no doubt that the latter is the rascal placing all these obstacles in the way of socialism. But capitalism furnishes besides the *obstacles* also the only *possibilities* of realizing the socialist program. The same can be said about democracy.

If democracy has become superfluous or annoying to the bourgeoisie, it is on the contrary necessary and indispensable to the working class. It is necessary to the working class because it creates the political forms (autonomous administration, electoral rights, etc.) that will serve the proletariat as fulcrums in its task of transforming bourgeois society. Democracy is indispensable to the working class, because only through the exercise of its democratic rights, in the struggle for democracy, can the proletariat become aware of its class interests and its historic task.

In a word, democracy is indispensable not because it renders superfluous the conquest of political power by the proletariat, but because it renders this conquest of power both *necessary* and *possible*. When Engels, in his preface to the *Class Struggles in France,* revised the tactics of the modern labor movement and urged the legal struggle as opposed to the barricades, he did not have in mind—this comes out of every line of the preface—the question of a definite conquest of political power, but the contemporary daily struggle. He did not have in mind the attitude that the proletariat must take toward the capitalist state at the time of the seizure of power, but the attitude of the proletariat while in the bounds of the capitalist state. Engels was giving directions to the proletariat *oppressed*, and not to the proletariat victorious.

On the other hand, Marx's well-known sentence on the agrarian question in England (Bernstein leans on it heavily) in which he says: "We shall probably succeed easier by buying the estates of the landlords," does not refer to the stand of the proletariat *before, but after its victory*. For there evidently can be a question of buying the property of the old dominant class only when the workers are in power. The possibility envisaged by Marx is of the *pacific exercise of the dictatorship of the proletariat* and not the replacement of the dictatorship with capitalist social reforms. There was no doubt for Marx and Engels about the necessity of having the proletariat conquer political power. It is left to Bernstein to consider the poultry yard of bourgeois parliamentarism as the organ by means of which we are to realize the most formidable social transformation of history, *the passage from capitalist society to socialism.*

Bernstein introduces his theory by warning the proletariat against the danger of acquiring power too early. That is, according to Bernstein, the proletariat ought to leave the bourgeois society in its present condition and itself suffer a frightful defeat. If the proletariat came to power, it could draw from Bernstein's theory the following "practical" conclusion: to go to sleep. His theory condemns the proletariat, at the most decisive moments of the struggle, to inactivity, to a passive betrayal of its own cause.

Our program would be a miserable scrap of paper if it could not serve us in *all* eventualities, at *all* moments of the struggle, and if it did not serve us by its *application* and not by its non-application. If our program contains the formula of the historical development of society from capitalism to socialism, it must also formulate, in all its characteristic fundamentals, all the transitory phases of this development, and it should, consequently, be able to indicate to the proletariat what ought to be its corresponding action at every moment on the road toward socialism. There can be no time for the proletariat when it will be obliged to abandon its program or be abandoned by it.

Practically, this is manifested in the fact that there can be no time when the proletariat, placed in power by the force of events, is not in the condition, or is not morally obliged, to take certain measures for the realization of its program, that is, take transitory measures in the direction of socialism. Behind the belief that the socialist program can collapse completely at any point of the dictatorship of the proletariat lurks the other belief that *the socialist program is, generally and at all times, unrealizable.*

And what if the transitory measures are premature? The question hides a great number of mistaken ideas concerning the real course of a social transformation.

In the first place, the seizure of political power by the proletariat, that is to say by a large popular class, is not produced artificially. It presupposes (with the exception of such cases as the Paris Commune, when the proletariat did not obtain power after a conscious struggle for its goal but fell into its hands like a good thing abandoned by everybody else) a definite degree of maturity of economic and political relations. Here we have the essential difference between coups d'etat along Blanqui's conception, which are accomplished by an "active minority," and burst out like pistol shot, always inopportunely, and the conquest of political power by a great conscious popular mass, which can only be the product of the decomposition of bourgeois society and therefore bears in itself the economic and political legitimization of its opportune appearance.

If, therefore, considered from the angle of political effect, the conquest of political power by the working class cannot materialize itself "too early," then from the angle of conservation of power, the premature revolution, the thought of which keeps Bernstein awake, menaces us like a sword of Damocles. Against that neither prayers nor supplication, neither scares nor any amount of anguish, are of any avail. And this for two very simple reasons.

In the first place, it is impossible to imagine that a transformation as formidable as the passage from capitalist society to socialist society can be realized in one happy act. To consider that as possible is again to lend color to conceptions that are clearly Blanquist. The socialist transformation supposes a long and stubborn struggle, in the course of which, it is quite probable, the proletariat will be repulsed more than once, so that for the first time, from the viewpoint of the final outcome of the struggle, it will have necessarily come to power "too early."

In the second place, it will be impossible to avoid the "premature" conquest of state power by the proletariat precisely because these "premature" attacks of the proletariat constitute a factor, and indeed a very important factor, creating the political conditions of the final victory. In the course of the political crisis accompanying its seizure of power, in the course of the long and stubborn struggles, the proletariat will acquire the degree of political maturity permitting it to obtain in time a definitive victory of the revolution. Thus these "premature" attacks of the proletariat against the state power are in themselves important historic factors helping to provoke and determine the *point* of the definite victory. Considered from this viewpoint, the idea of a "premature" conquest of political power by the laboring class appears to be a political absurdity derived from a mechanical conception of the development of society, and positing for the victory of the class struggle a point fixed *outside* and *independent of* the class struggle.

Since the proletariat is not in the position to seize political power in any other way than "prematurely," since the proletariat is absolutely obliged to seize power once or several times "too early" before it can maintain itself in power for good, the objection to the "premature" conquest of power is at bottom nothing more than a *general opposition to the aspiration of the proletariat to possess itself of state power.* Just as all roads lead to Rome, so too, do we logically arrive at the conclusion that the revisionist proposal to slight the final aim of the socialist movement is really a recommendation to renounce the socialist movement itself.

COLLAPSE

Bernstein began his revision of the social democracy by abandoning the theory of capitalist collapse. The latter, however, is the cornerstone of scientific socialism. Rejecting it, Bernstein also rejects the whole doctrine of socialism. In the course of his discussion, he abandons one after another of the positions of socialism in order to be able to maintain his first affirmation.

Without the collapse of capitalism the expropriation of the capitalist class is impossible. Bernstein therefore renounces expropriation and chooses a progressive realization of the "cooperative principle" as the aim of the labor movement.

But cooperation cannot be realized within capitalist production. Bernstein, therefore, renounces the socialization of production, and merely proposes to reform commerce and to develop consumers' co-operatives.

But the transformation of society through consumers' cooperatives, even by means of trade unions, is incompatible with the real material development of capitalist society. Therefore, Bernstein abandons the materialist conception of history.

But his conception of the march of economic development is incompatible with the Marxist theory of surplus value. Therefore, Bernstein abandons the theory of value and surplus value and, in this way, the whole economic system of Karl Marx.

But the struggle of the proletariat cannot be carried on without a given final aim and without an economic base found in the existing society. Bernstein, therefore, abandons the class struggle and speaks of reconciliation with bourgeois liberalism.

But in a class society, the class struggle is a natural and unavoidable phenomenon. Bernstein, therefore, contests even the existence of classes in society. The working class is for him a mass of individuals, divided politically and intellectually, but also economically. And the bourgeoisie, according to him, does not group itself politically in accordance with its inner economic interest, but only because of exterior pressure from above and below.

But if there is no economic base for the class struggle and if, consequently, there are no classes in our society, not only the future but even the past struggles of the proletariat against the bourgeoisie appear to be impossible and social democracy and its successes seem absolutely incomprehensible, or they can be understood only as the results of political pressure by the government—that is, not as the natural consequence of historic development but as the fortuitous consequences of the policy of Hohenzollern;* not as the legitimate offspring of capitalist society, but as the bastard children of reaction. Rigorously logical, in this respect, Bernstein passes from the materialist conception of history to the outlook of the *Frankfurter Zeitung* and the *Vossische Zeitung*.

---

* The Hohenzollern Dynasty ruled Prussia from 1415, and Germany after 1871, and held sway until Wilhelm II's forced abdication in November 1918. —H.S.

After rejecting the socialist criticism of capitalist society, it is easy for Bernstein to find the present state of affairs satisfactory—at least in a general way. Bernstein does not hesitate. He discovers that at the present time reaction is not very strong in Germany, that "we cannot speak of political reaction in the countries of Western Europe," and that in all the countries of the West "the attitude of the bourgeois classes toward the socialist movement is at most an attitude of defense but not one of oppression" (*Vorwärts*, March 26, 1899). Far from becoming worse, the situation of the workers is getting better. Indeed, the bourgeoisie is politically progressive and morally sane. We cannot speak either of reaction or oppression. It is for the best in the best of all possible worlds....

Bernstein thus travels in logical sequence from A to Z. He began by abandoning the *final aim* and supposedly keeping the movement. But as there can be no socialist movement without a socialist aim, he ends by renouncing the *movement*.

And thus Bernstein's conception of socialism collapses entirely. The proud and admirable symmetric construction of socialist thought becomes for him a pile of rubbish, in which the debris of all systems, the pieces of thought of various great and small minds, find a common resting place. Marx and Proudhon, Leon von Buch and Franz Oppenheimer, Friedrich Albert Lange and Kant, Herr Prokopovich and Dr. Ritter von Neupauer, Herkner and Schulze-Gaevernitz, Lassalle and Professor Julius Wolff:* all contribute something to Bernstein's system. From each he takes a little. There is nothing astonishing about that. For when he abandoned scientific socialism he lost the axis of intellectual crystallization around which isolated facts group themselves in the organic whole of a coherent conception of the world.

His doctrine, composed of bits of all possible systems, seems upon first consideration to be completely free from prejudices. For Bernstein does not like talk of "party science," or to be more exact, of class science, any more than he likes to talk of class liberalism or class morality. He thinks he succeeds in expressing human, general, abstract science, abstract liberalism, abstract morality. But since the society of reality is made up of classes, which have diametrically opposed

---

* Julius Wolff (1862–1937) was an Austrian academic economist. He taught Luxemburg and called her "the most gifted of the students during my Zurich years." —H.S.

interests, aspirations, and conceptions, a general human science in social questions, an abstract liberalism, an abstract morality, are at present illusions, pure utopia. The science, the democracy, the morality,
considered by Bernstein as general, human, are merely the dominant
science, dominant democracy, and dominant morality, that is, bourgeois science, bourgeois democracy, bourgeois morality.

When Bernstein rejects the economic doctrine of Marx in order to
swear by the teachings of Brentano,* Böhm-Bawerk, Jevons, Say, and
Julius Wolff, he exchanges the scientific base of the emancipation of
the working class for the apologetics of the bourgeoisie. When he
speaks of the generally human character of liberalism and transforms
socialism into a variety of liberalism, he deprives the socialist movement (generally) of its class character, and consequently of its historic
content, consequently of all content; and conversely, recognizes the
class representing liberalism in history, the bourgeoisie, as the cham-
pion of the general interests of humanity.

And when he was against "raising of the material factors to the
rank of an all-powerful force of development," when he protests
against the so-called contempt for the ideal that is supposed to rule
the social democracy, when he presumes to talk for idealism, for
morals, pronouncing himself at the same time against the only source
of the moral rebirth of the proletariat, a revolutionary class struggle—he does no more than the following: preach to the working class
the quintessence of the morality of the bourgeoisie, that is, reconciliation with the existing social order and the transfer of the hopes of the
proletariat to the limbo of ethical simulacra.

When he directs his keenest arrows against our dialectic system, he is
really attacking the specific mode of thought employed by the conscious
proletariat in its struggle for liberation. It is an attempt to break the
sword that has helped the proletariat to pierce the darkness of its future.
It is an attempt to shatter the intellectual arm with the aid of which the
proletariat, though materially under the yoke of the bourgeoisie, is yet
enabled to triumph over the bourgeoisie. For it is our dialectical system
that shows to the working class the transitory character of this yoke,
proving to the workers the inevitability of their victory, and is already
realizing a revolution in the domain of thought. Saying good-bye to our
system of dialectics, and resorting instead to the intellectual see-saw of

---

* Lujo Brentano (1844–1931) was a German academic economist and reformist, ally of Vollmar. —H.S.

the well-known "on one hand\on the other hand," "yes\but," "although\however," "more\less," etc., he quite logically lapses into a mode of thought that belongs historically to the bourgeoisie in decline, being the faithful intellectual reflection of the social existence and political activity of the bourgeoisie at that stage. The political "on one hand\on the other hand," "yes\but" of the bourgeoisie today resembles in a marked degree Bernstein's manner of thinking, which is the sharpest and surest proof of the bourgeois nature of his conception of the world.

But, as it is used by Bernstein, the word "bourgeois" itself is not a class expression but a general social notion. Logical to the end, he has exchanged, together with his science, politics, morals, and mode of thinking, the historic language of the proletariat for that of the bourgeoisie. When he uses, without distinction, the term "citizen" in reference to the bourgeois as well as to the proletarian, intending, thereby, to refer to man in general, he identifies man in general with the bourgeois, and human society with bourgeois society.

OPPORTUNISM IN THEORY AND PRACTICE

Bernstein's book is of great importance to the German and the international labor movement. It is the first attempt to give a theoretic base to the opportunist currents common in the social democracy.

These currents may be said to have existed for a long time in our movement, if we take into consideration such sporadic manifestations of opportunism as the question of subsidization of steamers. But it is only since about 1890, with the suppression of the antisocialist laws, that we have had a trend of opportunism of a clearly defined character. Vollmar's* "state socialism," the vote on the Bavarian budget, the "agrarian socialism" of south Germany, Heine's** policy of compensation, Schippel's*** stand on tariffs and militarism are the

---

* Georg Heinrich von Vollmar (1850–1922) was a revisionist anti-Marxist leader of the Bavarian SPD. He was at the forefront of the south German practice of voting for the local government's budget, in violation of official SPD policy. —H.S.

** Wolfgang Heine (1861–1944) was a supporter of Bernstein who advocated SPD acceptance of increased military spending in exchange for suffrage reform. —H.S.

*** Max Schippel (1859–1928) was a revisionist SPD leader who pulled the party away from its antimilitary position. —H.S.

high points in the development of our opportunist practice.

What appears to characterize this practice above all? A certain hostility to "theory." This is quite natural, for our "theory," that is, the principles of scientific socialism, impose clearly marked limitations to practical activity—insofar as it concerns the aims of this activity, the means used in attaining these aims, and the method employed in this activity. It is quite natural for people who run after immediate "practical" results to want to free themselves from such limitations and to render their practice independent of our "theory."

However, this outlook is refuted by every attempt to apply it in reality. State socialism, agrarian socialism, the policy of compensation, the question of the army all constituted defeats to our opportunism. It is clear that, if this current is to maintain itself, it must try to destroy the principles of our theory and elaborate a theory of its own. Bernstein's book is precisely an effort in that direction. That is why at Stuttgart all the opportunist elements in our party immediately grouped themselves around Bernstein's banner. If the opportunist currents in the practical activity of our party are an entirely natural phenomenon that can be explained in the light of the special conditions of our activity and its development, Bernstein's theory is no less natural an attempt to group these currents into a general theoretic expression, an attempt to elaborate its own theoretic conditions and to break with scientific socialism. That is why the published expression of Bernstein's ideas should be recognized as a theoretic test for opportunism and as its first scientific legitimization.

What was the result of this test? We have seen the result. Opportunism is not in a position to elaborate a positive theory capable of withstanding criticism. All it can do is to attack various isolated theses of Marxist theory and, just because Marxist doctrine constitutes one solidly constructed edifice, hope by this means to shake the entire system from the top to its foundation.

This shows that opportunist practice is essentially irreconcilable with Marxism. But it also proves that opportunism is incompatible with socialism (the socialist movement) in general, that its internal tendency is to push the labor movement into bourgeois paths, that opportunism tends to paralyze completely the proletarian class struggle. The latter, considered historically, has evidently nothing to do with Marxist doctrine. For, before Marx and independently from him, there have been labor movements and various socialist doctrines, each of which, in its way, was the theoretic expression, corresponding to the conditions of the time, of the struggle of the working class for emancipation. The theory that consists in basing socialism on the moral notion of justice, on a struggle against the mode of distribution, instead of basing it on a struggle against the mode of production, the conception of class antagonism as an antagonism between the poor and the rich, the effort to graft the "cooperative principle" on capitalist economy—all the nice notions found in Bernstein's doctrine—already existed before him. And these theories were, *in their time*, in spite of their insufficiency, effective theories of the proletarian class struggle. They were the children's seven-league boots, thanks to which the proletariat learned to walk upon the scene of history.

But after the development of the class struggle and its reflex in its social conditions had led to the abandonment of these theories and to the elaboration of the principles of scientific socialism, there could be no socialism—at least in Germany—outside of Marxist socialism, and there could be no socialist class struggle outside of the social democracy. From then on, socialism and Marxism, the proletarian struggle for emancipation and social democracy, were identical. That is why the return to pre-Marxist socialist theories no longer signifies today a return to the seven-league boots of the childhood of the proletariat, but a return to the puny worn-out slippers of the bourgeoisie.

Bernstein's theory was the *first*, and at the same time, the *last* attempt to give a theoretic base to opportunism. It is the last, because in Bernstein's system, opportunism has gone—negatively through its renunciation of scientific socialism, positively through its marshalling of every bit of theoretic confusion possible—as far as it can. In Bernstein's book, opportunism has crowned its theoretic development (just as it completed its practical development in the position taken by Schippel on the question of militarism) and has reached its ultimate conclusion.

Marxist doctrine cannot only refute opportunism theoretically. It alone can explain opportunism as a historic phenomenon in the development of the party. The forward march of the proletariat, on a world-historic scale, to its final victory is not, indeed, "so simple a thing." The peculiar character of this movement resides precisely in the fact that here, for the first time in history, the popular masses themselves, *in opposition* to the ruling classes, are to impose their will, but they must effect this outside of the present society, beyond the existing society. This *will* the masses can only form in a constant struggle against the existing order. The union of the broad popular masses with an aim reaching beyond the existing social order, the union of the daily struggle with the great world transformation, that is the task of the social democratic movement, which must logically grope on its road of development between the following two rocks: abandoning the mass character of the party or abandoning its final aim, falling into bourgeois reformism or into sectarianism, anarchism, or opportunism.

In its theoretic arsenal, Marxist doctrine furnished, more than half a century ago, arms that are effective against both of these two extremes. But because our movement is a mass movement and because the dangers menacing it are derived not from the human brain but from social conditions, Marxist doctrine could not assure us, in advance and once for always, against the anarchist and opportunist tendencies. The latter can be overcome only as we pass from the domain of theory to the domain of practice, but only with the help of the arms furnished us by Marx.

"Bourgeois revolutions," wrote Marx a half century ago, "like those of the eighteenth century, rush onward rapidly from success to success, their stage effects outbid one another, men and things seem to be set in flaming brilliants, ecstasy is the prevailing spirit; but they are short-lived, they reach their climax speedily, and then society relapses into a long fit of nervous reaction before it learns how to appropriate the fruits of its period of feverish excitement. Proletarian revolutions, on the contrary, such as those of the nineteenth century, criticize themselves constantly; constantly interrupt themselves in their own course; come back to what seems to have been accomplished, in order to start anew; scorn with cruel thoroughness the half-measures, weakness, and meanness of their first attempts; seem to throw down their adversary only to enable him to draw fresh strength from the earth and again to rise up against them in more gigantic stature; constantly recoil in fear before the undefined monster magnitude of their own objects—until finally that situation is created that renders all retreat impossible and conditions themselves cry out: 'Hic Rhodus, hic salta!' Here is the rose. And here we must dance!"*

---

* The first sentence is from an Aesop fable, *The Boastful Athlete*, and read originally "Here is the rod, jump here" and then in Latin translation became "Here is Rhodes, jump here." The second sentence is from the German "Hier ist die Rose. Hier tanze!" The meaning is basically "Show us what you can do!" or "So prove it!" (http://www.marxists.org/glossary/terms/h/i.htm) —H.S.

This has remained true even after the elaboration of the doctrine of scientific socialism. The proletarian movement has not as yet, all at once, become social democratic, even in Germany. But it is becoming more social democratic, surmounting continuously the extreme deviations of anarchism and opportunism, both of which are only determining phases of the development of the social democracy, considered as a process.

For these reasons, we must say that the surprising thing here is not the appearance of an opportunist current but rather its feebleness. As long as it showed itself in isolated cases of the practical activity of the party, one could suppose that it had a serious political base. But now that it has shown its face in Bernstein's book, one cannot help exclaim with astonishment:

"What? Is that all you have to say?" Not the shadow of an original thought! Not a single idea that was not refuted, crushed, reduced into dust by Marxism several decades ago!

It was enough for opportunism to speak out to prove it had nothing to say. In the history of our party that is the only importance of Bernstein's book.

Thus saying good-bye to the mode of thought of the revolutionary proletariat, to dialectics, and to the materialist conception of history, Bernstein can thank them for the attenuating circumstances they provide for his conversion. For only dialectics and the materialist conception of history, magnanimous as they are, could make Bernstein appear as an unconscious predestined instrument, by means of which the rising working class expresses its momentary weakness, but which, upon closer inspection, it throws aside contemptuously and with pride.

INTRODUCTION TO
THE MASS STRIKE

*A quiet heroism and a feeling of class solidarity are de-
veloping among the masses which I would very much
like to show to the dear Germans. Workers everywhere
are, by themselves, reaching agreements . . . the feeling
of solidarity and brotherhood with the Russian workers
is so strongly developed that you can't help but be
amazed even though you have personally worked for its
development. And then too, an interesting result of the
revolution: in all factories, committees, elected by the
workers, have arisen "on their own," which decide on
all matters relating to working conditions, hirings and
firings of workers, etc.*

—Letter to Karl and Luise Kautsky from Poland,
February 5, 1906

When Luxemburg wrote this letter the revolution that had
swept Russia was heading toward defeat, and within a
month she, along with countless revolutionary workers,
would be in prison. But her words nonetheless capture the life-chang-
ing experience of participating in a revolutionary movement that
both achieved great things and gave a taste of the possibilities of total
social transformation. Her desire to convey this experience, and to
draw out the lessons for the German movement, led to the publication of *The Mass Strike* later that year. That the revolutionary atmosphere had spread to Germany is evident in Luxemburg's tremendous
support among German workers:

A personal participant in the great events in Russia, she was naturally in great demand at local public meetings. At one meeting in Mannheim the crowd brushed aside the formal agenda with shouts of: "Tell us about Russia.". . .. These were the crowds, the masses who would ultimately make and unmake the party's policy. And what they wanted to hear was precisely what Rosa really wanted to talk about—the lessons of Russia.[1]

Luxemburg also wrote the pamphlet in response to socialists in Hamburg who wanted her to influence the discussion of the mass strike scheduled to take place at the party congress in Mannheim later that year. *The Mass Strike* was, further, an important intervention into a larger debate about the relationship between the trade unions and social democracy that continued the revolutionary critique of reformism launched in *Reform or Revolution*.

Following the repeal of the antisocialist laws in 1890 a newly legal trade union network grew exponentially in Germany: Union membership went from 300,000 in 1890 to more than 2.5 million in 1914; the total wealth of the unions increased from 425,845 to more than 88 million deutschmarks; the number of trade-union bureaucrats increased from 269 in 1900 to 2,867 in 1914.[2] In this period two major forces battled within the union movement. The increasingly powerful and well-funded bureaucracy favored a centralized structure oriented on material and economic issues, and a break from the movement's socialist roots in favor of political "neutrality." Radical union members, on the other hand, saw the development of this permanent bureaucracy of paid officials as a threat to the labor movement's independence. They feared the bureaucrats would rein in both the fight for immediate victories and for the socialist revolution necessary to end class exploitation and oppression for good.

By 1906 the increase in salaried trade-union functionaries, disconnected from the workers they formally represented, had changed the political character of the trade unions:

> The new bureaucracy viewed its successes not, like the party radicals, as part of the process of the organization of the proletariat for revolution, but as triumphs in and for themselves, to be further expanded within the framework of the capitalist order. The old intransigent hostility toward both the entrepreneur and the state yielded to a willingness to compromise differences.[3]

A series of trade-union conferences, and party and international congresses, tackled the question of the relationship between the party and the trade unions, and the attitude of both to the mass strike. At the SPD Congress in Jena in January 1905, August Bebel submitted a resolution endorsing the use of the mass strike in certain circumstances. Luxemburg gave radical speeches in favor of the mass strike—for which she was tried and given a prison sentence (two months, which she served in 1907)—and the measure passed. At the trade-union conference in Köln (Cologne) in May 1905 a resolution was passed, by 200 to 17, not only opposing the mass strike, but proscribing any discussion of it. Schorske explains what was at stake:

> If the party should adopt a mass strike tactic, the principle of gradual gains by centrally controlled but localized strikes would be jeopardized; the organizations and their treasuries might be wiped out in a revolutionary adventure for political ends, which the trade-union officials felt to be none of their concern; and the localists might gain strength among a rank and file infected with mass strike propaganda. For the union leaders, the mass strike question was dynamite.[4]

The SPD executive privately had similar fears, and entered secret negotiations with trade-union officials in February 1906, agreeing not to advocate a mass strike but to "'try to prevent one as much as possible.'"[5]

The debate over the mass strike and the trade unions precipitated the growing rift between the SPD executive and the revolutionaries. At the Mannheim Congress, Bebel, for the executive, advocated "parity" or "equal authority" between unions and the party. Against Bebel, Kautsky, at this point still an ally of Luxemburg, argued that the unions were limited to defending workers under the constraints of capitalism, strictly the "minor" platform of the Erfurt program. The party, on the other hand, represented the struggle for the complete emancipation of workers, only realizable in the final goal of socialist revolution. Therefore, the unions had to be subordinated to the party. Even though the congress favored Kautsky, the executive maneuvered a victory by adding parts of Kautsky's proposal to Bebel's. The result was a total reversal of the radical victory at the Jena Congress, and a decisive triumph for reformism.

But Luxemburg's firsthand revolutionary experience taught her that the power of the working class, both organized and unorganized, was beyond the scope of any trade union, no matter how firmly established, and capable of winning immense reforms in the here and now as well as forwarding the revolution. Luxemburg saw the mass strike as a crucial element of the revolutionary process, and something completely different from the dominant paradigms on offer. The mass strikes of 1905 undermined the idea of "pure trade-union" struggle—i.e., an exclusive focus on economic as opposed to political issues. Rather, history showed that economic struggles become political, and vice versa, as the two are inseparable and interdependent. So too did they refute the "parade-ground mentality" that represents strikes as things to be decreed or banned by trade-union officials. In a revolutionary situation, mass strikes slip the reins of such control and acquire a momentum all their own.

Luxemburg did not, as some have argued, suggest that mass strikes would spontaneously lead to revolution. Rather, she saw that only conscious socialist leadership is able to turn the latent power of the mass strike into successful revolution. In this she and Lenin were in absolute agreement: socialists must be the conscious vanguard that can lead the masses to revolutionary victory. Luxemburg effectively developed a vision of revolution, based on mass working-class self-activity and socialist leadership, that "laid the basis for the intellectual structure of the group, which after 1910 emerged as the 'left radical' wing of the Germany party that later provided the connecting link to Russian Bolshevism."[6]

There is one striking omission, however: the pamphlet does not address the soviet, or worker council, as a fundamental feature of socialist revolution. Yet this was an important part of the 1905 Revolution, one she remarked upon in her personal letters, and of course was to be central to the successful revolution of 1917.[7] This is perhaps less surprising when you consider that the emergence of soviets was treated with suspicion initially even by the Bolsheviks, who were to become their greatest advocates. Lenin, who recognized in them "the embryo of a provisional revolutionary government," argued, but "was unable to win the Bolshevik organization as a whole to this outlook until after the defeat of the 1905 revolution."[8]

Luxemburg's pamphlet failed in its ostensible goal of shaping the vote at the Mannheim Congress, but it succeeded in the far greater project of contributing to revolutionary theory, of generalizing from one historical time and place to the benefit of future moments. It is an inspiring account of a high point in working-class struggle, one that gives us a "glimpse of the magnificent revolutionary initiative and self-sacrifice that the workers rise to during a revolution."[9]

NOTES

Bronner, *Letters of Rosa Luxemburg,* 114
1 Nettl, *Rosa Luxemburg,* 369.
2 Howard, *Selected Political Writings of Rosa Luxemburg,* 264 n26.
3 Schorske, *German Social Democracy,* 15.
4 Ibid., 39.
5 Quoted in Schorske, *German Social Democracy,* 48.
6 Schorske, *German Social Democracy,* 55.
7 Dunayevskaya, *Rosa Luxemburg,* 19.
8 Quoted in Paul Le Blanc, *Lenin and the Revolutionary Party* (New Jersey: Humanities Press, 1990), 116.
9 Cliff, *Rosa Luxemburg,* 36.

THE MASS STRIKE, THE POLITICAL
PARTY, AND THE TRADE UNIONS

I. THE RUSSIAN REVOLUTION,
ANARCHISM, AND THE GENERAL STRIKE

Almost all works and pronouncements of international socialism on the subject of the mass strike date from the time before
the Russian Revolution [of 1905—Ed.], the first historical experiment on a very large scale with this means of struggle. It is therefore evident that they are, for the most part, out of date. Their standpoint is essentially that of Engels, who in 1873 wrote as follows in his
criticism of the revolutionary blundering of the Bakuninists* in Spain:

> The general strike, in the Bakuninists' program, is the lever which will
> be used for introducing the social revolution. One fine morning all
> the workers in every industry in a country, or perhaps in every coun-
> try, will cease work, and thereby compel the ruling classes either to
> submit in about four weeks, or to launch an attack on the workers so
> that the latter will have the right to defend themselves, and may use
> the opportunity to overthrow the old society. The proposal is by no
> means new: French and Belgian socialists have paraded it continually
> since 1848, but for all that it is of English origin. During the rapid
> and powerful development of Chartism among the English workers
> that followed the crisis of 1837, the "holy month"—a suspension of
> work on a national scale—was preached as early as 1839, and was re-
> ceived with such favor that in July 1842 the factory workers of the
> north of England attempted to carry it out. And at the Congress of
> the Alliancists at Geneva on September 1, 1873, the general strike
> played a great part, but it was admitted on all sides that to carry it

---

* Mikhail Bakunin (1814–1876) was a Russian emigrant to Germany, member of the First International and founder of the anarchist movement. —H.S.

out it was necessary to have a perfect organization of the working class and a full war chest. And that is the crux of the question. On the one hand, the governments, especially if they are encouraged by the workers' abstention from political action, will never allow the funds of the workers to become large enough, and on the other hand, political events and the encroachments of the ruling classes will bring about the liberation of the workers long before the proletariat gets the length of forming this ideal organization and this colossal reserve fund. But if they had these, they would not need to make use of the roundabout way of the general strike in order to attain their object.

Here we have the reasoning that was characteristic of the attitude of international social democracy towards the mass strike in the following decades. It is based on the anarchist theory of the general strike—that is, the theory of the general strike as a means of inaugurating the social revolution, in contradistinction to the daily political struggle of the working class—and exhausts itself in the following simple dilemma: either the proletariat as a whole are not yet in possession of the powerful organization and financial resources required, in which case they cannot carry through the general strike or they are already sufficiently well organized, in which case they do not need the general strike. This reasoning is so simple and at first glance so irrefutable that, for a quarter of a century, it has rendered excellent service to the modern labor movement as a logical weapon against the anarchist phantom and as a means of carrying out the idea of political struggle to the widest circles of the workers. The enormous strides taken by the labor movement in all capitalist countries during the last twenty-five years are the most convincing evidence of the value of the tactics of political struggle, which were insisted upon by Marx and Engels in opposition to Bakuninism; and German social democracy, in its position of vanguard of the entire international labor movement, is not in the least the direct product of the consistent and energetic application of these tactics.

The [1905] Russian Revolution has now effected a radical revision of the above piece of reasoning. For the first time in the history of the class struggle it has achieved a grandiose realization of the idea of the mass strike and—as we shall discuss later—has even matured the general strike and thereby opened a new epoch in the development of the labor movement. It does not, of course, follow from this that the tactics of political struggle recommended by Marx and Engels were false or that criticism applied by them to anarchism was incorrect. On the contrary, it is the same train of ideas, the same method, the Engels-

Marxian tactics, which lay at the foundation of the previous practice of the German social democracy, which now in the Russian Revolution are producing new factors and new conditions in the class struggle. The Russian Revolution, which is the first historical experiment on the model of the mass strike, does not merely provide no vindication of anarchism, but actually means *the historical liquidation of anarchism.* The sorry existence to which this cerebral tendency was condemned in recent decades by the powerful development of social democracy in Germany may, to a certain extent, be explained by the exclusive domination and long duration of the parliamentary period. A tendency patterned entirely upon the "first blow" and "direct action," a tendency "revolutionary" in the most naked, pitchfork sense, can only temporarily languish in the calm of parliamentarian day and, on a return of the period of direct open struggle, can come to life again and unfold its inherent strength.

Russia, in particular, appeared to have become the experimental field for the heroic deeds of anarchism. A country in which the proletariat had absolutely no political rights and extremely weak organizations, a many-colored complex of various sections of the population, a chaos of conflicting interests, a low standard of education among the masses of the people, extreme brutality in the use of violence on the part of the prevailing regime—all this seemed as if created to raise anarchism to a sudden if perhaps short-lived power. And finally, Russia was the historical birthplace of anarchism. But the fatherland of Bakunin was to become the burial place of his teachings. Not only did and do the anarchists in Russia not stand at the head of the mass strike movement; not only does the whole political leadership of revolutionary action and also of the mass strike lie in the hands of the social democratic organizations, which are bitterly opposed as "bourgeois parties" by Russian anarchists, or partly in the hands of such socialist organizations as are more or less influenced by the social democracy and more or less approximate to it—such as the terrorist party, the "socialist revolutionaries"—but the anarchists simply do not exist as a serious political tendency in the Russian Revolution. Only in a small Lithuanian town with particularly difficult conditions—a confused medley of different nationalities among the workers, an extremely scattered condition of small-scale industry, a very severely oppressed proletariat—in Bialystok, there is, among the seven or eight different revolutionary groups, a handful of half-grown "anarchists" who promote confusion and bewilderment among the workers to the best of their ability; and lastly in Moscow, and perhaps in two or three other towns, a handful of people of this ilk make themselves noticeable.

But apart from these few "revolutionary" groups, what is the actual role of anarchism in the Russian Revolution? It has become the sign of the common thief and plunderer; a large proportion of the innumerable thefts and acts of plunder of private persons are carried out under the name of "anarchist-communism"—acts that rise up like a troubled wave against the revolution in every period of depression and in every period of temporary defensive. Anarchism has become in the Russian Revolution, not the theory of the struggling proletariat, but the ideological signboard of the counterrevolutionary lumpenproletariat, who, like a school of sharks, swarm in the wake of the battleship of the revolution. And therewith the historical career of anarchism is well-nigh ended.

On the other hand, the mass strike in Russia has been realized not as means of evading the political struggle of the working class, and especially of parliamentarism, not as a means of jumping suddenly into the social revolution by means of a theatrical coup, but as a means, firstly, of creating for the proletariat the conditions of the daily political struggle and especially of parliamentarism. The revolutionary struggle in Russia, in which mass strikes are the most important weapon, is, by the working people, and above all by the proletariat, conducted for those political rights and conditions whose necessity and importance in the struggle for the emancipation of the working class Marx and Engels first pointed out, and in opposition to anarchism fought for with all their might in the International. Thus has historical dialectics, the rock on which the whole teaching of Marxian socialism rests, brought it about that today anarchism, with which the idea of the mass strike is indissolubly associated, has itself come to be opposed to the mass strike in practice; while on the contrary, the mass strike that, as the opposite of the political activity of the proletariat, was combated appears today as the most powerful weapon of the struggle for political rights. If, therefore, the Russian Revolution makes imperative a fundamental revision of the old standpoint of Marxism on the question of the mass strike, it is once again Marxism whose general method and points of view have thereby, in new form, carried off the prize. The Moor's beloved can die only by the hand of the Moor.

II. THE MASS STRIKE, A HISTORICAL AND NOT AN ARTIFICIAL PRODUCT

The first revision of the question of the mass strike that results from the experience of Russia relates to the general conception of the problem. Till the present time the zealous advocates of an "attempt with the mass strike" in Germany of the stamp of Bernstein, Eisner,* etc., and also the strongest opponents of such an attempt as represented in the trade-union camp by, for example, Bombelburg, stand, when all is said and done, on the same conception, and that is the anarchist one. The apparent polar opposites do not mutually exclude each other but, as always, condition, and at the same time, supplement each other. For the anarchist mode of thought is direct speculation on the "great Kladderadatsch,"** on the social revolution merely as an external and inessential characteristic. According to it, what is essential is the whole abstract, unhistorical view of the mass strike and of all the conditions of the proletarian struggle generally.

For the anarchist there exist only two things as material suppositions of his "revolutionary" speculations—first, imagination, and second, goodwill and courage to rescue humanity from the existing capitalist vale of tears. This fanciful mode of reasoning sixty years ago gave the result that the mass strike was the shortest, surest, and easiest means of springing into the better social future. The same mode of reasoning recently gave the result that the trade-union struggle was the only real "direct action of the masses" and also the only real revolutionary struggle—which, as is well known, is the latest notion of the French and Italian "syndicalists."*** The fatal thing for anarchism has always been that the methods of struggle improvised in the air were not only a reckoning without their host, that is, they

---

* Kurt Eisner (1867–1919) was a leading member of the SPD who edited the paper *Vorwärts* from 1898–1905. Initially a revisionist and opponent of Luxemburg, he moved leftward, opposed World War I as a pacifist, and helped found the independent SPD (U-SPD). —H.S.

** A loud noise or uproar. August Bebel often used the term in reference to the onset of capitalism's collapse. —H.S.

*** An anarchist trade unionism that opposes political organization and advocates working-class emancipation exclusively through independent trade union activity. —H.S.

were purely utopian, but that they, while not reckoning in the least with the despised evil reality, unexpectedly became in this evil reality, practical assistants to the reaction, where previously they had only been, for the most part, revolutionary speculations.

On the same ground of abstract, ahistorical methods of observation stand those today who would, in the manner of a board of directors, put the mass strike in Germany on the calendar on an appointed day, and those who, like the participants in the trade-union congress at Cologne, would by a prohibition of "propaganda" eliminate the problem of the mass strike from the face of the earth. Both tendencies proceed on the common, pure-anarchistic assumption that the mass strike is a purely technical means of struggle which can be "decided" at pleasure and strictly according to conscience, or "forbidden"—a kind of pocketknife that can be kept in the pocket clasped "ready for any emergency," and according to the decision, can be unclasped and used. The opponents of the mass strike do indeed claim for themselves the merit of taking into consideration the historical groundwork and the material conditions of the present situation in Germany in opposition to the "revolutionary romanticists" who hover in the air, and do not at any point reckon with the hard realities and the possibilities and impossibilities. "Facts and figures; figures and facts!" they cry, like Mr. Gadgrind in Dickens's *Hard Times*.

What the trade-union opponent of the mass strike understands by the "historical basis" and "material conditions" is two things—on the one hand the weakness of the proletariat, and on the other hand, the strength of Prussian-German militarism. The inadequate organization of the workers and the imposing Prussian bayonet—these are the facts and figures upon which these trade-union leaders base their practical policy in the given case. Now while it is quite true that the trade-union cash box and the Prussian bayonet are material and very historical phenomena, but the conception based upon them is not historical materialism in Marx's sense but a policemanlike materialism in the sense of Puttkammer.* The representatives of the capitalist police state reckon much, and indeed, exclusively, with the occasional real power of the organized proletariat as well as with the material might of the bayonet, and from the comparative example of these two rows of figures the

---

* Robert von Puttkammer (1828–1900) was a conservative German minister of the interior who upheld Bismarck's antisocialist laws in the 1870s and 1880s. —H.S.

comforting conclusion is always drawn that the revolutionary labor movement is produced by individual demagogues and agitators; and that therefore there is in the prisons and bayonets an adequate means of subduing the unpleasant "passing phenomena."

The class-conscious German workers have at last grasped the humor of the policemanlike theory that the whole modern labor movement is an artificial, arbitrary product of a handful of conscienceless "demagogues and agitators."

It is exactly the same conception, however, that finds expression when two or three worthy comrades unite in a voluntary column of night watchmen in order to warn the German working class against the dangerous agitation of a few "revolutionary romanticists" and their "propaganda of the mass strike"; or, when on the other side, a noisy indignation campaign is engineered by those who, by means of "confidential" agreements between the executive of the party and the general commission of the trade unions,* believe they can prevent the outbreak of the mass strike in Germany.

If it depended on the inflammatory "propaganda" of revolutionary romanticists or on confidential or public decisions of the party direction, then we should not even yet have had in Russia a single serious mass strike. In no country in the world—as I pointed out in March 1905 in the *Sächische Arbetierzeitung*—was the mass strike so little "propagated" or even "discussed" as in Russia. And the isolated examples of decisions and agreements of the Russian party executive, which really sought to proclaim the mass strike of their own accord—as, for example, the last attempt in August of this year after the dissolution of the Duma—are almost valueless.

If, therefore, the Russian Revolution teaches us anything, it teaches above all that the mass strike is not artificially "made," not "decided" at random, not "propagated," but that it is a historical phenomenon, which, at a given moment, results from social conditions with historical inevitability. It is not, therefore, by abstract speculations on the possibility or impossibility, the utility or the injuriousness of the mass strike, but only by an examination of those factors and social conditions out of which the mass strike grows in the present phase of the class struggle— in other words, it is not by *subjective criticism* of the mass strike from

---

* In Germany the "Free Trade Unions" (social democratic) coexisted with company unions, church unions, and "radical" bourgeois unions. The Catholic unions included opposition to social democracy in their statutes. —H.S.

the standpoint of what is desirable, but only by *objective investigation* of the sources of the mass strike from the standpoint of what is historically inevitable, that the problem can be grasped or even discussed.

In the unreal sphere of abstract logical analysis it can be shown with exactly the same force on either side that the mass strike is absolutely impossible and sure to be defeated, and that it is possible and that its triumph cannot be questioned. And therefore the value of the evidence led on each side is exactly the same—and that is nil. Therefore, the fear of the "propagation" of the mass strike, which has even led to formal anathemas against the persons alleged to be guilty of this crime, is solely the product of the droll confusion of persons. It is just as impossible to "propagate" the mass strike as an abstract means of struggle as it is to propagate the "revolution." "Revolution" like "mass strike" signifies nothing but an external form of the class struggle, which can have sense and meaning only in connection with definite political situations.

If anyone were to undertake to make the mass strike generally, as a form of proletarian action, the object of methodological agitation, and to go house to house canvassing with this "idea" in order to gradually win the working class to it, it would be as idle and profitless and absurd an occupation as it would be to seek to make the idea of the revolution or of the fight at the barricades the object of a special agitation. The mass strike has now become the center of the lively interest of the German and the international working class because it is a new form of struggle, and as such is the sure symptom of a thoroughgoing internal revolution in the relations of the classes and in the conditions of the class struggle. It is a testimony to the sound revolutionary instinct and to the quick intelligence of the mass of the German proletariat that, in spite of the obstinate resistance of their trade-union leaders, they are applying themselves to this new problem with such keen interest.

But it does not meet the case, in the presence of this interest and of this fine, intellectual thirst and desire for revolutionary deeds on the part of the workers, to treat them to abstract mental gymnastics on the possibility or impossibility of the mass strike; they should be enlightened on the development of the Russian Revolution, the international significance of that revolution, the sharpening of class antagonisms in Western Europe, the wider political perspectives of the class struggle in Germany, and the role and the tasks of the masses in the coming struggles. Only in this form will the discussion on the mass strike lead to the widening of the intellectual horizon of the proletariat, to the sharpening of their way of thinking, and to the steeling of their energy.

Viewed from this standpoint, however, the criminal proceedings desired by the enemies of "revolutionary romanticism" appear in all their absurdity, because, in treating of the problem, one does not adhere strictly to the text of the Jena resolution. The "practical politicians" agree to this resolution if need be, because they couple the mass strike chiefly with the fate of universal suffrage, from which it follows that they can believe two things—first, that the mass strike is of a purely defensive character, and second, that the mass strike is even subordinate to parliamentarism, that is, has been turned into a mere appendage of parliamentarism. But the real kernel of the Jena resolution in this connection is that in the present position of Germany an attempt on the part of the prevailing reaction on the parliamentary vote would in all probability be the moment for the introduction of, and the signal for, a period of stormy political struggles in which the mass strike as a means of struggle in Germany might well come into use for the first time.

But to seek to narrow and to artificially smother the social importance, and to limit the historical scope, of the mass strike as a phenomenon and as a problem of the class struggle by the wording of a congress resolution is an undertaking that for short-sightedness can only be compared with the veto on discussion of the trade-union congress at Cologne. In the resolution of the Jena Congress German social democracy has officially taken notice of the fundamental change that the Russian Revolution has effected in the international conditions of the proletarian class struggle, and has announced its capacity for revolutionary development and its power of adaptability to the new demands of the coming phase of the class struggle. Therein lies the significance of the Jena resolution. As for the practical application of the mass strike in Germany, history will decide that as it decided it in Russia—history in which German social democracy with its decisions is, it is true, an important factor, but, as the same time, only *one* factor among many.

III. DEVELOPMENT OF THE MASS STRIKE MOVEMENT IN RUSSIA

The mass strike, as it appears for the most part in the discussion in Germany, is a very clear and simply thought out, sharply sketched, isolated phenomenon. It is the political mass strike exclusively that is spoken of. What is meant by it is a single grand rising of the industrial proletariat springing from some political motive of the highest importance, and undertaken on the basis of an opportune and mutual understanding on the part of the controlling authorities of the party and of the trade unions, and carried through in the spirit of party discipline and in perfect order, and in still more perfect order brought to the directing committees as a signal given at the proper time, by which committees the regulation of support, the cost, the sacrifice—in a word, the whole material balance of the mass strike—is exactly determined in advance.

Now, when we compare this theoretical scheme with the real mass strike, as it appeared in Russia five years ago, we are compelled to say that this representation, which in the German discussion occupies the central position, hardly corresponds to a single one of the many mass strikes that have taken place, and on the other hand that the mass strike in Russia displays such a multiplicity of the most varied forms of action that it is altogether impossible to speak of "the" mass strike, of an abstract schematic mass strike. All the factors of the mass strike, as well as its character, are not only different in the different towns and districts of the country, but its general character has often changed in the course of the revolution. The mass strike has passed through a definite history in Russia, and is passing still further through it. Who, therefore, speaks of the mass strike in Russia must, above all things, keep its history before his eyes.

The present official period, so to speak, of the Russian Revolution is justly dated from the rising of the proletariat on January 22, 1905, when the demonstration of 200,000 workers ended in a frightful bloodbath before the tsar's palace. The bloody massacre in St. Petersburg was, as is well known, the signal for the outbreak of the first gigantic series of mass strikes, which spread over the whole of Russia within a few days and which carried the call to action of the revolution from St. Petersburg to every corner of the empire and among the widest sections of the proletariat. But the St. Petersburg rising of January 22 was only the critical moment of a mass strike that the proletariat of the tsarist capital had previously entered upon in January 1905. The January mass strike was without doubt carried through under the immediate influence of the gigantic general strike that in December 1904 broke out in the Caucasus, in Baku, and for a long time kept the whole of Russia in suspense. The events of December in Baku were on their part only the last and powerful ramification of those tremendous mass strikes, which, like a periodic earthquake, shook the whole of south Russia, and whose prologue was the mass strike in Batum in the Caucasus in March 1902.

This first mass strike movement in the continuous series of present revolutionary eruptions is finally separated by five or six years from the great general strike of the textile workers in St. Petersburg in 1896 and 1897, and if this movement is apparently separated from the present revolution by a few years of apparent stagnation and strong reaction, everyone who knows the inner political development of the Russian proletariat to their present stage of class consciousness and revolutionary energy will realize that the history of the present period of the mass struggles begins with those general strikes in St. Petersburg. They are therefore important for the problems of the mass strike because they already contain, in the germ, all the principal factors of later mass strikes.

Again, the St. Petersburg general strike of 1896 appears as a purely economic partial wage struggle. Its causes were the intolerable working conditions of the spinners and weavers in St. Petersburg; a working day of thirteen, fourteen, or fifteen hours, miserable piece-work rates, and a whole series of contemptible chicaneries on the part of the employers. This condition of things, however, was patiently endured by workers for a long time till an apparently trivial circumstance filled the cup to overflowing. The coronation of the present tsar, Nicholas II, which had been postponed for two years for fear of the revolutionaries, was celebrated in May 1896, and on that occasion the St. Petersburg employers displayed their patriotic zeal by giving their workers three days of compulsory holidays, for which, curious to relate, they did not desire to pay their employees. The workers, angered by this, began to move. After a conference of about three hundred of the intelligent workers in the Ekaterinhof Garden, a strike was decided upon, and the following demands were formulated: first, payment of wages for the coronation holidays; second, a working day of ten hours; third, increased rates for piecework. This happened on May 24. In a week every weaving and spinning establishment was at a standstill and 40,000 workers were in the general strike. Today this event, measured by the gigantic mass strike of the revolution, may appear a little thing. In the political polar rigidity of the Russia of that time a general strike was something unheard of; it was even a complete revolution in miniature. There began, of course,

the most brutal persecution. About one thousand workers were arrested and the general strike was suppressed.

Here already we see all the fundamental characteristics of the later
mass strikes. The next occasion of the movement was wholly accidental, even unimportant, its outbreak elementary; but in the success of
the movement the fruits of the agitation, extending over several years,
of the social democracy were seen and in the course of the general
strike the social democratic agitators stood at the head of the movement, directed it, and used it to stir up revolutionary agitation. Furthermore the strike was outwardly a mere economic struggle for
wages, but the attitude of the government and the agitation of the social democracy made it a political phenomenon of the first rank. And
lastly, the strike was suppressed; the workers suffered a "defeat." But
in January of the following year the textile workers of St. Petersburg
repeated the general strike once more and this time achieved a remarkable success: the legal introduction of a working day of eleven hours
throughout the whole of Russia. What was nevertheless a much more
important result was this: since that first general strike of 1896, which
was entered upon without a trace of organization or of strike funds, an
intensive trade-union fight began in Russia proper that spread from St.
Petersburg to the other parts of the country and opened up entirely
new vistas to social democratic agitation and organization, through
which, in the apparently death-like peace of the following period, the
revolution was prepared by underground work.

The outbreak of the Caucasian strike in March 1902 was apparently as accidental and as much due to pure economic partial causes
(although produced by quite other factors) as that of 1896. It was connected with the serious industrial and commercial crisis that in Russia
was the precursor of the Japanese war, which, combined, were the most
powerful factors of the nascent revolutionary ferment. The crisis produced an enormous mass of unemployment that nourished the agitation among the proletarian masses, and therefore the government, to
restore tranquility among the workers, undertook to transport the "superfluous hands" in batches to their respective home districts. One such
measure, which was to affect about four hundred petroleum workers,
called forth a mass protest in Batum, which led to demonstrations, arrests, a massacre, and finally to a political trial in which the purely economic and partial affair suddenly became a political and revolutionary
event. The reverberation of the wholly "fruitless" expiring and

suppressed strike in Batum was a series of revolutionary mass demonstrations of workers in Nizhni-Novgorod, Saratov, and other towns, and therefore a mighty surge forward of the general wave of the revolutionary movement.

Already in November 1902 the first genuine revolutionary echo followed in the shape of a general strike at Rostov-on-Don. Disputes about the rates of pay in the workshops of the Vladicaucasus Railway gave the impetus to this movement. The management sought to reduce wages and therefore the Don committee of social democracy issued a proclamation with a summons to strike for the following demands: a nine-hour day, increase of wages, abolition of fines, dismissal of obnoxious engineers, etc. Entire railway workshops participated in the strike. Presently all other industries joined in and suddenly an unprecedented state of affairs prevailed in Rostov: all industrial work was at a standstill, and every day monster meetings of fifteen thousand to twenty thousand were held in the open air, sometimes surrounded by a cordon of Cossacks, at which for the first time social democratic popular speakers appeared publicly, inflammatory speeches on socialism and political freedom were delivered and received with immense enthusiasm, and revolutionary appeals were distributed by tens of thousands of copies. In the midst of rigid absolutist Russia the proletariat of Rostov won for the first time the right of assembly and freedom of speech by storm. It goes without saying that there was a massacre here. The disputes over wages in the Vladicaucasus Railway workshops grew in a few days into a political general strike and a revolutionary street battle. As an echo to this there followed immediately a general strike at the station of Tichoretzkaia on the same railway. Here too a massacre took place and also a trial, and thus even Tichoretzkaia has taken its place in the indissoluble chain of the factors of the revolution.

The spring of 1903 gave the answer to the defeated strikes in Rostov and Tichoretzkaia; the whole of south Russia in May, June, and July was aflame. Baku, Tiflis, Batum, Elisavetgrad, Odessa, Kiev, Nikolaev, and Ekaterinoslav were in a general strike in the literal meaning of those words. But here again the movement did not arise on any preconceived plan from one another; it flowed together from individual points in each one from different causes and in a different form. The beginning was made by Baku where several partial wage struggles in individual factories and departments culminated in a general strike.

In Tiflis the strike was begun by 2,000 commercial employees who had a working day from six o'clock in the morning to eleven at night. On the fourth of July they all left their shops and made a circuit of the town to demand from the proprietors of the shops that they close their premises. The victory was complete; the commercial employees won a working day from eight in the morning to eight in the evening, and they were immediately joined by all the factories, workshops, and offices, etc. The newspapers did not appear, and tramway traffic could not be carried on under military protection.

In Elisavetgrad on July 4 a strike began in all the factories with purely economic demands. These were mostly conceded, and the strike ended on the fourteenth. Two weeks later, however, it broke out again. The bakers this time gave the word and the bricklayers, the joiners, the dyers, the mill-workers, and finally all factory workers joined them.

In Odessa the movement began with a wage struggle in the course of which the "legal" workers' union, founded by government agents according to the program of the famous gendarme Zubatov,* was developed. Historical dialectics had again seized the occasion to play one of its malicious little pranks. The economic struggles of the earlier period (among them the great St. Petersburg general strike of 1896) had misled Russian social democracy into exaggerating the importance of so-called economics, and in this way the ground had been prepared among the workers for the demagogic activities of Zubatov. After a time, however, the great revolutionary stream turned round the little ship with the false flag, and compelled it to ride right at the head of the revolutionary proletarian flotilla. The Zubatovian unions gave the signal for the great general strike in Odessa in the spring of 1904, as for the general strike in St. Petersburg in January 1905. The workers of Odessa, who were not to be deceived by the appearance of friendliness on the part of the government for the workers, and of its sympathy with purely economic strikes, suddenly demanded proof by example, and compelled the Zubatovian "workers union" in a factory to declare a strike for very moderate demands. They were immediately thrown on the streets, and when they demanded the protection of the authorities that was promised them by their leader, the gentleman vanished and left the workers in the wildest excitement.

---

* Zubatov, Sergey Vasilyevich (1864–1917) was the tsar's chief of secret police (the Okhrana) who after 1901 organized alternative worker associations to counter the impact of the social democratic unions. He committed suicide after the 1917 revolution. —H.S.

The social democrats at once placed themselves at the head of affairs, and the strike movement extended to other factories. On the first day of July 2,500 dockers struck work for an increase of wages from eighty kopecks to two rubles, and the shortening of the workday by half an hour. On the sixteenth of July the seamen joined the movement. On the thirteenth the tramway staff began a strike. Then a meeting took place of all the strikers, seven thousand or eight thousand men; they formed a procession that went from factory to factory, growing like an avalanche, and presently a crowd of forty thousand to fifty thousand betook themselves to the docks in order to bring all work there to a standstill. A general strike soon reigned throughout the whole city.

In Kiev, a strike began in the railway workshops on July 21. Here also the immediate cause was miserable conditions of labor, and wage demands were presented. On the following day the foundry men followed the example. On July 23, an incident occurred that gave the signal for the general strike. During the night two delegates of the railwaymen were arrested. The strikers immediately demanded their release, and as this was not conceded, they decided not to allow trains to leave the town. At the station all the strikers with their wives and families sat down on the railway track—a sea of human beings. They were threatened with rifle salvoes. The workers bared their breasts and cried, "Shoot!" A salvo was fired into the defenseless seated crowd, and thirty to forty corpses, among them women and children, remained on the ground. On this becoming known the whole town of Kiev went on strike on the same day. The corpses of the murdered workers were raised on high by the crowd and carried round in a mass demonstration. Meetings, speeches, arrests, isolated street fights—Kiev was in the midst of the revolution. The movement was soon at an end. But the printers had won a shortening of the working day by one hour and a wage increase of one ruble; in a yeast factory the eight-hour day was introduced; the railway workshops were closed by order of the ministry; other departments continued partial strikes for their demands.

In Nikolaev the general strike broke out under the immediate influence of news from Odessa, Baku, Batum, and Tiflis, in spite of the opposition of the social democratic committee, who wanted to postpone the outbreak of the movement till the time came when the military should have left the town for maneuvers. The masses refused to hold back; one factory made a beginning, the strikes went from one workshop to another, the resistance of the military only poured oil on the fire. Mass processions with revolutionary songs were formed, in which all workers, employees, tramway officials, men, and women took part. The cessation of work was complete. In Ekaterinoslav the bakers came out on strike on August 5, on the seventh the men in the railway workshops, and then all the other factories on August 8. Tramway traffic stopped, and the newspapers did not appear.

Thus the colossal general strike in south Russia came into being in the summer of 1903. By many small channels of partial economic struggles and little "accidental" occurrences it flowed rapidly to a raging sea, and changed the entire south of the tsarist empire for some weeks into a bizarre revolutionary workers' republic. "Brotherly embraces, cries of delight and of enthusiasm, songs of freedom, merry laughter, humor, and joy were seen and heard in the crowd of many thousands of persons which surged through the town from morning till evening. The mood was exalted; one could almost believe that a new, better life was beginning on the earth. A most solemn and at the same time an idyllic, moving spectacle." So wrote at the time the correspondent of the liberal *Osvoboshdenye* of Peter Struve.

The year 1904 brought with it war, and for a time, an interval of quiet in the mass strike movement. At first a troubled wave of "patriotic" demonstrations arranged by the police authorities spread over the country. The "liberal" bourgeois society was for the time being struck to the ground by the tsarist official chauvinism. But soon the social democrats took possession of the arena; revolutionary workers' demonstrations were opposed to the demonstrations of the patriotic lumpenproletariat, which were organized under police patronage. At last the shameful defeats of the tsarist army woke the liberal society from its lethargy; then began the era of democratic congresses, banquets, speeches, addresses, and manifestos. Absolutism, temporarily suppressed through the disgrace of the war, gave full scope to these gentlemen, and by and by they saw everything in rosy colors. For six months bourgeois liberalism occupied the center of the stage, and the proletariat remained in the shadows. But after a long depression absolutism again roused itself, the camarilla gathered all its strength, and by a single powerful movement of the Cossack's heel the whole liberal movement was driven into a corner. Banquets, speeches, and congresses were prohibited out of hand as "intolerable presumption," and liberalism suddenly found itself at the end of its tether.

But exactly at the point where liberalism was exhausted, the action of the proletariat began. In December 1904 the great general strike, due to unemployment, broke out in Baku; the working class was again on the field of battle. As speech was forbidden and rendered impossible, action began. In Baku for some weeks in the midst of the general strike the social democrats ruled as absolute masters of the situation; and the peculiar events of December in the Caucasus would have caused an immense sensation if they had not been so quickly put in the shade by the rising tide of the revolution that they themselves had set into motion. The fantastic confused news of the general strike in Baku had not reached all parts of the tsarist empire when in January 1905 the mass strike in St. Petersburg broke out.

Here also, as is well known, the immediate cause was trivial. Two men employed at the Putilov Works were discharged on account of their membership in the legal Zubatovian union. This measure called forth a solidarity strike on January 16 of the whole of the twelve thousand employees in this works. The social democrats seized the occasion of the strike to begin a lively agitation for the extension of the demands and set forth demands for the eight-hour day, the right of combination, freedom of speech and of the press, etc. The unrest among the Putilov workers communicated itself quickly to the remainder of the proletariat, and in a few days 140,000 workers were on strike. Joint conferences and stormy discussions led to the working out of that proletarian charter of bourgeois freedom with the eight-hour day at its head with which, on January 22, 200,000 workers, led by Father Gapon,* marched to the tsar's palace. The conflict of the two Putilov workers who had been subjected to disciplinary punishment had changed within a week into the prologue of the most violent revolution in modern times.

The events that followed upon this are well known; the bloodbath in St. Petersburg called forth gigantic mass strikes and a general strike in the month of January and February in all the industrial centers and towns in Russia, Poland, Lithuania, the Baltic Provinces, the Caucasus, Siberia, from north to south and east to west. On closer inspection, however, it can be seen that the mass strike was appearing in other forms than those of the previous period. Everywhere at that time the social democratic organizations went before with appeals;

---

* The orthodox priest and tsarist police informer who led the workers' protest to the tsar's palace in St. Petersburg marking the start of the 1905 Revolution. Tsarist troops attacked the crowd in what came to be known as the "Bloody Sunday" massacre. —H.S.

everywhere revolutionary solidarity with the St. Petersburg proletariat was expressly stated as the cause and aim of the general strike; everywhere, at the same time, there were demonstrations, speeches, conflicts with the military.

But even here there was no predetermined plan, no organized action, because the appeals of the parties could scarcely keep pace with the spontaneous risings of the masses; the leaders scarcely had time to formulate the watchwords of the onrushing crowd of the proletariat. Furthermore, the earlier mass and general strikes had originated from individual coalescing wage struggles, which, in the general temper of the revolutionary situation and under the influence of the social democratic agitation, rapidly became political demonstrations; the economic factor and the scattered condition of trade unionism were the starting point; all-embracing class action and political direction the result. The movement was now reversed.

The general strikes of January and February broke out as unified revolutionary actions to begin with under the direction of the social democrats; but this action soon fell into an unending series of local, partial, economic strikes in separate districts, towns, departments, and factories. The entire spring of 1905 and into the middle of the summer there fermented throughout the whole of the immense empire an uninterrupted economic strike of almost the entire proletariat against capital—a struggle that embraced, on the one hand, all the petty bourgeois and liberal professions, commercial employees, technicians, actors, and members of artistic professions, and on the other hand, penetrated to the domestic servants, the minor police officials, and even to the stratum of the lumpenproletariat, and simultaneously surged from the towns to the country districts and even knocked at the iron gates of the military barracks.

This is a gigantic, many-colored picture of a general arrangement of labor and capital that reflects all the complexity of social organization and of the political consciousness of every section and of every district; and the whole long scale runs from the regular trade-union struggle of a tried and tested troop of the proletariat drawn from large-scale industry to the formless protest of a handful of rural proletarians, to the first slight stirrings of an agitated military garrison; from the well-educated and elegant revolt in cuffs and white collars in the counting house of a bank to the shy-bold murmurings of a clumsy meeting of dissatisfied policemen in a smoke-grimed dark and dirty guardroom.

According to the theory of the lovers of "orderly and well-disci-plined" struggles, according to plan and scheme, according to those especially who always ought to know better from afar "how it should have been done," the decay of the great political general strike of January 1905 into a number of economic struggles was probably "a great mistake," which crippled that action and changed it into a "straw fire." But social democracy in Russia, which had taken part in the revolution but had not "made" it, and which had even to learn its law from its course itself, was at the first glance put out of counte-nance for a time by the apparently fruitless ebb of the storm-flood of the general strike. History, however, which had made that "great mis-take," thereby accomplished, heedless of the reasonings of its offi-cious schoolmaster, a gigantic work for the revolution that was as in-evitable as it was, in its consequences, incalculable.

The sudden general rising of the proletariat in January under the powerful impetus of the St. Petersburg events was outwardly a politi-cal act of the revolutionary declaration of war on absolutism. But this first general direct action reacted inwardly all the more powerfully as it for the first time awoke class feeling and class consciousness in mil-lions upon millions as if by an electric shock. And this awakening of class feeling expressed itself forthwith in the circumstances that the proletarian mass, counted by millions, quite suddenly and sharply came to realize how intolerable was the social and economic existence that they had patiently endured for decades in the chains of capitalism. Thereupon, there began a spontaneous general shaking of and tugging at these chains. All the innumerable sufferings of the modern prole-tariat reminded them of the old bleeding wounds. Here was the eight-hour day fought for, there piecework was resisted, here were brutal foremen "driven off" in a sack on a handcar, at another place infa-mous systems of fines were fought against, everywhere better wages were striven for, and here and there the abolition of homework. Back-ward, degraded occupations in large towns, small provincial towns, which had hitherto dreamed in an idyllic sleep, the village with its legacy from feudalism—all these, suddenly awakened by the January lightning, bethought themselves of their rights and now sought fever-ishly to make up for their previous neglect.

The economic struggle was not here really a decay, a dissipation of action, but merely change of front, a sudden and natural alteration of the first general engagement with absolutism, in a general reckon-ing with capital, which in keeping with its character, assumed the form of individual, scattered wage struggles. Political class action was not broken in January by the decay of the general strike into economic strikes, rather the reverse; after the possible content of political action in the given situation and at the given stage of the revolution was exhausted, it broke, or rather changed, into economic action.

In point of fact, what more could the general strike in January have achieved? Only complete thoughtlessness could expect that absolutism could be destroyed at one blow by a single "long-drawn" general strike after the anarchist plan. Absolutism in Russia must be overthrown by the proletariat. But in order to be able to overthrow it, the proletariat requires a high degree of political education, of class consciousness and organization. All these conditions cannot be fulfilled by pamphlets and leaflets, but only by the living political school, by the fight and in the fight, in the continuous course of the revolution. Further, absolutism cannot be overthrown at any desired moment in which only adequate "exertion" and "endurance" is necessary. The fall of absolutism is merely the outer expression of the inner social and class development of Russian society.

Before absolutism can, and so that it may be overthrown, the bourgeois Russia in its interior, in its modern class divisions, must be formed. That requires the drawing together of the various social layers and interests, besides the education of the proletarian revolutionary parties, and not less of the liberal, radical, petty bourgeois, conservative, and reactionary parties; it requires self-consciousness, self-knowledge and the class consciousness not merely of the layers of the people, but also of the layers of the bourgeoisie. But this also can be achieved and come to fruition in no way but in the struggle, in the process of revolution itself, through the actual school of experience, in collision with the proletariat as well as with one another, in incessant mutual friction. This class division and class maturity of bourgeois society, as well as its action in the struggle against absolutism, is on the one hand hampered and made difficult by the peculiar leading role of the proletariat and, on the other hand, is spurred on and accelerated. The various undercurrents of the social process of the revolution cross one another, check one another, and increase the internal contradictions of the revolution, but in the end accelerate and thereby render still more violent its eruptions.

This apparently simple and purely mechanical problem may therefore be stated thus; the overthrow of absolutism is a long, continuous social process, and its solution demands a complete undermining of the soil of society; the uppermost part be placed lowest and the lowermost part highest, the apparent "order" must be changed to a chaos, and the apparently "anarchistic" chaos must be changed into a new order. Now in this process of the social transformation of the old Russia, not only the January lightning of the first general strike, but also the spring and summer thunderstorms that followed it played an indispensable part. The embittered general relations of wage labor and capital contributed in equal measure to the drawing together of the various layers of the people and those of the bourgeoisie, to the class consciousness of the revolutionary proletariat and to that of the liberal and conservative bourgeoisie. And just as the urban wage struggle contributed to the formation of a strong monarchist industrial party in Moscow, so the conflagration of the violent rural rising in Livonia led to the rapid liquidation of the famous aristocratic-agrarian *zemstvo** liberalism.

But at the same time, the period of the economic struggles of the spring and summer of 1905 made it possible for the urban proletariat, by means of active social democratic agitation and direction, to assimilate later all the lessons of the January prologue and to grasp clearly all the further tasks of the revolution. There was connected with this too, another circumstance of an enduring social character: *a general raising of the standard of life of the proletariat*—economic, social, and intellectual.

The January strikes of 1905 ended victoriously almost throughout. As proof of this, some data from the enormous, and for the most part still inaccessible, mass of material may be cited here relating to a few of the most important strikes carried through in Warsaw alone by the social democrats of Poland and Lithuania. In the great factories of the metal industry of Warsaw: Lilpop, Ltd.; Ran and Löwenstein; Rudzki and Co.; Borman, Schwede, and Co.; Handtke, Gerlach, and Pulst; Geisler Bros.; Eberherd, Wolski, and Co.; Konrad and Yarnuszkiewicz, Ltd.; Weber and Daehu; Ewizdzinski and Co.; Wolonski Wire Works; Gostynski and Co., Ltd.; Brun and Son; Fraget; Norblin; Werner; Buch; Kenneberg Bros.; Labor; Dittunar Lamp Factory; Serkowski; Weszk—twenty-two factories in all—the workers won after a strike of four to five weeks (starting January 25–

---

* Zemstvos were rural political assemblies in tsarist Russia formed in 1864, dominated by landowners. —H.S.

26) a nine-hour day, a 25 percent increase of wages, and obtained various smaller concessions. In the large workshops of the timber industry of Warsaw, namely Karmanski, Damieki, Gromel, Szerbinskik, Twemerowski, Horn, Devensee, Tworkowski, Daab, and Martens—twelve workshops in all—the strikes had won by the twenty-third of February the nine-hour day; they were not satisfied with this but insisted upon the eight-hour day, which they also won, together with an increase in wages, after a further strike of a week.

The entire bricklaying industry began a strike on February 27 and demanded, in conformity with the watchword of social democracy, the eight-hour day; they won the ten-hour day on March 11 together with an increase of wages for all categories, regular weekly payment of wages, etc. The painters, the cartwrights, the saddlers, and the smiths all won the eight-hour day without decrease of wages.

The telephone workshops struck for ten days and won the eight-hour day and an increase of wages of 10 percent to 15 percent. The large linen-weaving establishment of Hielle and Dietrich (ten thousand workers) after a strike lasting nine weeks, obtained a decrease of the working day by one hour and a wage increase of 5 percent to 10 percent. And similar results in endless variation were to be seen in the older branches of industry in Warsaw, Lodz, and Sosnovitz.

In Russia proper the eight-hour day was won in December 1904 by a few categories of oil workers in Baku; in May 1905 by the sugar workers of the Kiev district; in January 1905 all the printing works in Samara (where at the same time an increase of piecework rates was obtained and fines were abolished); in February in the factory in which medical instruments for the army are manufactured, in a furniture factory, and in the cartridge factory in St. Petersburg. Further, the eight-hour day was introduced in the mines at Vladivostock, in March in the government mechanical workshops dealing with government stock, and in May among the employees of the Tiflis electric town railway. In the same month a working day of eight and a half hours was introduced in the large cotton-weaving factory of Marosov (and at the same time the abolition of night work and a wage increase of 8 percent were won); in June an eight-hour day in a few oil works in St. Petersburg and Moscow; in July a working day of eight and a half hours among the smiths at the St. Petersburg docks; and in November in all the private printing establishments of the town of Orel (and at the same time an increase of time rates of 20 percent and piecework rates of 100 percent, as well as the setting up of a conciliation board on which workers and employer were equally represented.)

The nine-hour day in all the railway workshops (in February), in many government, military, and naval workshops, in most of the factories of the town of Berdiansk, in all the printing works of the towns of Poltava and Minsk; nine and a half hours in the shipyards, mechanical workshops, and foundries in the town of Nikolaev; in June, after a general strike of waiters in Warsaw, in many restaurants and cafes (and at the same time a wage increase of 20 percent to 40 percent, with a two-week holiday in the year).

The ten-hour day in almost all the factories of the towns of Lodz, Sosnovitz, Riga, Kovno, Oval, Dorfat, Minsk, Kharkov, in the bakeries of Odessa, among the mechanics in Kishinev, at a few smelting works in St. Petersburg, in the match factories of Kovno (with an increase of wages of 10 percent), in all the government marine workshops, and among all the dockers.

The wage increases were in general smaller than the shortening of hours but always more significant: in Warsaw in the middle of March 1905 a general increase of wages of 15 percent was fixed by the municipal factories department; in the center of the textile industry, Ivanovo Vosnesensk, the wage increase amounted to 7 percent to 15 percent, in Kovno the increase affected 73 percent of the workers. A fixed minimum wage was introduced in some of the bakeries in Odessa, in the Neva shipbuilding yards in St. Petersburg, etc.

It goes without saying that these concessions were withdrawn again, now here and now there. This however was only the cause of renewed strife and led to still more bitter struggles for revenge, and thus the strike period of the spring of 1905 has of itself become the prologue to an endless series of ever-spreading and interlacing economic struggles that have lasted to the present day. In the period of the outward stagnation of the revolution, when the telegraph carried no sensational news from the Russian theater of war to the outside world, and when the West European laid aside his newspaper in disappointment with the remark there "was nothing doing" in Russia, the great underground work of the revolution was in reality being carried on without cessation, day by day and hour by hour, in the very heart of the empire. The incessant intensive economic struggle effected, by rapid and abbreviated methods, the transition of capitalism from the stage of primitive accumulation, of patriarchal unmethodical methods of working, to a highly modern, civilized one.

At the present time the actual working day in Russian industry leaves behind not only the Russian factory legislation (that is, the legal working day of eleven hours) but even the actual conditions of Germany. In most departments of large-scale industry in Russia the ten-hour day prevails, which in Germany is declared in social legislation to be an unattainable goal. And what is more, that longed-for "industrial constitutionalism," for which there is so much enthusiasm in Germany, and for the sake of which the advocates of opportunist tactics would keep every keen wind from the stagnant waters of their all-suffering parliamentarism, has already been born, together with political "constitutionalism," in the midst of the revolutionary storm, from the revolution itself! In actual fact it is not merely a general raising of the standard of life, or the cultural level of the working class that has taken place. The material standard of life as a permanent stage of well-being has no place in the revolution. Full of contradictions and contrasts it brings simultaneously surprising economic victories and the most brutal acts of revenge on the part of the capitalists; today the eight-hour day, and tomorrow wholesale lockouts and actual starvation for millions.

The most precious, because lasting, thing in this rapid ebb and flow of the wave is its mental sediment: the intellectual, cultural growth of the proletariat, which proceeds by fits and starts, and which offers an inviolable guarantee of their further irresistible progress in the economic as in the political struggle. And not only that. Even the relations of the worker to the employer are turned round; since the January general strike and the strikes of 1905 that followed upon it, the principle of the capitalist "mastery of the house" is de facto abolished. In the larger factories of all important industrial centers the establishment of workers' committees has, as if by itself, taken place, with which alone the employer negotiates and which decide all disputes.

And finally another thing, the apparently "chaotic" strikes and the "disorganized" revolutionary action after the January general strike are becoming the starting point of a feverish *work of organization*. Dame History, from afar, smilingly hoaxes the bureaucratic lay figures who keep grim watch at the gate over the fate of the German trade unions. The firm organizations, which, as the indispensable hypothesis for an eventual German mass strike, should be fortified like an impregnable citadel—these organizations are in Russia, on the contrary, already born from the mass strike. And while the guardians of the German trade unions for the most part fear that the organizations will fall in pieces in a revolutionary whirlwind like rare porcelain, the Russian Revolution shows us the exactly opposite picture; from the whirlwind and the storm, out of the fire and glow of the mass strike and the street fighting rise again, like Venus from the foam, fresh, young, powerful, buoyant trade unions.

Here again a little example, which, however, is typical of the whole empire. At the second conference of the Russian trade unions, which took place at the end of February 1906 in St. Petersburg, the representative of the Petersburg trade unions, in his report on the development of trade-union organizations, said of the tsarist capital:

> January 22, 1905, which washed away the Gapon union, was a turning point. The workers in large numbers have learned by experience to appreciate and understand the importance of organization, and that only they themselves can create these organizations. The first trade union—that of the printers—originated in direct connection with the January movement. The commission appointed to work out the tariffs framed the statutes, and on July 19 the union began its existence. Just about this time the union of office-workers and bookkeepers was called into existence.
>
> In addition to those organizations, which extend almost openly, there arose from January to October 1905 semi-legal and illegal trade unions. To the former belonged, for example, the union of chemists' assistants and commercial employees. Among the illegal unions special attention must be drawn to the watchmakers' union, whose first secret session was held on April 24. All attempts to convene a general open meeting were shattered on the obstinate resistance of the police and the employers in the form of the Chamber of Commerce. This mischance has not prevented the existence of the union. It held secret meetings of members on June 9 and August 14, apart from the sessions of the executive of the union. The tailors and tailoresses union was founded in 1905 at a meeting in a wood at which seventy tailors were present. After the question of forming the union was discussed a commission was appointed which was entrusted with the task of working out the statutes. All attempts of the commission to obtain a legal existence for the union were unsuccessful. Its activities were confined to agitation and the enrolling of new members in the individual workshops. A similar fate was in store for the shoemakers' union. In July, a secret night meeting was convened in a wood near the city. Over 100 shoemakers attended; a report was read on the importance of trade unionism, on its history in Western Europe, and its tasks in Russia. It was then decided to form a trade union; a commission of twelve was appointed to work out the statutes and call a

general meeting of shoemakers. The statutes were drawn up, but in the meantime it had not been found possible to print them nor had the general meeting been convened.

These were the first difficult beginnings. Then came the October days, the second general strike, the tsar's manifesto of October 30, and the brief "constitution period." The workers threw themselves with fiery zeal into the waves of political freedom in order to use it forthwith for the purpose of the work of organization. Besides daily political meetings, debates, and the formation of clubs, the development of trade unionism was immediately taken in hand. In October and November *forty* new trade unions appeared in St. Petersburg. Presently a "central bureau," that is, a trade-union council, was established, various trade-union papers appeared, and since November a central organ has also been published, the *Trade Union.*

What was reported above concerning Petersburg was also true on the whole of Moscow and Odessa, Kiev and Nikolaev, Saratov and Voronezh, Samara and Nizhni-Novgorod, and all the larger towns of Russia and, to a still higher degree, of Poland. The trade unions of different towns seek contact with one another and conferences are held. The end of the "constitution period," and the return to reaction in December 1905 put a stop for the time being to the open widespread activity of the trade unions, but did not, however, altogether extinguish them. They operate as organizations in secret and occasionally carry on quite open wage struggles. A peculiar mixture of the legal and illegal condition of trade-union life is being built up, corresponding to the highly contradictory revolutionary situation.

But in the midst of the struggle the work of organization is being more widely extended, in a thoroughgoing, not to say pedantic fashion. The trade unions of the social democracy of Poland and Lithuania, for example, which at the last congress (in July 1906) were represented by five delegates from a membership of 10,000, are furnished with the usual statutes, printed membership cards, adhesive stamps, etc. And the same bakers and shoemakers, engineers, and printers of Warsaw and Lodz, who in June 1905 stood on the barricades and in December only awaited the word from Petersburg to begin street fighting, find time and are eager, between one mass strike and another, between prison and lockout, and under the conditions of a siege, to go into their trade-union statutes and discuss them earnestly. These barricade fighters of yesterday and tomorrow have indeed more than once at meetings severely reprimanded their leaders and threatened them with withdrawal from the party because the unlucky trade-union membership cards could not be printed quickly enough—in secret, printing works under incessant police persecution. This zeal and this earnestness continue to this day. For example, in the first two weeks of July 1906 fifteen new trade unions appeared in Ekaterinoslav, six in Kostroma, several in Kiev, Poltava, Smolensk, Cherkassy, Proskurvo, down to the most insignificant provincial towns.

In the session of the Moscow trade-union council of June 4 this year, after the acceptance of the reports of individual trade-union delegates, it was decided "that the trade unions should discipline their members and restrain from street rioting because the time is not considered opportune for the mass strike. In the face of possible provocation on the part of the government, care should be taken that the masses do not stream out in the streets." Finally, the council decided that if at any time one trade union began a strike, the others should hold back from any wages movement. Most of the economic struggles are now directed by the trade unions.

Thus the great economic struggle that proceeded from the January general strike, and which has not ceased to the present day, has formed a broad background of the revolution from which, in ceaseless reciprocal action with the political agitation and the external events of the revolution, there ever arise here and there now isolated explosions, and now great actions of the proletariat. Thus there flame up against this background the following events one after the other; at the May Day demonstration there was an unprecedented, absolute general strike in Warsaw, which ended in a bloody encounter between the defenseless crowd and the soldiers. At Lodz in June a mass outing, which was scattered by the soldiers, led to a demonstration of one hundred thousand workers at the funeral of some of the victims of the brutal soldiery and to a renewed encounter with the military, and finally, on June 23, 24, and 25, passed into the first barricade fight in the tsarist empire. Similarly in June the first great revolt of the sailors of the Black Sea Fleet exploded in the harbor at Odessa from a trifling incident on board the armored vessel *Potemkin,* which reacted immediately on Odessa and Nikolaev in the form of a violent mass strike. As a further echo followed the mass strike and the sailors' revolts in Kronstadt, Libau, and Vladivostok.

In the month of October the grandiose experiment of St. Petersburg was made with the introduction of the eight-hour day. The general council of workers' delegates decided to achieve the eight-hour day in a revolutionary manner. That means that on the appointed day all the workers of Petersburg should inform their employers that they are not willing to work more than eight hours a day, and should leave their places of work at the end of eight hours. The idea was the occasion of lively agitation, was accepted by the proletariat with enthusiasm and carried out, but very great sacrifices were not thereby avoided. Thus, for example, the eight-hour day meant an enormous fall in wages for the textile workers who had hitherto worked eleven hours and that on a system of piecework. This, however, they willingly accepted. *Within a week the eight-hour day prevailed in every factory and workshop in Petersburg,* and the joy of the workers knew no bounds. Soon, however, the employers, stupefied at first, prepared their defenses; everywhere they threatened to close their factories. Some of the workers consented to negotiate and obtained here a working day of ten hours and there one of nine hours. The elite of the Petersburg proletariat, however—the workers in the large government engineering establishments—remained unshaken, and a lockout ensued, which threw forty-five thousand to fifty thousand men on the streets for a month. At the settlement the eight-hour day movement was carried into the general strike of December, which the great lockout had hampered to a great extent.

Meanwhile, however, the second tremendous general strike throughout the whole empire follows in October as a reply to the project of the Bulygin Duma*—the strike to which the railwaymen gave the summons. This second great action of the proletariat already bears a character essentially different from that of the first one in January. The element of political consciousness already plays a much bigger role. Here also, to be sure, the immediate occasion for the outbreak of the mass strike was a subordinate and apparently accidental thing: the conflict of the railwaymen with the management over the pension fund. But the general rising of the industrial proletariat that followed upon it was conducted in accordance with clear political ideas. The prologue of the January strike was a procession to the tsar to ask for political freedom: the watchword of the October strike ran away with the constitutional comedy of tsarism!

---

* The first Russian parliament, named for the tsar's minister for the interior, set up in response to the 1905 Revolution. It never in fact convened, and gave way to a more democratic Duma as the tsar was forced to make further concessions to the workers. —H.S.

And thanks to the immediate success of the general strike, to the tsar's manifesto of October 30, the movement does not flow back on itself as in January, but rushes over outwardly in the eager activity of newly acquired political freedom. Demonstrations, meetings, a young press, public discussions, and bloody massacres as the end of the story, and thereupon new mass strikes and demonstrations—such is the stormy picture of the November and December days. In November, at the insistence of the social democrats in Petersburg the first demonstrative mass strike is arranged as a protest demonstration against the bloody deeds and the proclamation of a state of siege in Poland and Livonia.

The fermentation after the brief constitutional period and the gruesome awakening finally leads in December to the outbreak of the third general mass strike throughout the empire. This time its course and its outcome are altogether different from those in the two earlier cases. Political action does not change into economic action as in January, but it no longer achieves a rapid victory as in October. The attempts of the tsarist camarilla with real political freedom are no longer made, and revolutionary action therewith, for the first time, and along its whole length, knocked against the strong wall of the physical violence of absolutism. By the logical internal development of progressive experience the mass strike this time changes into an open insurrection, to armed barricades, and street fighting in Moscow. The December days in Moscow close the first eventful year of the revolution as the highest point in the ascending line of political action and of the mass strike movement.

The Moscow events show a typical picture of the logical development and at the same time of the future of the revolutionary movement on the whole: their inevitable close in a general open insurrection, which again on its part cannot come in any other way than through the school of a series of preparatory partial insurrections, which therefore meantime end in partial outward "defeats" and, considered individually, may appear to be "premature."

The year 1906 brings the elections to the Duma and the Duma incidents. The proletariat, from a strong revolutionary instinct and clear knowledge of the situation, boycotts the whole tsarist constitutional farce, and liberalism again occupies center stage for a few months. The situation of 1904 appears to have come again, a period of speeches instead of acts, and the proletariat for a time walk in shadow in order to devote themselves the more diligently to the trade-union struggle and the work of the organization. The mass strikes are no longer spoken of, while the clattering rockets of liberal rhetoric are fired off day after day. At last, the iron curtain is torn down, the actors are dispersed, and nothing remains of the liberal rockets but smoke and vapor. An attempt of the central committee of the Russian social democracy to call forth a mass strike, as a demonstration for the Duma and the reopening of the period of liberal speechmaking, falls absolutely flat. The role of the political mass strike alone is exhausted, but, at the same time, the transition of the mass strike into a general popular rising is not yet accomplished. The liberal episode is past, the proletarian episode is not yet begun. The stage remains empty for the time being.

IV. THE INTERACTION OF THE POLITICAL AND THE ECONOMIC STRUGGLE

We have attempted in the foregoing to sketch the history of the mass strike in Russia in a few strokes. Even a fleeting glance at this history shows us a picture that in no way resembles the one usually formed by discussions in Germany on the mass strike. Instead of the rigid and hollow scheme of an arid political action carried out by the decision of the highest committees and furnished with a plan and panorama, we see a bit of pulsating like of flesh and blood, which cannot be cut out of the large frame of the revolution but is connected with all parts of the revolution by a thousand veins.

The mass strike, as the Russian Revolution shows it to us, is such a changeable phenomenon that it reflects all phases of the political and economic struggle, all stages and factors of the revolution. Its adaptability, its efficiency, the factors of its origin are constantly changing. It suddenly opens new and wide perspectives on the revolution when it appears to have already arrived in a narrow pass and where it is impossible for anyone to reckon upon it with any degree of certainty. It flows now like a broad billow over the whole kingdom, and now divides into a gigantic network of narrow streams; now it bubbles forth from under the ground like a fresh spring and now is completely lost under the earth. Political and economic strikes, mass strikes and partial strikes, demonstrative strikes and fighting strikes, general strikes of individual branches of industry and general strikes in individual towns, peaceful wage struggles and street massacres, barricade fighting—all these run through one another, run side by side, cross one another, flow in and over one another—it is a ceaselessly moving, changing sea of phenomena. And the law of motion of these phenomena is clear: it does not lie in the mass strike itself nor in its technical details, but in the political and social proportions of the forces of the revolution.

The mass strike is merely the form of the revolutionary struggle and every disarrangement of the relations of the contending powers, in party development and in class division, in the position of counter-revolution—all this immediately influences the action of the strike in a thousand invisible and scarcely controllable ways. But strike action itself does not cease for a single moment. It merely alters its forms, its dimensions, its effect. It is the living pulse of the revolution and at the same time its most powerful driving wheel. In a word, the mass strike, as shown to us in the Russian Revolution, is not a crafty method discovered by subtle reasoning for the purpose of making the proletarian struggle more effective, *but the method of motion of the proletarian mass,* the phenomenal form of the proletarian struggle in the revolution.

Some general aspects may now be examined that may assist us in forming a correct estimate of the problem of the mass strike:

1. It is absurd to think of the mass strike as one act, one isolated action. The mass strike is rather the indication, the rallying idea, of a whole period of the class struggle lasting for years, perhaps for decades. Of the innumerable and highly varied mass strikes that have taken place in Russia during the last four years, the scheme of the mass strike was a purely political movement, begun and ended after a cut-and-dried plan, a short single act of one variety only and at that a subordinate variety—pure demonstration strike. In the whole course of the five-year period we see in Russia only a few demonstration strikes, which, be it noted, were generally confined to single towns. Thus the annual May Day general strike in Warsaw and Lodz in Russia proper on the first of May has not yet been celebrated to any appreciable extent by abstention from work; the mass strike in Warsaw on September 11, 1905, as a memorial service in honor of the executed Martin Kasprzak;* that of November 1905 in Petersburg as

---

* A leader of the Polish Proletariat Party who worked with Luxemburg and helped her to escape Poland in 1889. The government executed him for his involvement in the 1905 Revolution. —H.S.

protest demonstration against the declaration of a state of siege in Poland and Livonia; that of January 22, 1906, in Warsaw, Lodz, Czentochon, and in Dombrowa coal basin, as well as, in part, those in a few Russian towns as anniversary celebrations of the Petersburg bloodbath; in addition, in July 1906 a general strike in Tiflis as demonstration of sympathy with soldiers sentenced by court-martial on account of the military revolt; and finally from the same cause, in September 1906, during the deliberations of the court-martial in Reval. All the above great and partial mass strikes and general strikes were not demonstration strikes but fighting strikes, and as such they originated for the most part spontaneously, in every case from specific local accidental causes, without plan and undesignedly, and grew with elemental power into great movements, and then they did not begin an "orderly retreat," but turned now into economic struggles, now into street fighting, and now collapsed into themselves.

In this general picture the purely political demonstration strike plays quite a subordinate role—isolated small points in the midst of a mighty expanse. Thereby, temporarily considered, the following characteristic discloses itself: the demonstration strikes, which, in contradistinction to the fighting strikes, exhibit the greatest mass of party discipline, conscious direction, and political thought, and therefore must appear as the highest and most mature form of the mass strike, play in reality the greatest part in the *beginnings* of the movement. Thus, for example, the absolute cessation of work on May 1, 1905, in Warsaw, as the first instance of a decision of the social democrats carried throughout in such an astonishing fashion, was an experience of great importance for the proletarian movement in Poland. In the same way the sympathetic strike of the same year in Petersburg made a great impression as the first experiment of conscious systematic mass action in Russia. Similarly the "trial mass strike" of the Hamburg comrades* on January 17, 1906, will play a prominent part in the history of the future German mass strike as the first vigorous attempt with the much disputed weapon, and also a very successful and convincingly striking test of the fighting temper and the lust for battle of the Hamburg working class. And just as surely will the period of the mass strike in Germany, when it has once begun in real earnest, lead of itself to a

---

* Hamburg's SPD was among the most radical in Germany. Hamburg workers held a successful "trial mass strike" on January 17, 1906. —H.S.

real, general cessation of work on May first. The May Day festival may naturally be raised to a position of honor as the first great demonstration under the aegis of the mass struggle. In this sense the "lame horse,"* as the May Day festival was termed at the trade-union congress at Cologne, still has a great future before it and an important part to play in the proletarian class struggle in Germany.

But with the development of the earnest revolutionary struggle the importance of such demonstrations diminishes rapidly. It is precisely those factors that objectively facilitate the realization of the demonstration strike after a preconceived plan and at the party's word of command—namely, the growth of political consciousness and the training of the proletariat—make this kind of mass strike impossible; today the proletariat in Russia, the most capable vanguard of the masses, does not want to know about mass strikes; the workers are no longer in a mood for jesting and will now think only of a serious struggle with all its consequences. And when, in the first great mass strike in January 1905, the demonstrative element, not indeed in an intentional, but more in an instinctive, spontaneous form, still played a great part, on the other hand, the attempt of the central committee of the Russian social democrats to call a mass strike in August as a demonstration for the dissolved Duma was shattered by, among other things, the positive disinclination of the educated proletariat to engage in weak half-actions and mere demonstrations.

2. When, however, we have in view the less important strike of the demonstrative kind, instead of the fighting strike as it represents in Russia today the actual vehicle of proletarian action, we see still more clearly that it is impossible to separate the economic factors from one another. Here also the reality deviates from the theoretical scheme, and the pedantic representation in which the pure political mass strike is logically derived from the trade-union general strike as the ripest and highest stage, but at the same time is kept distinct from it, is shown to be absolutely false. This is expressed not merely in the fact that the mass strikes, from that first great wage struggle of the Petersburg textile workers in 1896–97 to the last great mass strike in December

---

* Unlike in Poland, May Day did not play a major role in Germany's socialist traditions. The first attempt at a workers' celebration of May Day in 1890 was marred by fears from SPD leaders of a return to illegality. The trade unions explicitly opposed May Day worker celebrations after 1906. —H.S.

1905, passed imperceptibly from the economic field to the political, so that it is almost impossible to draw a dividing line between them.

Again, every one of the great mass strikes repeats, so to speak, on a small scale, the entire history of the Russian mass strike, and begins with a pure economic, or at all events, a partial trade-union conflict, and runs through all the stages to the political demonstration. The great thunderstorm of mass strikes in south Russia in 1902 and 1903 originated, as we have seen, in Baku from a conflict arising from the disciplinary punishment of the unemployed, in Rostov from disputes about wages in the railway workshops, in Tiflis from a struggle of the commercial employees for reduction of working hours, in Odessa from a wage dispute in a single small factory. The January mass strike of 1905 developed from an internal conflict in the Putilov Works, the October strike from the struggle of the railway workers for a pension fund, and finally the December strike from the struggle of the postal and telegraph employees for the right of combination. The progress of the movement on the whole is not expressed in the circumstances that the economic initial stage is omitted, but much more in the rapidity with which all the stages to the political demonstration are run through and in the extremity of the point to which the strike moves forward.

But the movement on the whole does not proceed from the economic to the political struggle, nor even the reverse. Every great political mass action, after it has attained its political highest point, breaks up into a mass of economic strikes. And that applies not only to each of the great mass strikes, but also to the revolution as a whole. With the spreading, clarifying, and involution of the political struggle, the economic struggle not only does not recede, but extends, organizes, and becomes involved in equal measure. Between the two there is the most complete reciprocal action.

Every new onset and every fresh victory of the political struggle is transformed into a powerful impetus for the economic struggle, extending at the same time its external possibilities and intensifying the inner urge of the workers to better their position, and their desire to struggle. After every foaming wave of political action a fructifying deposit remains behind from which a thousand stalks of economic struggle shoot forth. And conversely, the workers' condition of ceaseless economic struggle with the capitalists keeps their fighting energy alive in every political interval; it forms, so to speak, the permanent fresh reservoir of the strength of the proletarian classes, from which the political fight ever renews its strength, and at the same time leads the indefatigable economic sappers of the proletariat at all times, now here and now there, to isolated sharp conflicts, out of which political conflicts on a large scale unexpectedly explode.

In a word: the economic struggle is the transmitter from one political center to another; the political struggle is the periodic fertilization of the soil for the economic struggle. Cause and effect here continually change places; and thus the economic and the political factor in the period of the mass strike, now widely removed, completely separated, or even mutually exclusive, as the theoretical plan would have them, merely form the two interlacing sides of the proletarian class struggle in Russia. And *their unity* is precisely the mass strike. If the sophisticated theory proposes to make a clever logical dissection of the mass strike for the purpose of getting at the "purely political mass strike," it will by this dissection, as with any other, not perceive the phenomenon in its living essence, but will kill it altogether.

3. Finally, the events in Russia show us that the mass strike is inseparable from the revolution. The history of the Russian mass strikes is the history of the Russian Revolution. When, to be sure, the representatives of our German opportunism hear of "revolution," they immediately think of bloodshed, street fighting, or powder and shot, and the logical conclusion thereof is: the mass strike leads inevitably to the revolution, therefore we dare not have it. In actual fact we see in Russia that almost every mass strike in the long run leads to an encounter with the armed guardians of tsarist order, and therein the so-called political strikes exactly resemble the larger economic struggle. The revolution, however, is something other and something more than bloodshed. In contradiction to the police interpretation, which views the revolution exclusively from the standpoint of street disturbances and rioting, that is, from the standpoint of "disorder," the interpretation of scientific socialism sees in the revolution above all a thoroughgoing internal reversal of social class relations. And from this standpoint an altogether different connection exists between revolution and mass strike in Russia from that contained in the commonplace conception that the mass strike generally ends in bloodshed.

We have seen above the inner mechanism of the Russian mass strike, which depends upon the ceaseless reciprocal action of the political and economic struggles. But this reciprocal action is conditioned during the revolutionary period. Only in the sultry air of the period of revolution can any partial little conflict between labor and capital grow into a general explosion. In Germany the most violent, most brutal collisions between the workers and employers take place every year and every day without the struggle overleaping the bounds of the individual departments or individual towns concerned, or even those of the individual factories. Punishment of organized workers in Petersburg and unemployment as in Baku, wage struggles as in Odessa, struggles for the right of combination as in Moscow are the order of the day in Germany. No single one of these cases, however, changes suddenly into a common class action. And when they grow into isolated mass strikes, which have without question a political coloring, they do not bring about a general storm. The general strike of Dutch railwaymen, which died away in spite of the warmest sympathy, in the midst of the complete impassivity of the proletariat of the country, affords a striking proof of this.

And conversely, only in the period of revolution, when the social foundations and the walls of class society are shaken and subjected to a constant process of disarrangement, can any political class action of the proletariat arouse from their passive condition in a few hours whole sections of the working class who have hitherto remained unaffected, and this is immediately and naturally expressed in a stormy economic struggle. The worker, suddenly aroused to activity by the electric shock of political action, immediately seizes the weapon lying nearest his hand for the fight against his condition of economic slavery: the stormy gesture of the political struggle causes him to feel with unexpected intensity the weight and the pressure of his economic chains. And while, for example, the most violent political struggle in Germany—the electoral struggle or the parliamentary struggle over the customs tariff—exercised a scarcely perceptible direct influence upon the course and the intensity of the wage struggles being conducted at the same time in Germany, every political action of the proletariat in Russia immediately expresses itself in the extension of the area and the deepening of the intensity of the economic struggle.

The revolution thus first creates the social conditions in which this sudden change of the economic struggle into the political and of the political struggle into the economic is possible, a change that finds its expression in the mass strike. And if the vulgar scheme sees the connection between mass strike and revolution only in bloody street encounters with which the mass strikes conclude, a somewhat deeper look into the Russian events shows an exactly opposite connection: in reality the mass strike does not produce the revolution, but the revolution produces the mass strike.

4. It is sufficient in order to comprehend the foregoing to obtain an explanation of the question of the conscious direction and initiative in the mass strike. If the mass strike is not an isolated act but a whole period of the class struggle, and if this period is identical with a period of revolution, it is clear that the mass strike cannot be called at will, even when the decision to do so may come from the highest committee of the strongest social democratic party. As long as the social democracy has not the power to stage and countermand revolutions according to its fancy, even the greatest enthusiasm and impatience of the social democratic troops will not suffice to call into being a real period of mass strike as a living, powerful movement of the people. On the basis of a decision of the party leadership and of party discipline, a single short demonstration may well be arranged similar to the Swedish mass strike, or to the latest Austrian strike, or even to the Hamburg mass strike of January 17. These demonstrations, however, differ from an actual period of revolutionary mass strikes in exactly the same way that the well-known demonstrations in foreign ports during a period of strained diplomatic relations differ from a naval war. A mass strike born of pure discipline and enthusiasm will, at best, merely play the role of an episode, of a symptom of the fighting mood of the working class upon which, however, the conditions of a peaceful period are reflected.

Of course, even during the revolution, mass strikes do not exactly fall from heaven. They must be brought about in some way or another by the workers. The resolution and determination of the workers also play a part and indeed the initiative and the wider direction naturally fall to the share of the organized and most enlightened kernel of the proletariat. But the scope of this initiative and this direction, for the most part, is confined to application to individual acts, to individual strikes, when the revolutionary period is already begun, and indeed, in most cases, is confined within the boundaries of a single town. Thus, for example, as we have seen, the social democrats have already, on several occasions, successfully issued a direct summons for a mass strike in Baku, in Warsaw, in Lodz, and in Petersburg. But this succeeds much less frequently when applied to general movements of the whole proletariat.

Further, there are quite definite limits set to initiative and conscious direction. During the revolution it is extremely difficult for any directing organ of the proletarian movement to foresee and to calculate which occasions and factors can lead to explosions and which cannot. Here also initiative and direction do not consist in issuing commands according to one's inclinations, but in the most adroit adaptability to the given situation, and the closest possible contact with the mood of the masses. The element of spontaneity, as we have seen, plays a great part in all Russian mass strikes without exception, be it as a driving force or as a restraining influence. This does not occur in Russia, however, because social democracy is still young or weak, but because in every individual act of the struggle so very many important economic, political and social, general and local, material and psychical factors react upon one another in such a way that no single act can be arranged and resolved as if it were a mathematical problem. The revolution, even when the proletariat, with the social democrats at their head, appears in the leading role, is not a maneuver of the proletariat in the open field, but a fight in the midst of the incessant crashing, displacing, and crumbling of the social foundation. In short, in the mass strikes in Russia the element of spontaneity plays such a predominant part not because the Russian proletariat is "uneducated," but because revolutions do not allow anyone to play the schoolmaster with them.

On the other hand, we see in Russia that the same revolution that rendered the social democrats' command of the mass strike so difficult, and which struck the conductor's baton from, or pressed into, their hand at all times in such a comical fashion—we see that it resolved of itself all those difficulties of the mass strike that, in the theoretical scheme of German discussion, are regarded as the chief concerns of the "directing body": the question of "provisioning," "discovery of cost," and "sacrifice." It goes without saying that it does not resolve them in the way that they would be resolved in a quiet confidential discussion between the higher directing committees of the labor movement, the members sitting pencil in hand. The "regulation" of all these questions consists in the circumstance that the revolution brings such an enormous mass of people upon the stage that any computation or regulation of the cost of the movement such as can be effected in a civil process, appears to be an altogether hopeless undertaking.

The leading organizations in Russia certainly attempt to support the direct victims to the best of their ability. Thus, for example, the brave victims of the gigantic lockout in St. Petersburg, which followed the eight-hour-day campaign, were supported for weeks. But all these measures are, in the enormous balance of the revolution, but as a drop in the ocean. At the moment that a real, earnest period of mass strikes begins, all these "calculations" of "cost" become merely projects for exhausting the ocean with a tumbler. And it is a veritable ocean of frightful privations and sufferings that is brought by every revolution to the proletarian masses. And the solution that a revolutionary period makes of this apparently invincible difficulty consists, under the circumstances, of such an immense volume of mass idealism being simultaneously released that the masses are insensible to the bitterest sufferings. With the psychology of a trade unionist who will not stay off his work on May Day unless he is assured in advance of a definite amount of support in the event of his being victimized, neither revolution nor mass strike can be made. But in the storm of the revolutionary period even the proletarian is transformed from a provident paterfamilias demanding support into a "revolutionary romanticist," for whom even the highest good, life itself, to say nothing of material well-being, possesses but little in comparison with the ideals of the struggle.

If, however, the direction of the mass strike in the sense of command over its origin, and in the sense of the calculating and reckoning of the cost, is a matter of the revolutionary period itself, the directing of the mass strike becomes, in an altogether different sense, the duty of social democracy and its leading organs. Instead of puzzling their heads with the technical side, with the mechanism, of the mass strike, the social democrats are called upon to assume *political* leadership in the midst of the revolutionary period.

To give the cue for, and the direction to, the fight; to so regulate the tactics of the political struggle in its every phase and at its every moment that the entire sum of the available power of the proletariat, which is already released and active, will find expression in the battle array of the party; to see that the tactics of the social democrats are decided according to their resoluteness and acuteness and that they never fall below the level demanded by the actual relations of forces, but rather rise above it—that is the most important task of the directing body in a period of mass strikes. And this direction changes of itself, to a certain extent, into technical direction. A consistent, resolute, progressive tactic on the part of the social democrats produces in the masses a feeling of security, self-confidence, and desire for struggle; a vacillating weak tactic, based on an underestimation of the proletariat, has a crippling and confusing effect upon the masses. In the first case mass strikes break out "of themselves" and "opportunely"; in the second case they remain ineffective amid direct summonses of the directing body to mass strikes. And of both the Russian Revolution affords striking examples.

V. LESSONS OF THE WORKING CLASS MOVEMENT IN RUSSIA APPLICABLE TO GERMANY

Let us now see how far all these lessons that can be learned from the Russian mass strikes are applicable to Germany. The social and political conditions, the history and status of the labor movement are widely different in Germany and Russia. At first sight the inner law of the Russian mass strikes as sketched above may appear to be solely the product of specifically Russian conditions, which need not be taken into account by the German proletariat. Between the political and the economic struggle in the Russian Revolution there is a very close internal connection; their unity becomes an actual fact in the period of mass strikes. But is not that simply a result of Russian absolutism? In a state in which every form and expression of the labor movement is forbidden, in which the simplest strike is a political crime, it must logically follow that every economic struggle will become a political one.

Further, when contrariwise, the first outbreak of the political revolution has drawn after it a general reckoning of the Russian working class with the employers, that is likewise a simple result of the circumstances that the Russian worker has hitherto had a very low standard of life, and has never yet engaged in a single economic struggle for an improvement of his condition. The proletariat in Russia has first, to a certain extent, to work their way out of these miserable conditions, and what wonder that they eagerly availed themselves, with the eagerness of youth, of the first means to that end as soon as the revolution brought the first fresh breeze into the heavy air of absolutism?

And finally, the stormy revolutionary course of the Russian mass strike as well as their preponderant spontaneous, elementary character is explained on the one hand by the political backwardness of Russia, by the necessity of first overthrowing the oriental despotism, and on the other hand, by the want of organization and of discipline of the Russian proletariat. In a country in which the working class has had thirty years' experience of political life, a strong social democratic party of three million members, and a quarter of a million selected troops organized in trade unions, neither the political struggle nor the mass strike can possibly assume the same stormy and elemental character as in a semi-barbarous state that has just made the leap from the Middle Ages into the modern bourgeois order. This is the current conception among those who would read the stage of maturity of the social conditions of a country from the text of the written laws.

Let us examine the questions in their order. To begin with it is going the wrong way about the matter to date the beginning of the economic struggle in Russia only from the outbreak of the revolution. As a matter of fact, the strikes and wage disputes in Russia proper were increasingly the order of the day since the nineties of the last century, and in Russian Poland even since the eighties, and had eventually won civic rights for the workers. Of course, they were frequently followed by brutal police measures, but nevertheless they were daily phenomena. For example, in both Warsaw and Lodz as early as 1891, there was a considerable strike fund, and the enthusiasm for trade unionism in these years had even created that "economic" illusion in Poland for a short time, which a few years later prevailed in Petersburg and the rest of Russia.

In the same way there is a great deal of exaggeration in the notion that the proletarian in the tsarist empire had the standard of life of a pauper before the revolution. The layer of workers in large industries in the great towns who had been the most active and zealous in the economic as in the political struggle are, as regards the material conditions of life, on a scarcely lower plane than the corresponding layer of the German proletariat, and in some occupations as high wages are to be met with in Russia as in Germany, and here and there, even higher. And as regards the length of the working day, the difference in the large-scale industries in the two countries is here and there insignificant. The notion of the presumed material and cultural condition of helotry of the Russian working class is similarly without justification in fact. This notion is contradicted, as a little reflection will show, by the facts of the revolution itself and the prominent part that was played therein by the proletariat. With paupers no revolution of this political maturity and cleverness of thought can be made, and the industrial workers of St. Petersburg and Warsaw, Moscow and Odessa, who stand in the forefront of the struggle, are culturally and mentally much nearer to the West European type than is imagined by those who regard bourgeois parliamentarism and methodical trade-union practice as the indispensable, or even the only, school of culture for the proletariat. The modern large capitalist development of Russia and the intellectual influence, exerted for a decade and a half, of social democracy, which has encouraged and directed the economic struggle, have accomplished an important piece of cultural work without the outward guarantees of the bourgeois legal order.

The contrast, however, grows less when, on the other hand, we look a little further into the actual standard of life in the German working class. The great political mass strikes in Russia have from the first aroused the widest layers of the proletariat and thrown them into a feverish economic struggle. But are there not in Germany whole unenlightened sections among the workers to which the warm light of the trade unions has hitherto scarcely penetrated, whole layers that up to the present have never attempted, or vainly attempted, to raise themselves out of their social helotry by means of daily wage struggles?

Let us consider the *poverty of the miners*. Already in the quiet working day, in the cold atmosphere of the parliamentary monotony of Germany—as also in other countries, and even in the El Dorado of trade unionism, Great Britain—the wage struggle of the mine workers hardly ever expresses itself in any other way than by violent eruptions from time to time in mass strikes of typical, elemental character. This only shows that the antagonism between labor and capital is too sharp and violent to allow of its crumbling away in the form of quiet systematic, partial trade-union struggles. The misery of the miners, with its eruptive soil, which even in "normal" times is a storm center of the greatest violence, must immediately explode in a violent economic socialist struggle with every great political mass action of the working class, with every violent sudden jerk that disturbs the momentary equilibrium of everyday social life.

Let us take further the case of the *poverty of the textile workers*. Here also the bitter, and for the most part fruitless, outbreaks of the wage struggle that raged through Vogtland every few years, give but a faint idea of the vehemence with which the great agglomerate mass of helots of trustified textile capital must explode during a political convulsion, during a powerful, daring mass action of the German proletariat. Again, let us take the *poverty of the home-workers, of the ready-made clothing workers, of the electricity workers*, veritable storm centers in which violent struggles will be the more certain to break out with every political atmospheric disturbance in Germany; the less frequently the proletariat take up the struggle in tranquil times, and the more unsuccessfully they fight at any time, the more brutally will capital compel them to return, gnashing their teeth to the yoke of slavery.

Now, however, whole great categories of the proletariat have to be taken into account, which, in the "normal" course of things in Germany, cannot possibly take part in a peaceful economic struggle for the improvement of their condition and cannot possibly avail themselves of the right of combination. First and foremost we give the example of the glaring *poverty of the railway and the postal employees*. For these government workers there exist Russian conditions in the midst of the parliamentary constitutional state of Germany, that is to say, Russian conditions as they existed only before the revolution, during the untroubled splendor of absolutism. Already in the great October strike of 1905 the Russian railwaymen in the then-formally absolutist Russia, were, as regards the economic and social freedom of their movement, head and shoulders above the Germans. The Russian railway and postal employees won the de facto right of combination in the storm, and if momentarily trial upon trial and victimization were the rule, they were powerless to affect the inner unity of workers.

However, it would be an altogether false psychological reckoning if one were to assume, with the German reaction, that the slavish obedience of the German railway and postal employees will last forever, that it is a rock that nothing can wear away. When even the German trade-union leaders have become accustomed to the existing conditions to such an extent that they, untroubled by an indifference almost without parallel in the whole of Europe, can survey with complete satisfaction the results of the trade-union struggle in Germany, then the deep-seated, long-suppressed resentment of the uniformed state slaves will inevitably find vent with a general rising of the industrial workers. And when the industrial vanguard of the proletariat, by means of mass strikes, grasps at new political rights or attempts to defend existing ones, the great army of railway and postal employees must of necessity bethink themselves of their own special disgrace, and at last rouse themselves for their liberation from the extra share of Russian absolutism that is specially reserved for them in Germany.

The pedantic conception that would unfold great popular movements according to plan and recipe regards the acquisition of the right of combination for the railway workers as necessary before anyone will "dare to think" of a mass strike in Germany. The actual and natural course of events can only be the opposite of this: only from a spontaneous, powerful mass strike action can the right of combination from the German railway workers, as well as for the postal employees, actually be born. And the problems, which in the existing conditions of Germany are insoluble, will suddenly find their solution under the influence and the pressure of a universal political mass action of the proletariat.

And finally, the greatest and most important: *the poverty of the land workers.* If the British trade unions are composed exclusively of industrial workers, that is quite understandable in view of the special character of the British national economy, and of the unimportant part that agriculture plays, on the whole, in the economic life of Britain. In Germany, a trade-union organization, be it ever so well constructed, if it comprises only industrial workers, and is inaccessible to the great army of land workers, will give only a weak, partial picture of the conditions of the proletariat. But again it would be a fatal illusion to think that conditions in the country are unalterable and immovable and that the indefatigable educational work of the social democracy, and still more, the whole internal class politics of Germany, does not continually undermine the outward passivity of the agricultural workers and that any great general class action of the German proletariat, for whatever object undertaken, may not also draw the rural proletariat into the conflict.

Similarly, the picture of the alleged economic superiority of the German over the Russian proletariat is considerably altered when we look away from the tables of the industries and departments organized in trade unions and bestow a look upon those great groups of the proletariat who are altogether outside the trade-union struggle, or whose special economic condition does not allow for their being forced into the narrow framework of the daily guerrilla warfare of the trade unions. We see there one important sphere after another, in which the sharpening of antagonisms has reached the extreme point, in which inflammable material in abundance is heaped up, in which there is a great deal of "Russian absolutism" in its most naked form, and in which economically the most elementary reckonings with capital have first to be made.

In a general political mass strike of the proletariat, then, all these outstanding accounts would inevitably be presented to the prevailing system. An artificially arranged demonstration of the urban proletariat, taking place once, a mere mass strike action arising out of discipline, and directed by the conductor's baton of a party executive, could therefore leave the broad masses of the people cold and indifferent. But a powerful and reckless fighting action of the industrial proletariat, born of a revolutionary situation, must surely react upon the deeper-lying layers, and ultimately draw all those into a stormy general economic struggle who, in normal times, stand aside from the daily trade-union fight.

But when we come back to the organized vanguard of the German industrial proletariat, on the other hand, and keep before our eyes the objects of the economic struggle that have been striven for by the Russian working class, we do not at all find that there is any tendency to look down upon the things of youth, as the oldest German trade unions had reason to do. Thus the most important general demand of the Russian strikes since January 22—the eight-hour day—is certainly not an unattainable platform for the German proletariat, but rather in most cases, a beautiful, remote ideal. This applies also to the struggle for the "mastery of the household" platform, to the struggle for the introduction of workers' committees into all the factories, for the abolition of piecework, for the abolition of homework in handicraft, for the complete observance of Sunday rest, and for the recognition of the right of combination. Yes, on closer inspection all the economic objects of struggle of the Russian proletariat are also for the German proletariat very real, and touch a very sore spot in the life of the workers.

It therefore inevitably follows that the pure political mass strike, which operates to one's advantage, is, in Germany, a mere lifeless theoretical plan. If mass strikes result, in a natural way from a strong revolutionary ferment, in a determined political struggle of the urban workers, they will equally naturally, exactly as in Russia, change into a whole period of elementary economic struggles. The fears of the trade-union leaders, therefore, that the struggle for economic interests in a period of stormy political strife, in a period of mass strikes, can simply be pushed aside and suppressed rest upon an utterly baseless, schoolboy conception of the course of events. A revolutionary period in Germany would also so alter the character of the trade-union struggle and develop its potentialities to such an extent that the present guerrilla warfare of the trade unions would be child's play in comparison. And on the other hand, from this elementary economic tempest of mass strikes, the political struggle would derive always new impetus and fresh strength. The reciprocal action of economic and political struggle, which is the mainspring of present-day strikes in Russia, and at the same time the regulating mechanism, so to speak, of the revolutionary action of the proletariat, would result also in Germany, and quite naturally, from the conditions themselves.

VI. COOPERATION OF ORGANIZED AND UNORGANIZED WORKERS NECESSARY FOR VICTORY

In connection with this, the question of organization in relation to the problem of the mass strike in Germany assumes an essentially different aspect.

The attitude of many trade-union leaders to this question is generally summed up in the assertion: "We are not yet strong enough to risk such a hazardous trial of strength as a mass strike." Now this position is so far untenable that it is an insoluble problem to determine the time, in a peaceful fashion by counting heads, when the proletariat is "strong enough" for any struggle. Thirty years ago the German trade unions had 50,000 members. That was obviously a number with which a mass strike on the above scale was not to be thought of. Fifteen years later the trade unions were four times as strong, and counted 237,000 members. If, however, the present trade-union leaders had been asked at the time if the organization of the proletariat was then sufficiently ripe for a mass strike, they would assuredly have replied that it was still far from it and that the number of those organized in trade unions would first have to be counted by millions.

Today the number of trade unionists already runs into the second million, but the views of the leaders are still exactly the same, and may very well be the same to the end. The tacit assumption is that the entire working class of Germany, down to the last man and the last woman, must be included in the organization before it "is strong enough" to risk a mass action, which then, according to the old formula, would probably be represented as "superfluous." This theory is nevertheless absolutely utopian, for the simple reason that it suffers from an internal contradiction that goes in a vicious circle. Before the workers can engage in any direct class struggle they must all be organized. The circumstances, the conditions, of capitalist development and of the bourgeois state make it impossible that, in the normal course of things, without stormy class struggles, certain sections and these the greatest, the most important, the lowest and the most oppressed by capital, and by the state—can be organized at all. We see even in Britain, which has had a whole century of indefatigable trade-union effort without any "disturbances"—except at the beginning in the period of the Chartist movement—without any "romantic revolutionary" errors or temptations, it has not been possible to do more than organize a minority of the better-paid sections of the proletariat.

On the other hand the trade unions, like all fighting organizations of the proletariat, cannot permanently maintain themselves in any other way than by struggle, and not struggles of the same kind as the war between the frogs and the mice in the stagnant waters of the bourgeois parliamentary period, but struggle in the troubled revolutionary periods of the mass strike. The rigid, mechanical-bureaucratic conception cannot conceive of the struggle save as the product of organization at a certain stage of its strength. On the contrary, the living, dialectical explanation makes the organization arise as a product of the struggle. We have already seen a grandiose example of this phenomenon in Russia, where a proletariat almost wholly unorganized created a comprehensive network of organizational appendages in a year and a half of stormy revolutionary struggle.

Another example of this kind is furnished by the history of the German unions. In the year 1878 the number of trade-union members amounted to 50,000. According to the theory of the present-day trade-union leaders this organization, as stated above, was not nearly "strong enough" to enter upon a violent political struggle. The German trade unions however, weak as they were at the time, did take up the struggle—namely the struggle against the antisocialist laws—and showed that they were "strong enough," not only to emerge from the struggle victorious, but to increase their strength fivefold: in 1891, after the repeal of the antisocialist laws, their membership was 277,659. It is true that the methods by which the trade unions conquered in the struggle against the antisocialist laws do not correspond to the ideal of a peaceful, beelike, uninterrupted process: they went first into the fight absolutely in ruins, to rise again on the next wave and to be born anew. But this is precisely the specific method of growth corresponding to the proletarian class organizations: to be tested in the struggle and to go forth from the struggle with increased strength.

On a closer examination of German conditions and of the condition of the different sections of the working class, it is clear that the coming period of stormy political mass struggles will not bring the dreaded, threatening downfall of the German trade unions, but on the contrary, will open up hitherto unsuspected prospects of the extension of their sphere of power—an extension that will proceed rapidly by leaps and bounds. But the question has still another aspect. The plan of undertaking mass strikes as a serious political class action with organized workers only is absolutely hopeless. If the mass strike, or rather, mass strikes, and the mass struggle are to be successful they must become a real *people's movement*, that is, the widest sections of the proletariat must be drawn into the fight. Already in the parliamentary form the might of the proletarian class struggle rests not on the small organized group, but on the surrounding periphery of the revolutionary-minded proletariat. If the social democrats were to enter the electoral battle with their few hundred thousand organized members alone, they would condemn themselves to futility. And although it is the tendency of social democracy, wherever possible, to draw the whole great army of its voters into the party organization, its mass of voters after thirty years experience of social democracy is not increased through the growth of the party organization, but on the contrary, the new sections of the proletariat, won for the time being through the electoral struggle, are the fertile soil for the subsequent seed of organization. Here the organization does not supply the troops for the struggle, but the struggle, to an ever-growing degree, supplies recruits for the organization.

In a much greater degree does this obviously apply to direct political mass action than to the parliamentary struggle. If the social democrats, as the organized nucleus of the working class, are the most important vanguard of the entire body of the workers and if the political clarity, the strength, and the unity of the labor movement flow from this organization, then it is not permissible to visualize the class movement of the proletariat as a movement of the organized minority.

Every real, great class struggle must rest upon the support and cooperation of the widest masses, and a strategy of class struggle that does not reckon with this cooperation, that is based upon the idea of the finely stage-managed march out of the small, well-trained part of the proletariat, is foredoomed to be a miserable fiasco.

Mass strikes and political mass struggles cannot, therefore, possibly be carried through in Germany by the organized workers alone, nor can they be appraised by regular "direction" from the central committee of a party. In this case, again—exactly as in Russia—they depend not so much upon "discipline" and "training" and upon the most careful possible regulation beforehand of the questions of support and cost, as upon a real revolutionary, determined class action, which will be able to win and draw into the struggle the widest circles of the unorganized workers, according to their mood and their conditions.

The overestimate and the false estimate of the role of organizations in the class struggle of the proletariat is generally reinforced by the underestimate of the unorganized proletarian mass and of their political maturity. In a revolutionary period, in the storm of great unsettling class struggles, the whole educational effect of the rapid capitalist development and of social democratic influences first shows itself upon the widest sections of the people, of which, in peaceful times the tables of the organized, and even election statistics, give only a faint idea.

We have seen that, in Russia, in about two years a great general action of the proletariat can forthwith arise from the smallest partial conflict of the workers with the employers, from the most insignificant act of brutality of the government organs. Everyone, of course, sees and believes that, because in Russia "the revolution" is there. But what does that mean? It means that class feeling, the class instinct, is alive and very active in the Russian proletariat, so that immediately they regard every partial question of any small group of workers as a general question, as a class affair, and quick as lightning they react to its influence as a unity. While in Germany, France, Italy, and Holland the most violent trade-union conflicts call forth hardly any general action of the working class—and when they do, only the organized part of the workers moves—in Russia the smallest dispute raises a storm. That means nothing else, however, than that at present—paradoxical as it may sound—the class instinct of the youngest, least-trained, badly educated, and still worse-organized Russian proletariat is immeasurably stronger than that of the organized, trained, and enlightened working class of Germany or of any other West European country. And that is not to be reckoned a special virtue of the "young, unexhausted East" as compared with the "sluggish West," but is simply a result of direct revolutionary mass action.

In the case of the enlightened German worker the class consciousness implanted by the social democrats is *theoretical and latent*: in the period ruled by bourgeois parliamentarism it cannot, as a rule, actively participate in a direct mass action; it is the ideal sum of the four hundred parallel actions of the electoral sphere during the election struggle, of the many partial economic strikes and the like. In the revolution when the masses themselves appear upon the political battlefield this class consciousness becomes *practical and active*. A year of revolution has therefore given the Russian proletariat that "training" that thirty years of parliamentary and trade-union struggle cannot artificially give to the German proletariat. Of course, this living, active class feeling of the proletariat will considerably diminish in intensity, or rather change into a concealed and latent condition, after the close of the period of revolution and the erection of a bourgeois-parliamentary constitutional state.

And just as surely, on the other hand, will the living revolutionary class feeling, capable of action, affect the widest and deepest layers of the proletariat in Germany in a period of strong political engagement, and that the more rapidly and more deeply, more energetically the educational work of social democracy is carried on among them. This educational work and the provocative and revolutionizing effect of the whole present policy of Germany will express itself in the circumstances that all those groups, which at present, in their apparent political stupidity, remain insensitive to all the organizing attempts of the social democrats and of the trade unions, will suddenly follow the flag of social democracy in a serious revolutionary period. Six months of a revolutionary period will complete the work of the training of these as yet unorganized masses that ten years of public demonstrations and distribution of leaflets would be unable to do. And when conditions in Germany have reached the critical stage for such a period, the sections that are today unorganized and backward will, in the struggle, prove themselves the most radical, the most impetuous element, and not one that will have to be dragged along. If it should come to mass strikes in Germany, it will almost certainly not be the best organized workers—and most certainly not the printers—who will develop the greatest capacity for action, but the worst organized or totally unorganized—the miners, the textile workers, and perhaps even the land workers.

In this way we arrive at the same conclusions in Germany in relation to the peculiar tasks of *direction* as it relates to the role of social democracy in mass strikes, as in our analysis of events in Russia. If we now leave the pedantic scheme of demonstrative mass strikes artificially brought about by order of parties and trade unions, and turn to the living picture of a peoples' movement arising with elementary energy from the culmination of class antagonisms and the political situation—a movement that passes, politically as well as economically, into mass struggles and mass strikes—it becomes obvious that the task of social democracy does not consist in the technical preparation and direction of mass strikes, but, first and foremost, in the *political leadership* of the whole movement.

The social democrats are the most enlightened, most class-conscious vanguard of the proletariat. They cannot and dare not wait, in a fatalist fashion, with folded arms for the advent of the "revolutionary situation," to wait for that which, in every spontaneous peoples' movement, falls from the clouds. On the contrary, they must now, as always, hasten the development of things and endeavor to accelerate events. This they cannot do, however, by suddenly issuing the "slogan" for a mass strike at random at any odd moment, but first and foremost, by making clear to the widest layers of the proletariat the *inevitable advent* of this revolutionary period, the inner *social factors* making for it, and the *political consequences* of it. If the widest proletarian layer should be won for a political mass action of the social democrats, and if, vice versa, the social democrats should seize and maintain the real leadership of a mass movement—should they become, in a *political sense*, the rulers of the whole movement, then they must, with the utmost clearness, consistency and resoluteness, inform the German proletariat of their tactics and aims in the period of coming struggle.

VII. THE ROLE OF THE MASS STRIKE IN THE REVOLUTION

We have seen that the mass strike in Russia does not represent an artificial product of premeditated tactics on the part of the social democrats, but a natural historical phenomenon on the basis of the present revolution. Now what are the factors that in Russia have brought forth this new phenomenal form of the revolution?

The Russian Revolution has for its next task the abolition of absolutism and the establishment of a modern bourgeois-parliamentary constitutional state. It is exactly the same in form as that which confronted Germany in the March [1848] Revolution, and France at the great French Revolution of the end of the eighteenth century. But the condition, the historical milieu, in which these formally analogous revolutions took place, are fundamentally different from those of present-day Russia. The most decisive difference is the circumstances that between those bourgeois revolutions of the West and the present bourgeois revolution in the East, the whole cycle of capitalist development has run its course. And this development had seized not only the West European countries, but also absolutist Russia. Large-scale industry with all its consequences—modern class divisions, sharp social contrasts, modern life in large cities, and the modern proletariat—has become in Russia the prevailing form, that is, in social development, the decisive form of production.

The remarkable, contradictory, historical situation results from this that the bourgeois revolution, in accordance with its formal tasks will, in the first place, be carried out by a modern class-conscious proletariat, and in an international milieu whose distinguishing characteristic is the ruin of bourgeois democracy. It is not the bourgeoisie that is now the leading revolutionary element, as in the earlier revolutions of the West, while the proletarian masses, disorganized among the petty bourgeoisie, furnish material for the army of the bourgeoisie, but on the contrary, it is the class-conscious proletariat that is the active and driving element, while the big bourgeois sections are partly directly counterrevolutionary, partly weakly liberal, and only rural petty bourgeoisie and the urban petty bourgeois intelligentsia are definitively oppositional and even revolutionary minded.

The Russian proletariat, however, who are destined to play the leading part in the bourgeois revolution, enter the fight free from all illusions of bourgeois democracy, with a strongly developed consciousness of their own specific class interests, and at a time when the antagonism between capital and labor has reached its height. This contradictory situation finds expression in the fact that in this formally bourgeois revolution, the antagonism of bourgeois society to absolutism is governed by the antagonism of the proletariat to bourgeois society, that the struggle of the proletariat is directed simultaneously and with equal energy against both absolutism and capitalist exploitation, and that the program of the revolutionary struggle concentrates with equal emphasis on political freedom, the winning of the eight-hour day, and a human standard of material existence for the proletariat. This twofold character of the Russian Revolution is expressed in that close union of the economic with the political struggle and in their mutual interaction, which we have seen is a feature of the Russian events and which finds its appropriate expression in the mass strike.

In the earlier bourgeois revolutions where, on the one hand, the political training and the leadership of the revolutionary masses were undertaken by the bourgeois parties, and where, on the other hand, it was merely a question of overthrowing the old government, the brief battle at the barricades was the appropriate form of the revolutionary struggle. Today, when the working classes are being enlightened in the course of the revolutionary struggle, when they must marshal their forces and lead themselves, and when the revolution is directed as much against the old state power as against capitalist exploitation, the mass strike appears as the natural means of recruiting the widest proletarian layers for the struggle, as well as being at the same time a means of undermining and overthrowing the old state power, and of stemming capitalist exploitation. The urban industrial proletariat is now the soul of the revolution in Russia. But in order to carry through a direct political struggle as a mass, the proletariat must first be assembled as a mass, and for this purpose they must come out of the factory and workshop, mine and foundry, must overcome the levigation and the decay to which they are condemned under the daily yoke of capitalism.

The mass strike is the first natural, impulsive form of every great revolutionary struggle of the proletariat and the more highly developed the antagonism is between capital and labor, the more effective and decisive must mass strikes become. The chief form of previous bourgeois revolutions, the fight at the barricades, the open conflict with the armed power of the state, is in the revolution today only the culminating point, only a moment on the process of the proletarian mass struggle. And therewith in the new form of the revolution there is reached that civilizing and mitigating of the class struggle that was prophesied by the opportunists of German social democracy— the Bernsteins, Davids,* etc. It is true that these men saw the desired civilizing and mitigating of

---

* Eduard David (1863–1930) was a right-wing, prowar German social democrat. —H.S.

the class struggle in the light of petty bourgeois democratic illusions—they believed that the class struggle would shrink to an exclusively parliamentary contest and that street fighting would simply be done away with. History has found the solution in a deeper and finer fashion: in the advent of revolutionary mass strikes, which, of course, in no way replaces brutal street fights or renders them unnecessary, but which reduces them to a moment in the long period of political struggle, and which at the same time unites with the revolutionary period an enormous cultural work in the most exact sense of the words: the material and intellectual elevation of the whole working class through the "civilizing" of the barbaric forms of capitalist exploitation.

The mass strike is thus shown to be not a specifically Russian product, springing from absolutism, but a universal form of the proletarian class struggle resulting from the present stage of capitalist development and class relations. From this standpoint the three bourgeois revolutions—the great French Revolution, the German Revolution of March, and the present Russian Revolution—form a continuous chain of development in which the fortunes and the end of the capitalist century are to be seen. In the great French Revolution the still wholly underdeveloped internal contradictions of bourgeois society gave scope for a long period of violent struggles, in which all the antagonisms that first germinated and ripened in the heat of the revolution raged unhindered and unrestrained in a spirit of reckless radicalism. A century later the revolution of the German bourgeoisie, which broke out midway in the development of capitalism, was already hampered on both sides by the antagonism of interests and the equilibrium of strength between capital and labor, and was smothered in a bourgeois-feudal compromise, and shortened to a brief, miserable episode ending in words.

Another half century, and the present Russian Revolution stands at a point of the historical path that is already over the summit, that is on the other side of the culminating point of capitalist society, at which the bourgeois revolution cannot again be smothered by the antagonism between bourgeoisie and proletariat, but, will, on the contrary, expand into a new lengthy period of violent social struggles, at which the balancing of the account with absolutism appears a trifle in comparison with the many new accounts that the revolution itself opens up. The present revolution realizes in the particular affairs of absolutist Russia the general results of international capitalist development, and appears not so much as the last successor of the old bourgeois revolutions as the forerunner of the new series of proletarian revolutions of the West. The most backward country of all, just because it has been so unpardonably late with its bourgeois revolution, shows ways and methods of further class struggle to the proletariat of Germany and the most advanced capitalist countries.

Accordingly it appears, when looked at in this way, to be entirely wrong to regard the Russian Revolution as a fine play, as something specifically "Russian," and at best to admire the heroism of the fighting men, that is, the last accessories of the struggle. It is much more important that the German workers should learn to look upon the Russian Revolution *as their own affair*, not merely as a matter of international solidarity with the Russian proletariat, but first and foremost, as a *chapter of their own social and political history*. Those trade-union leaders and parliamentarians who regard the German proletariat as "too weak" and German conditions "as not ripe enough" for revolutionary mass struggles have obviously not the least idea that the measure of the degree of ripeness of class relations in Germany and of the power of the proletariat does not lie in the statistics of German trade unionism or in election figures—but in the events of the Russian Revolution. Exactly as the ripeness of French class antagonisms under the July monarchy and the June battle of Paris was reflected in the German March Revolution, in its course and its fiasco, so today the ripeness of German class antagonisms is reflected in the events and in the power of the Russian Revolution. And while the bureaucrats of the German labor movement rummage in their office drawers for information as to their strength and maturity, they do not see that what they seek is lying before their eyes in a great historical revolution, because, historically considered, the Russian Revolution is a reflex of the power and the maturity of the International, and therefore, in the first place, of the German labor movement.

It would therefore be a too pitiable and grotesquely insignificant result of the Russian Revolution if the German proletariat should merely draw from it the lesson—as is desired by Comrades Frohme, Elm, and others—of using the extreme form of the struggle, the mass strike, and so weaken themselves as to be merely a reserve force in the event of the withdrawal of the parliamentary vote, and therefore a passive means of parliamentary defensive. When the parliamentary vote is taken from us there we will not resist. That is a self-evident decision. But for this it is not necessary to adopt the heroic pose of a

Danton as was done, for example, by Comrade Elm in Jena, because
the defense of the modest measure of parliamentary right already pos-
sessed is less a Heaven-storming innovation, for which the frightful
hecatombs of the Russian Revolution were first necessary as a means
of encouragement, than the simplest and first duty of every opposition
party. But the mere defensive can never exhaust the policy of the proletariat in a period of revolution. And if it is, on the one hand, difficult
to predict with any degree of certainty whether the destruction of universal suffrage would cause a situation in Germany that would call
forth an immediate mass strike action, so on the other hand, it is absolutely certain that when we in Germany enter upon the period of
stormy mass actions, it will be impossible for the social democrats to
base their tactics upon a mere parliamentary defensive.

To fix beforehand the cause and the moment from and in which
the mass strikes in Germany will break out is not in the power of social democracy, because it is not in its power to bring about historical
situations by resolutions at party congresses. But what it can and
must do is to make clear the political tendencies, once they appear,
and to formulate them as resolute and consistent tactics. Man cannot
keep historical events in check while making recipes for them, but he
can see in advance their apparent calculable consequences and
arrange his mode of action accordingly.

The first threatening political danger with which the German proletariat have concerned themselves for a number of years is a coup d'état
of the reaction that will wrest from the wide masses of the people of
the most important political right—universal suffrage. In spite of the
immense importance of this possible event, it is, as we have already
said, impossible to assert with certainty that an open popular movement would immediately break out after the coup d'état, because
today innumerable circumstances and factors have to be taken into account. But when we consider the present extreme acuteness of conditions in Germany, and on the other hand, the manifold international
reactions of the Russian Revolution and of the future rejuvenated Russia, it is clear that the collapse of German politics that would ensue
from the repeal of universal suffrage could not alone call a halt to the
struggle for this right. This coup d'état would rather draw after it, in a
longer or shorter period and with elementary power, a great general
political reckoning of the insurgent and awakened mass of the people—a reckoning with bread usury, with artificially caused dearness of

meat, with expenditure on a boundless militarism and "navalism," with the corruption of colonial policy, with the national disgrace of the Königsberg trial, with the cessation of social reform, with the discharging of railway workers, the postal officials, and the land workers, with the tricking and mocking of the miners, with the judgement of Lobtau and the whole system of class justice, with the brutal lockout system—in short, with the whole thirty-year-old oppression of the combined dominion of Junkerdom and large trustified capital.

But once the ball is set rolling, social democracy, whether it wills it or not, can never again bring it to a standstill. The opponents of the mass strike are in the habit of denying that the lessons and examples of the Russian Revolution can be a criterion for Germany because, in the first place, in Russia the great step must first be taken from an Oriental despotism to a modern bourgeois legal order. The formal distance between the old and the new political order is said to be a sufficient explanation of the vehemence and the violence of the revolution in Russia. In Germany we have long had the most necessary forms and guarantees of a constitutional state, from which it follows that such an elementary raging of social antagonisms is impossible here.

Those who speculate thus forget that in Germany, when it comes to the outbreak of open political struggles, even the historically determined goal will be quite different from that in Russia today. Precisely because the bourgeois legal order in Germany has existed for a long time, because therefore it has had time to completely exhaust itself and to draw to an end, because bourgeois democracy and liberalism have had time to die out—because of this there can no longer be any talk of a *bourgeois* revolution in Germany. And therefore in a period of open political popular struggles in Germany, the last historically necessary goal can only be the *dictatorship of the proletariat*. The distance, however, of this task from the present conditions of Germany is still greater than that of the bourgeois legal order from Oriental despotism, and therefore, the task cannot be completed at one stroke, but must similarly be accomplished during a long period of gigantic social struggles.

But is there not a gross contradiction in the picture we have drawn? On the one hand it means that in an eventual future period of political mass action the most backward layers of the German proletariat—the land workers, the railwaymen, and the postal slaves—will first of all win the right of combination, and that the worst excrescences of exploitation must first be removed, and on the other hand, the political task of this period is said to be the conquest of power by the proletariat! On the one hand, economic, trade-union struggles for the most immediate interests, for the material elevation of the working class; on the other hand, the ultimate goal of social democracy! Certainly these are great contradictions, but they are not contradictions due to our reasoning, but contradictions due to capitalist development. It does not proceed in a beautiful straight line but in a lightning-like zig-zag. Just as the various capitalist countries represent the most varied stages of development, so within each country the different layers of the same working class are represented. But history does not wait patiently till the backward countries and the most advanced layers have joined together so that the whole mass can move symmetrically forward like a compact column. It brings the best prepared parts to explosion as soon as conditions there are ripe for it, and then in the storm of the revolutionary period, lost ground is recovered, unequal things are equalized, and the whole pace of social progress changed at one stroke to the double-quick.

Just as in the Russian Revolution all the grades of development and all the interests of the different layers of workers are united in the social democratic program of the revolution, and the innumerable partial struggles united in the great common class action of the proletariat, so will it also be in Germany when the conditions are ripe for it. And the task of social democracy will then be to regulate its tactics, not by the most backward phases of development but by the most advanced.

VIII. NEED FOR UNITED ACTION OF TRADE UNIONS AND SOCIAL DEMOCRACY

The most important desideratum that is to be hoped for from the German working class in the period of great struggles that will come sooner or later is, after complete resoluteness and consistency of tactics, the utmost capacity for action, and therefore the utmost possible unity of the leading social democratic part of the proletarian masses. Meanwhile the first weak attempts at the preparation of great mass actions have discovered a serious drawback in this connection: the total separation and independence of the two organizations of the labor movement, the social democracy and the trade unions.

It is clear on a closer consideration of the mass strikes in Russia as well as of the conditions in Germany itself that any great mass action, if it is not confined to a mere one-day demonstration but is intended to be a real fighting action, cannot possibly be thought of as a so-called political mass strike. In such an action in Germany the trade unions would be implicated as much as the social democrats. Not because the trade-union leaders imagine that the social democrats, in view of their smaller organization, would have no other resources than the cooperation of one and a quarter million trade unionists and without them would be unable to do anything, but because of a much more deep-lying motive: because every direct mass action of the period of open class struggles would be at the same time both political and economic. If in Germany, from any cause and at any time, it should come to great political struggles, to mass strikes, then at that time an era of violent trade-union struggles would begin in Germany, and events would not stop to inquire whether the trade-union leaders had given their consent to the movement or not. Whether they stand aside or endeavor to resist the movement, the result of their attitude will only be that the trade-union leaders, like the party leaders in the analogous case, will simply be swept aside by the rush of events, and the economic and the political struggles of the masses will be fought out without them.

As a matter of fact the separation of the political and the economic struggle and the independence of each is nothing but an artificial product of the parliamentarian period, even if historically determined. On the one hand in the peaceful, "normal" course of bourgeois society, the economic struggle is split into a multitude of individual struggles in every undertaking and dissolved in every branch of production. On the other hand the political struggle is not directed by the masses themselves in a direct action, but in correspondence with the form of the bourgeois state, in a representative fashion, by the presence of legislative representation. As soon as a period of revolutionary struggles commences, that is, as soon as the masses appear upon the scene of conflict, the breaking up, the economic struggle, as well as the indirect parliamentary form of the political struggle, ceases; in a revolutionary mass action the political and economic struggle are one, and the artificial boundary between trade union and social democracy as two separate, wholly independent forms of the labor movement, is simply swept away. But what finds concrete expression in the revolutionary mass movement finds expression also in the parliamentary period as an actual state of affairs.

There are not two different class struggles of the working class, an economic and a political one, but only *one* class struggle, which aims at one and the same time at the limitation of capitalist exploitation within bourgeois society, and at the abolition of exploitation together with bourgeois society itself.

When these two sides of the class struggle are separated from one another for technical reasons in the parliamentary period, they do not form two parallel, concurrent actions, but merely two phases, two stages of the struggle for emancipation of the working class. The trade-union struggle embraces the immediate interests, and the social democratic struggle the future interests, of the labor movement. The communists, says the *Communist Manifesto*, represent, as against various group interests, national or local, as a whole of the proletariat, and in the various stages of development of the class struggle, the interests of the whole movement, that is, the ultimate goal—the liberation of the proletariat. The trade unions represent only the group interests and only one stage of development of the labor movement. Social democracy represents the working class and the cause of its liberation as a whole. The relation of the trade unions to social democracy is therefore a part of the whole, and when, among the trade-union leaders, the theory of "equal authority" of trade unions and social democracy finds so much favor, it rests upon a fundamental misconception of the essence of trade unionism itself and of its role in the general struggle for freedom of the working class.

This theory of the parallel action of social democracy and the trade unions and of their "equal authority" is nevertheless not altogether without foundation, but has its historical roots. It rests upon the illusion of the peaceful, "normal" period of bourgeois society, in which the political struggle of social democracy appears to be consumed in the parliamentary struggle. The parliamentary struggle, however, the counterpart of the trade-union struggle, is equally with it, a fight conducted exclusively on the basis of the bourgeois social order. It is by its very nature political reform work, as that of the trade unions is economic reform work. It represents political work for the present, as trade unions represent economic work for the present. It is, like them, merely a phase, a stage of development in the complete process of the proletarian class struggle whose ultimate goal is as far beyond the parliamentary struggle as it is beyond the trade-union struggle. The parliamentary struggle is, in relation to social democratic policy, also a part of the whole, exactly as trade-union work is. Social democracy today comprises the parliamentary and the trade-union struggle in one class struggle aiming at the abolition of the bourgeois social order.

The theory of the "equal authority" of trade unions and social democracy is likewise not a mere theoretical misunderstanding, not a mere case of confusion but an expression of the well-known tendency of that opportunist wing of social democracy that reduces the political struggle of the working class to the parliamentary contest, and desires to change social democracy from a revolutionary proletarian party into a petty bourgeois reform one.* If social democracy should accept the theory of the "equal authority" of the trade unions, it would thereby accept, indirectly and tacitly, that transformation which has long been striven for by the representatives of the opportunist tendency.

In Germany, however, there is such a shifting of relations within the labor movement as is impossible in any other country. The theoretical

---

* As the existence of such a tendency within German social democracy is generally denied, one must be grateful for the candor with which the opportunist trend has recently formulated its real aims and wishes. At a party meeting in Mayence on September 10, 1909, the following resolution, proposed by Dr. David, was carried:

Whereas the Social Democratic Party interprets the term "revolution" not in the sense of violent overthrow, but in the peaceful sense of development, that is, the gradual realization of a new economic principle, the public party meeting at Mayence repudiates every kind of revolutionary romance.

The meeting sees in the conquest of political power nothing but the winning over of the majority of the people to the ideas and demands of the social democracy; a conquest that cannot be achieved by means of violence, but only by the revolutionizing of the mind by means of intellectual propaganda and practical reform work in all spheres of political, economic, and social life.

In the conviction that social democracy flourishes far better when it employs legal means than when it relies on illegal means and revolution, the meeting repudiates *"direct mass action"* as a tactical principle, and holds fast to the principle of "parliamentary reform action," that is, it desires that the party in the future as in the past, shall earnestly endeavor *to achieve its aims by legislation and gradual organizational development.*

The indispensable condition for this reformist method of struggle is that *the possibility of participation of the dispossessed masses of the people in the legislation* of the empire and of the individual states shall not be lessened but *increased to the fullest possible extent.* For this reason, the meeting declares it to be an incontestable right of the working class to withhold its labor for a longer or shorter period to ward off attacks on its legal rights and to gain further rights, when all other means fail. [cont.]

conception, according to which the trade unions are merely a part of social democracy, finds its classic expression in Germany in fact, in actual practice, and that in three directions. First, the German trade unions are a direct product of social democracy; it was social democracy that created the beginnings of the present trade-union movement in Germany and that enabled it to attain such great dimensions, and it is social democracy that supplies it to this day with its leaders and the most active promoters of its organization.

Second, the German trade unions are a product of social democracy also in the sense that social democratic teaching is the soul of trade-union practice, as the trade unions owe their superiority over all bourgeois and denominational trade unions to the idea of the class struggle; their practical success, their power, is a result of the circumstance that their practice is illuminated by the theory of scientific socialism and they are thereby raised above the level of a narrow-minded socialism. The strength of the "practical policy" of the German trade unions lies in their insight into the deeper social and economic connections of the capitalist system; but they owe this insight entirely to the theory of scientific socialism upon which their practice is based. Viewed in this way, any attempt to emancipate the trade unions from the social democratic theory in favor of some other "trade-union theory" opposed to social democracy is, from the standpoint of the trade unions themselves and of their future, nothing but an attempt to commit suicide. The separation of trade-union practice from the theory of scientific socialism would mean to the German trade unions the immediate loss of all their superiority over all kinds of bourgeois trade unions, and their fall from their present height to the level of unsteady groping and mere dull empiricism.

Thirdly and finally, the trade unions are, although their leaders have gradually lost sight of the fact, even as regards their numerical

[cont.] But as the political mass strike can only be victoriously carried through when kept within *strictly legal limits* and when the strikers give no reasonable excuse to the authorities to resort to armed force, the meeting perceives the only necessary and real preparation for the exercise of this method of struggle in the further extension of the political, trade-union, and cooperative organizations. Because only in this way can the conditions be created among the wide masses of the people that can guarantee the successful prosecution of a mass strike: conscious discipline and adequate economic support. —R.L.

strength, a direct product of the social democratic movement and the social democratic agitation. It is true that in many districts trade-union agitation precedes social democratic agitation, and that everywhere trade-union work prepares the way for party work. From the point of view of effect, party and trade unions assist each other to the fullest extent. But when the picture of the class struggle in Germany is looked at as a whole and its more deep-seated associations, the proportions are considerably altered. Many trade-union leaders are in the habit of looking down triumphantly from the proud height of their membership of one and a quarter million on the miserable organized members of the Social Democratic Party, not yet half a million strong, and of recalling the time, ten or twelve years ago, when those in the ranks of social democracy were pessimistic as to the prospects of trade-union development.

They do see that between these two things—the large number of organized trade unionists and the small number of organized social democrats—*there exists in a certain degree a direct causal connection*. Thousands and thousands of workers do not join the party organizations precisely because they join the trade unions. According to the theory, all the workers must be doubly organized, must attend two kinds of meetings, pay double contributions, read two kinds of workers' papers, etc. But for this it is necessary to have a higher standard of intelligence and of that idealism, which, from a pure feeling of duty to the labor movement, is prepared for the daily sacrifice of time and money, and finally, a higher standard of that passionate interest in the actual life of the party that can only be engendered by membership of the party organization. All this is true of the most enlightened and intelligent minority of social democratic workers in the large towns, where party life is full and attractive and where the workers' standard of living is high. Among the wider sections of the working masses in the large towns, however, as well as in the provinces, in the smaller and the smallest towns where political life is not an independent thing but a mere reflex of the course of events in the capital, where consequently, party life is poor and monotonous, and where, finally, the economic standard of life of the workers is, for the most part, miserable, it is very difficult to secure the double form of organization.

For the social democratically minded worker from the masses the question will be solved by his joining his trade union. The immediate interests of his economic struggle that are conditioned by the nature of the struggle itself cannot be advanced in any other way than by membership in a trade-union organization. The contribution that he pays, often amid considerable sacrifice of his standard of living, brings him immediate, visible results. His social democratic inclinations, however, enable him to participate in various kinds of work without belonging to a special party organization; by voting at parliamentary elections, by attendance at social democratic public meetings, by following the reports of social democratic speeches in representatives bodies, and by reading the party press. Compare in this connection the number of social democratic electors or the number of subscribers to *Vorwärts* with the number of organized party members in Berlin!

And what is most decisive, the social democratically minded average worker who, as a simple man, can have no understanding of the intricate and fine so-called two-soul theory,* feels that he is, even in the trade union, *social democratically* organized. Although the central committees of the unions have no official party label, the workman from the masses in every city and town sees at the head of his trade union as the most active leaders, those colleagues whom he knows also as comrades and social democrats in public life, now as Reichstag, Landtag, or local representatives, now as trusted men of the social democracy, members of election committees, party editors and secretaries, or merely as speakers and agitators. Further, he hears expressed in the agitational work of his trade union much the same ideas, pleasing and intelligible to him, of capitalist exploitation, class relations, etc., as those that have come to him from social democratic agitation. Indeed, the most and best loved of the speakers at trade-union meetings are those same social democrats.

Thus everything combines to give the average class-conscious worker the feeling that he, in being organized in his trade union, is also a member of his labor party and is social democratically organized, *and therein lies the peculiar recruiting strength of the German trade unions.* Not because of the appearance of neutrality, but because of the social democratic reality of their being, have the central unions been enabled to attain their present strength. This is simply through the coexistence of the various unions—Catholic, Hirsch-Dunker,*

---

* An allusion to a line from Goethe's *Faust*: "Two souls, alas! are lodg'd within my breast." —H.S.

etc.—founded by bourgeois parties by which it was sought to establish the necessity for that political "neutrality." When the German worker who has full freedom of choice to attach himself to a Christian, Catholic, Evangelical, or Free-thinking trade union, chooses none of these but the "free trade union" instead, or leaves one of the former to join the latter, he does so only because he considers that the central unions are the avowed organizations of the modern class struggle, or, what is the same thing in Germany, that they are social democratic trade unions.

In a word the appearance of "neutrality," which exists in the minds of many trade-union leaders, does not exist for the mass of organized trade unionists. And that is the good fortune of the trade-union movement. If the appearance of "neutrality," that alienation and separation of the trade unions from social democracy, really and truly becomes a reality in the eyes of the proletarian masses, then the trade unions would immediately lose all their advantages over competing bourgeois unions, and therewith their recruiting power, their living fire. This is conclusively proved by facts that are generally known. The appearance of party-political "neutrality" of the trade unions could, as a means of attraction, render inestimable service in a country in which social democracy itself has no credit among the masses, in which the odium attaching a workers' organization injures it in the eyes of the masses rather than advantages it—where, in a word, the trade unions must first of all recruit their troops from a wholly unenlightened, bourgeois-minded mass.

The best example of such a country was, throughout the whole of the last century and is to a certain extent today, Great Britain. In Germany, however, party relations are altogether different. In a country in which social democracy is the most powerful political party, in which its recruiting power is represented by an army of over three million proletarians, it is ridiculous to speak of the deterrent effect of social democracy and of the necessity for a fighting organization of the workers to ensure political neutrality. The mere comparison of the figures of social democratic voters with the figures of the trade-union organizations in Germany is sufficient to prove to the most

---

* This was the only legal union during the time of the antisocialist laws. It opposed strikes and functioned as a working-class self-help organization. —H.S.

simple-minded that the trade unions in Germany do not, as in England, draw their troops from the unenlightened bourgeois-minded mass, but from the mass of proletarians already aroused by the social democracy and won by it to the idea of the class struggle. Many trade-union leaders indignantly reject the idea—a requisite of the "theory of neutrality"—and regard the trade unions as a recruiting school for social democracy. This apparently insulting, but in reality, highly flattering presumption is in Germany reduced to mere fancy by the circumstance that the positions are reversed; it is the social democracy that is the recruiting school for the trade unions.

Moreover, if the organizational work of the trade unions is for the most part of a very difficult and troublesome kind, it is, with the exception of a few cases and some districts, not merely because on the whole, the soil has not been prepared by the social democratic plough, but also because the trade-union seed itself, and the sower as well, must also be "red," social democratic, before the harvest can prosper. But when we compare in this way the figures of trade-union strength, not with those of the social democratic organizations, but—which is the only correct way—with those of the mass of social democratic voters, we come to a conclusion that differs considerably from the current view of the matter. The fact then comes to light that the "free trade unions" actually represent today but a minority of the class-conscious workers of Germany, that even with their one and a quarter million organized members they have not yet been able to draw into their ranks one-half of those already aroused by social democracy.

The most important conclusion to be drawn from the facts cited above is that the *complete unity* of the trade-union and the social democratic movements, which is absolutely necessary for the coming mass struggles in Germany, *is actually here*, and that it is incorporated in the wide mass that forms the basis at once of social democracy and trade unionism, and in whole consciousness both parts of the movement are mingled in a mental unity. The alleged antagonism between social democracy and trade unions shrinks to an antagonism between social democracy and a certain part of the trade-union officials, which is, however, at the same time an antagonism within the trade unions between this part of the trade-union leaders and the proletarian mass organized in trade unions.

The rapid growth of the trade-union movement in Germany in the course of the last fifteen years, especially in the period of great economic prosperity from 1895 to 1900, has brought with it a great independence of the trade unions, a specializing of their methods of struggle, and finally the introduction of a regular trade-union official-dom. All these phenomena are quite understandable and natural historical products of the growth of the trade unions in this fifteen-year period, and of the economic prosperity and political calm of Germany. They are, although inseparable from certain drawbacks, without doubt a historically necessary evil. But the dialectics of development also brings with it the circumstance that these necessary means of promoting trade-union growth become, on the contrary, obstacles to its further development at a certain stage of organization and at a certain degree of ripeness of conditions.

The specialization of professional activity as trade-union leaders, as well as the naturally restricted horizon that is bound up with disconnected economic struggles in a peaceful period, leads only too easily, among trade-union officials, to bureaucratism and a certain narrowness of outlook. Both, however, express themselves in a whole series of tendencies that may be fateful in the highest degree for the future of the trade-union movement. There is first of all the overvaluation of the organization, which from a means has gradually been changed into an end in itself, a precious thing, to which the interests of the struggles should be subordinated. From this also comes that openly admitted need for peace, which shrinks from great risks and presumed dangers to the stability of the trade unions, and further, the overvaluation of the trade-union method of struggle itself, its prospects, and its successes.

The trade-union leaders, constantly absorbed in the economic guerrilla war whose plausible task it is to make the workers place the highest value on the smallest economic achievement, every increase in wages and shortening of the working day, gradually lose the power of seeing the larger connections and of taking a survey of the whole position. Only in this way can one explain why many trade-union leaders refer with the greatest satisfaction to the achievements of the last fifteen years, instead of, on the contrary, emphasizing the other side of the medal; the simultaneous and immense reduction of the proletarian standard of life by land usury, by the whole tax and customs policy, by landlord rapacity, which has increased house rents to such an exorbitant extent, in short, by all the objective tendencies of bourgeois policy that have largely neutralized the advantages of the fifteen years of trade-union struggle. From the *whole* social democratic truth, which, while emphasizing the importance of the present work and its absolute necessity, attaches the chief importance to the criticism and the limits to this work, the *half* trade-union truth is taken that emphasizes only the positive side of the daily struggle.

And finally, from the concealment of the objective limits drawn by the bourgeois social order to the trade-union struggle, there arises a hostility to every theoretical criticism that refers to these limits in connection with the ultimate aims of the labor movement. Fulsome flattery and boundless optimism are considered to be the duty of every "friend of the trade-union movement." But as the social democratic standpoint consists precisely in fighting against uncritical trade-union optimism, as in fighting against uncritical parliamentary optimism, a front is at last made against the social democratic theory: men grope for a "new trade-union theory," that is, a theory that would open an illimitable vista of economic progress to the trade-union struggle within the capitalist system, in opposition to the social democratic doctrine. Such a theory has indeed existed for some time—the theory of Professor Sombart, which was promulgated with the express intention of driving a wedge between the trade unions and the social democracy in Germany, and of enticing the trade unions over to the bourgeois position.

In close connection with these theoretical tendencies is a revolution in the relations of leaders and rank and file. In place of the direction by colleagues through local committees, with their admitted inadequacy, there appears the businesslike direction of the trade-union officials. The initiative and the power of making decisions thereby devolve upon trade-union specialists, so to speak, and the more passive virtue of discipline upon the mass of members. This dark side of officialdom also assuredly conceals considerable dangers for the party, as from the latest innovation, the institution of local party secretaries; it can quite easily result, if the social democratic mass is not careful, that these secretariats may remain mere organs for carrying out decisions and not be regarded in any way the appointed bearers of the initiative and of the direction of local party life. But by the nature of the case, by the character of the political struggle, there are narrow bounds drawn to bureaucratism in social democracy as in trade-union life.

But here the technical specializing of wage struggles as, for example, the conclusion of intricate tariff agreements and the like, frequently means that the mass of organized workers are prohibited from taking a "survey of the whole industrial life," and their incapacity for taking decisions is thereby established. A consequence of this conception is the argument with which every theoretical criticism of the prospects and possibilities of trade-union practice is tabooed and which alleges that it represents a danger to the pious trade-union sentiment of the masses. From this the point of view has been developed that it is only by blind, childlike faith in the efficacy of the trade-union struggle that the working masses can be won and held for the organization. In contradistinction to social democracy, which bases its influence on the unity of the masses amid the contradictions of the existing order and in the complicated character of its development, and on the critical attitude of the masses to all factors and stages of their own class struggle, the influence and the power of the trade unions are founded upon the upside-down theory of the incapacity of the masses for criticism and decision. "The faith of the people must be maintained"—that is the fundamental principle, acting upon which many trade-union officials stamp as attempts on the life of this movement all criticisms of the objective inadequacy of trade unionism.

And finally, a result of all this specialization and this bureaucratism among trade-union officials is the great independence and the "neutrality" of the trade unions in relation to social democracy. The extreme independence of the trade-union organization is a natural result of its growth, as a relation that has grown out of the technical division of work between the political and the trade-union forms of struggle. The "neutrality" of the German trade unions, on its part, arose as a product of the reactionary trade-union legislation of the Prusso-German police state. With time, both aspects of their nature have altered. From the condition of political "neutrality" of the trade unions imposed by the police, a theory of their voluntary neutrality has been evolved as a necessity founded upon the alleged nature of the trade-union struggle itself. And the technical independence of the trade unions, which should rest upon the division of work in the unified social democratic class struggle, the separation of the trade unions from social democracy, from its views and its leadership, has been changed into the so-called equal authority of trade unions and social democracy.

The appearance of separation and equality of trade unions and social democracy is, however, incorporated chiefly in the trade-union officials, and strengthened through the managing apparatus of the trade unions. Outwardly, by the coexistence of a complete staff of trade-union officials, of a wholly independent central committee, of numerous professional press, and finally of a trade-union congress, the illusion is created of an exact parallel with the managing apparatus of the social democracy, the party executive, the party press, and the party conference. This illusion of equality between social democracy and the trade union had led to, among other things, the monstrous spectacle that, in part, quite analogous agendas are discussed at social democratic conferences and trade-union congresses, and that on the same questions different, and even diametrically opposite, decisions are taken. From the natural division of work between the party conference, which represents the general interests and tasks of the labor movement, and the trade-union congress (which deals with the much narrower sphere of social questions and interests), the artificial division has been made of a pretended trade-union and a social democratic outlook in relation to the same general questions and interests of the labor movement.

Thus the peculiar position has arisen that this same trade-union movement, which below, in the wide proletarian masses, is absolutely one with social democracy, parts abruptly from it above, in the superstructure of management, and sets itself up as an independent great power. The German labor movement therefore assumes the peculiar form of a double pyramid whose base and body consist of one solid mass but whose apices are wide apart.

It is clear from this presentation of the case in what way alone in a natural and successful manner that compact unity of the German labor movement can be attained, which, in view of the coming political class struggles and of the peculiar interests of the further development of the trade unions, is indispensably necessary. Nothing could be more perverse or more hopeless than to desire to attain the unity desired by means of sporadic and periodical negotiations on individual questions affecting the labor movement between the Social Democratic Party leadership and the trade-union central committees. It is just the highest circles of both forms of the labor movement, which as we have seen, incorporate their separation and self-sufficiency, that are themselves, therefore, the promoters of the illusion of the "equal authority" and of the parallel existence of social democracy and trade unionism.

To desire the unity of these through the union of the party executive and the general commission is to desire to build a bridge at the very spot where the distance is greatest and the crossing most difficult. Not above, among the heads of the leading directing organizations and in their federative alliance, but below, among the organized proletarian masses, lies the guarantee of the real unity of the labor movement. In the consciousness of the million trade unionists, the party and the trade unions are actually *one*, they represent in different forms the *social democratic* struggle for the emancipation of the proletariat. And the necessity automatically arises therefrom of removing any causes of friction that have arisen between the social democracy and a part of the trade unions, of adapting their mutual relation to the consciousness of the proletarian masses, that is, of *rejoining the trade unions to social democracy*. The synthesis of the real development that led from the original incorporation of the trade unions to their separation from social democracy will thereby be expressed, and the way will be prepared for the coming period of great proletarian mass struggles during the period of vigorous growth of both trade unions and social democracy, and their reunion, in the interests of both, will become a necessity.

It is not, of course, a question of the merging of the trade-union organization in the party, but of the restoration of the unity of social democracy and the trade unions, which corresponds to the actual relation between the labor movement as a whole and its partial trade-union expression. Such a revolution will inevitably call forth a vigorous opposition from a part of the trade-union leadership. But it is high time for the working masses of social democracy to learn how to express their capacity for decision and action, and therewith to demonstrate their ripeness for that time of great struggles and great tasks in which they, the masses, will be the actual chorus and the directing bodies will merely act the "speaking parts," that is, will only be the interpreters of the will of the masses.

The trade-union movement is not that which is reflected in the quite understandable *but irrational* illusion of a minority of the trade-union leaders, but that which lives in the consciousness of the mass of proletarians who have been won for the class struggle. In this consciousness the trade-union movement is part of social democracy. "And what it is, that should it dare to appear."*

---

* Also translated as "And what she is, that dares she to appear." This quotation is from the 1800 play *Maria Stuart* by the German author Friedrich Schiller (1759–1805). Bernstein used the line as a section header in chapter three of his book *Evolutionary Socialism*. —H.S.

FURTHER READING

P aul Frölich's *Rosa Luxemburg* is the most important biography. It has the advantage of being an "eyewitness account" by a contemporary and political comrade. However, this also produces some problems, as Frölich is largely uncritical of Luxemburg and at times too much inside events to provide a reasonably objective analysis. J. P. Nettl's two-volume *Rosa Luxemburg* is a good companion piece, as the author relies on archival material and is scrupulous in his documentation, despite his hostility to revolutionary socialism. His condescending tone can be rather irritating, but the record he provides is nonetheless rich and detailed. The 1986 film *Rosa Luxemburg* by German director Margarethe von Trotta draws heavily on Luxemburg's writings, speeches, and letters and is an emotionally powerful complement to the written biographies.

Mary-Alice Waters's *Rosa Luxemburg Speaks* is the single best English language collection of Luxemburg's works, and is the source for many later editions. The more recent *Rosa Luxemburg Reader*, edited by Peter Hudis and Kevin Anderson, is a useful supplement, and many other works can be found on the Rosa Luxemburg Internet Archive.

Paul Le Blanc's *Rosa Luxemburg: Reflections and Writings* features a well-chosen selection of essays critically assessing her political contribution, as well as a thoughtful assortment of short pieces and extracts from longer works by Luxemburg.

For political context, Carl Schorske's *German Social Democracy, 1905–1917* is outstanding, providing a clear narrative of the SPD's development and an illuminating analysis of the social and economic forces behind it. Pierre Broué's *The German Revolution 1917–1923* is essential reading for understanding the period and Luxemburg's place in it; for those who are daunted by its dense 900-plus pages, Chris Harman's *The Lost Revolution* offers a pithy and insightful historical overview.

WORKS ABOUT ROSA LUXEMBURG

Basso, Lelio. *Rosa Luxemburg, a Reappraisal.* New York: Praeger, 1975.

Bronner, Stephen E. *Rosa Luxemburg: A Revolutionary for Our Times.* New York: Columbia University Press, 1987.

Cliff, Tony. *Rosa Luxemburg.* London: Bookmarks, 1983.

Dunayevskaya, Raya. *Rosa Luxemburg, Women's Liberation, and Marx's Philosophy of Revolution.* Urbana: University of Illinois Press, 1991.

Frölich, Paul. *Rosa Luxemburg: Ideas in Action.* Translated by Joanna Hoornweg. London: Pluto, 1972, 21.

Geras, Norman. *The Legacy of Rosa Luxemburg.* London: New Left Books, 1976.

Jacob, Mathilde. *Rosa Luxemburg: An Intimate Portrait.* London: Lawrence and Wishart, 2000.

Le Blanc, Paul, ed. *Rosa Luxemburg: Reflections and Writings.* Amherst: Humanity Books, 1999.

Löwy, Michael. "Rosa Luxemburg's Conception of 'Socialism or Barbarism.'" *On Changing the World, Essays in Political Philosophy, from Karl Marx to Walter Benjamin.* Atlantic Highlands, NJ: Humanities Press, 1993.

Lukács, Georg. "The Marxism of Rosa Luxemburg" and "Critical Observations on Rosa Luxemburg's 'Critique of the Russian Revolution.'" *History and Class Consciousness: Studies in Marxist Dialectics.* 1922. Cambridge, MA: MIT Press, 1988. 27–45, 272–294.

Nettl, J. P. *Rosa Luxemburg.* 2 vols. London: Oxford University Press, 1966.

Trotta, Margarethe von. *Rosa Luxemburg.* 1986. Starring Barbara Sukowa. In German with English subtitles. Bioskop Film, Munich.

HISTORICAL AND POLITICAL BACKGROUND

Braunthal, Julius. *History of the International, 1864–1943.* 2 vols. New York: Frederick A. Praeger, 1967.

Broué, Pierre. *The German Revolution 1917–1923.* 1971. Chicago: Haymarket Books, 2006.

Harman, Chris. *The Lost Revolution: Germany 1918–1923.* London: Bookmarks, 1982.

Le Blanc, Paul. *Lenin and the Revolutionary Party.* New Jersey: Humanities Press, 1990.

———. *From Marx to Gramsci: An Introduction to Revolutionary Marxist Politics.* Amherst, NY: Humanity Books, 1996.

Schorske, Carl E. *German Social Democracy, 1905–1917.* 1955. Cambridge: Harvard University Press, 1983.

WORKS BY ROSA LUXEMBURG

Bronner, Stephen E., ed. *The Letters of Rosa Luxemburg.* Boulder, CO: Westview Press, 1978.

Davis, Horace B. *The National Question: Selected Writings by Rosa Luxemburg.* New York: Monthly Review Press, 1976.

Howard, Dick. *Selected Political Writings of Rosa Luxemburg.* New York: Monthly Review Press, 1971.

Hudis, Peter and Kevin B. Anderson, eds. *The Rosa Luxemburg Reader.* New York: Monthly Review Press, 2004.

Le Blanc, Paul, ed. *Rosa Luxemburg: Reflections and Writings.* Amherst: Humanity Books, 1999.

Looker, Robert, ed. *Rosa Luxemburg: Selected Political Writings.* New York: Grove Press, 1974.

Luxemburg, Rosa. *The Accumulation of Capital.* London: Routledge, 2003.

———. *The Accumulation of Capital: An Anti-Critique.* New York: Monthly Review Press, 1972.

———. *The Crisis in the German Social-Democracy.* New York: Howard Fertig, 1969.

———. *The Industrial Development of Poland.* Translated by Tessa De Carlo. New York: Campaigner Publications, 1977.

Rosa Luxemburg Internet Archive. www.marxists.org/archive/luxemburg/index.htm.

Waters, Mary-Alice, ed. *Rosa Luxemburg Speaks*. New York: Pathfinder Press, 1970.

INDEX

8-hour workday, 125, 127, 129, 132, 137–138, 149, 163; "not an unattainable platform," 155
8.5-hour workday, 132
9-hour workday, 123, 132, 133, 138
10-hour workday, 121, 132, 133, 134, 138
11-hour workday, 122, 134
12-hour workday, 124
13-, 14-, and 15-hour workday, 121
17-hour workday, 124

Accumulation of Capital (Luxemburg), 18
Adler, Max, 14
Aesop, 103n
agricultural workers, 154, 161, 167
agriculture, 62
Alliancists, 111
anarchism, 111–116 passim
Anti-Düring (Engels), 53
anti-Semitism, 12
antisocialist laws, 6, 7, 10, 11, 106, 116n, 157–158
antiwar demonstrations, 25
antiwar pamphlets, 24–25, 30
arrests of workers, 122
Austria, 2

bakers, 124, 126, 133
Baku, 132; general strikes, 120–121, 123–124, 126–127, 144
Bakunin, Mikhail, 6, 111–113 passim
Barnimstrasse Military Women's Prison, 24
Batum, 121–123 passim

Bebel, August, 32n31, 33n59, 107, 115n
Berdiansk, 133
Berlin, 12, 17, 24, 25; demonstrations, 28
Bernstein, Eduard, 13, 19–20, 36n101, 37–39, 41–104 passim; *Evolutionary Socialism*, 37, 41, 72–104, 181n
Bialystok, 113
"big capitalists": Marx on, 55
Bismarck, 6, 10, 32n32
Blanqui, Louis Auguste, 6, 75n, 76n, 95
Blanquism, 76, 89
Böhm-Bawerk, Eugen von, 77, 78
Bolsheviks, 1, 7, 10, 22, 108; call for new International, 23; Luxemburg on, 26
Bonaparte, Louis, 33n54
bookkeepers, 135
bourgeoisie, 61, 62, 64, 65, 69; Bernstein and, 97–100 passim; Germany, 27, 86, 164; petite bourgeoisie, 43, 89, 91, 162, 164; Poland, 8; revolution and, 162; Russia, 130, 131
"bourgeoisie" (word), 100
Braun, Otto, 22
Bremen, 26
Brentano, Lujo, 99
Breslau prison, 24, 25
bricklayers, 124, 132
Broué, Pierre, 10–11, 17, 26–27, 28, 36n101; *The German Revolution 1917–1923*, 183

ABOUT HAYMARKET BOOKS

Haymarket Books is a nonprofit, progressive book distributor and publisher, a project of the Center for Economic Research and Social Change. We believe that activists need to take ideas, history, and politics into the many struggles for social justice today. Learning the lessons of past victories, as well as defeats, can arm a new generation of fighters for a better world. As Karl Marx said, "The philosophers have merely interpreted the world; the point however is to change it."

We take inspiration and courage from our namesakes, the Haymarket Martyrs, who gave their lives fighting for a better world. Their 1886 struggle for the eight-hour day, which gave us May Day, the international workers' holiday, reminds workers around the world that ordinary people can organize and struggle for their own liberation. These struggles continue today across the globe—struggles against oppression, exploitation, hunger, and poverty.

It was August Spies, one of the Martyrs who was targeted for being an immigrant and an anarchist, who predicted the battles being fought to this day. "If you think that by hanging us you can stamp out the labor movement," Spies told the judge, "then hang us. Here you will tread upon a spark, but here, and there, and behind you, and in front of you, and everywhere, the flames will blaze up. It is a subterranean fire. You cannot put it out. The ground is on fire upon which you stand."

We could not suceed in our publishing efforts without the generous financial support of our readers. Many people contribute to our project through the Haymarket Sustainers program, where donors receive free books in return for their monetary support. If you would like to be a part of this program, please contact us at info@haymarketbooks.org.

Order these titles and more through our online store available at:
www.haymarketbooks.org or call 773-583-7884.

ALSO FROM HAYMARKET BOOKS

Beyond the Green Zone:
Dispatches from an Unembedded Journalist in Occupied Iraq
Dahr Jamail • Foreword by Amy Goodman • Independent jouralist Dahr Jamail presents never-before printed details of siege of Fallujah and examines the origins of the Iraqi resistance, bringing us inside the Iraq we never see. $20, hardcover. ISBN 978-1-931859-47-9.

Welcome to the Terrordome: The Pain, Politics, and Promise of Sports
Dave Zirin • This much-anticipated sequel to *What's My Name, Fool?* by acclaimed sportswriter Dave Zirin breaks new ground in sportswriting, looking at the controversies and trends now shaping sports in the United States—and abroad. Always insightful, never predictable. $16. ISBN 978-1-931859-41-7.

In Praise of Barbarians: Essays Against Empire
Mike Davis • No writer in the United States today brings together analysis and history as comprehensively and elegantly as Mike Davis. In these contemporary, interventionist essays, Davis goes beyond critique to offer real solutions and concrete possibilities for change. $15. ISBN 978-1-931859-42-4.

Sin Patrón: Stories from Argentia's Occupied Factories
The lavaca collective, with a foreword by Naomi Klein and Avi Lewis • The inside story of Argentina's remarkable movement to create factories run democratically by workers themselves. $16. ISBN 978-1-931859-43-1.

Between the Lines: Readings on Israel, the Palestinians,
and the U.S. "War on Terror"
Tikva Honig-Parnass and Toufic Haddad • This compilation of essays—edited by a Palestinian and an Israeli—constitutes a challenge to critially rethink the Israeli-Palestinian conflict. $17. ISBN 978-1-931859-44-8.

No One Is Illegal: Fighting Racism and State Violence
on the U.S./Mexico Border
Justin Akers Chacón and Mike Davis • Countering the chorus of anti-immigrant voices, Davis and Akers Chacón expose the racism of anti-immigration vigilantes and put a human face on the immigrants who risk their lives to cross the border to work in the United States. $16. ISBN 978-1-931859-35-3.

A Little Piece of Ground
Elizabeth Laird • Growing up in occupied Palestine through the eyes of a twelve-year-old boy. $9.95. ISBN 978-1-931859-38-7.

The Communist Manifesto:
A Road Map to History's Most Important Political Document
Karl Marx and Frederick Engels, edited by Phil Gasper • This beautifully organized and presented edition of *The Communist Manifesto* is fully annotated, with clear historical references and explication, additional related texts, and a glossary that will bring the text to life. $12. ISBN 978-1-931859-25-7.

Subterranean Fire: A History of Working-Class Radicalism in the U.S.
Sharon Smith • Workers in the United States have a rich tradition of fighting back and achieving gains previously thought unthinkable, but that history remains largely hidden. *In Subterranean Fire*, Sharon Smith brings that history to light and reveals its lessons for today. $16. ISBN 978-1-931859-23-3.

Soldiers in Revolt: GI Resistance During the Vietnam War
David Cortright with a new introduction by Howard Zinn • "An exhaustive account of rebellion in all the armed forces, not only in Vietnam but throughout the world."— *New York Review of Books*. $16. ISBN 978-1-931859-27-1.

Friendly Fire: The Remarkable Story of a Journalist Kidnapped in Iraq, Rescued by an Italian Secret Service Agent, and Shot by U.S. Forces
Giuliana Sgrena • The Italian journalist, whose personal story was featured on *60 Minutes*, describes the real story of her capture and shooting in 2004. Sgrena also gives invaluable insight into the reality of life in occupied Iraq, exposing U.S. war crimes there. $20, hard cover. ISBN 978-1-931859-39-4.

The Meaning of Marxism
Paul D'Amato • A lively and accessible introduction to the ideas of Karl Marx, with historical and contemporary examples. $12. ISBN 978-1-931859-29-5.

Revolution and Counterrevolution: Class Struggle in a Moscow Metal Factory
Kevin Murphy • Murphy's wealth of research and insight deliver an exciting contribution to the discussion about class and the Russian Revolution. $20. ISBN 978-1-931859-50-9.

The Women Incendiaries: The Inspiring Story of the Women of the Paris Commune Who Took up Arms in the Fight for Liberty and Equality

Edith Thomas • *The Women Incendiaries* tells the often over-looked story of the crucial role played by women during the Paris Commune of 1871, one of history's most important emxperiments in working-class democracy. $16. ISBN 978-1-931859-46-2.

The Dispossessed: Chronicles of the *Desterrados* of Colombia

Alfredo Molano • Here in their own words are the stories of the Desterrados, or "dispossessed"—the thousands of Colombians displaced by years of war and state-backed terrorism, funded in part through U.S. aid to the Colombian government. With a preface by Aviva Chomsky. $14. ISBN 978-1-931859-17-2.

Vive la Revolution: A Stand-up History of the French Revolution

Mark Steel • An actually interesting, unapologetically sympathetic and extremely funny history of the French Revolution. $14. ISBN 978-1-931859-37-0.

Poetry and Protest: A Dennis Brutus Reader

Aisha Karim and Lee Sustar, editors • A vital original collection of the interviews, poetry, and essays of the much-loved anti-apartheid leader. $16. ISBN 978-1-931859-22-6.

The Bending Cross: A Biography of Eugene Victor Debs

Ray Ginger, with a new introduction by Mike Davis • The classic biography of Eugene Debs, one of the most important thinkers and activists in the United States. $18. ISBN 978-1-931859-40-0.

What's My Name, Fool? Sports and Resistance in the United States

Dave Zirin • *What's My Name, Fool?* offers a no-holds-barred look at the business of sports today. In humorous and accessible language, Zirin shows how sports express the worst, as well as the most creative and exciting, features of American society. $15. ISBN 978-1-931859-20-5.

Literature and Revolution

Leon Trotsky, William Keach, editor • A new, annotated edition of Leon Trotsky's classic study of the relationship of politics and art. $16. ISBN 978-1931859-16-5.

ABOUT THE EDITOR

Helen Scott is an associate professor of English at the University of Vermont where she teaches postcolonial studies and Caribbean literature. She worked on the union drive that won faculty representation with United Academics (AFT-AAUP), and she is currently a union delegate. She has published articles in *Callaloo, International Socialist Review, Journal of Haitian Studies, Postcolonial Text*; has chapters in anthologies including *Marxism, Modernity, and Postcolonial Studies*, and *Haiti: Writing Under Siege*; and a book, *Caribbean Women Writers and Globalization: Fictions of Independence*, published by Ashgate. Originally from Britain, she has lived in the U.S. since 1988 and is a longtime socialist activist who frequently speaks on panels and at rallies against imperialism and racism, and for labor and immigrant rights.